D1526843

AFFLUENCE,

ALTRUISM, AND ATROPHY

AFFLUENCE, ALTRUISM, AND ATROPHY
The Decline of Welfare States

Morris Silver
Professor of Economics
City College of the City University of New York

New York University Press
New York *and* London

Library of Congress Cataloging in Publication Data
Silver, Morris.
    Affluence, altruism, and atrophy.

    Bibliography: p.
    Includes index.
    1. Welfare state. 2. Wealth. 3. Altruism.
4. Social policy. I. Title.
HN18.S547   361.6'5   79-3528
ISBN 0-8147-7810-0

Published in the United States of America

To the memory of my father
and friend, Julius

CONTENTS

PREFACE

The purport of this study is to make the relationship between affluence and altruism the central point of a general consideration of the problem of decline, or atrophy, of welfare states.

Because of the importance of the topic and because so many disciplines border it, I have tried to discuss it in ordinary language. Some technical terms in economics and an indifference curve analysis are used, but the nonspecialist can easily skip over these parts without in any way losing the central thread of the argument. Originally, *Affluence, Altruism, and Atrophy* was a much longer book, including materials on such peripheral problems as the relationship between income and happiness and the origins of the market system. The book also included a survey of the "doomsday" literature of the 1970s. These were removed in the interests of sharpening the focus on the problem of the decline of welfare states.

A few words are in order concerning my extensive use of remote historical experience. This may trouble the novice (or ideologue) who believes in the existence of steady advances and fixed stages of historical evolution. The economic historian, however, knows better. Admittedly it is dangerous to draw lessons for today from data that are not only alien and complex but often rather sketchy. One is liable to see exactly what one wishes to see. Nevertheless, I know of no other method by which disturbing trends in our own welfare state can be placed in context and thereby more fully illuminated. Unlike the overly particularistic historians or the social voluntarist, I believe that comparative history not only is possible but teaches lessons we can ignore only at our peril.

If sometimes a note of personal antagonism intrudes itself into the analysis, it is because the analyst finds it difficult to remain aloof from a historical process in which he and his loved ones are potential victims.

There is another point. I am an economist, not a professional historian. I have relied entirely on secondary rather than on original sources. For this approach, which one practitioner has styled the practice of predatory scholarship, I apologize. Nothing else was possible. Hopefully, I have not made any major errors of fact.

Finally, I would like to urge the reader to read the notes. In the interests of production economy these have been placed at the end of the book rather than on page bottoms. I trust that they will not be overlooked.

I would like to thank Armen Alchian, James Buchanan, Malcolm Galatin, Roger McCain, George Schwab, Arthur Tiedemann, and Gordon Tullock for their helpful comments. Thanks are also due to Georgia Capel and Lynn Harris for their efforts beyond the call of duty in transforming my scribbles into a clearly typed manuscript. Above all, as ever, I am thankful to my wife Sandy and to our sons Gerry and Ron.

Morris Silver
Woodbury, New York
July 13, 1979

INTRODUCTION

I feel sure that we will not be able to understand fully the decline of empires until a combined effort of historians and biologists has clarified the effects of protracted well-being and high standards of living on the psychological structure of a population and the feedback effects of these changes on the cultural behavior of the same population.

—Carlo M. Cipolla

There can be no doubt that moral and religious beliefs can destroy a civilization and that, where such doctrines prevail, not only the most revered moral leaders, sometimes saintly figures whose unselfishness is beyond question, may become grave dangers to the values which the same people regard as unshakeable. Against this threat we can protect ourselves only by subjecting even our dearest dreams of a better world to ruthless dissection. . . . We must make our rational insight dominate over our inherited instincts.

—F. A. Hayek

A specter is haunting the United States—the specter of decline. Anthony J. Wiener, a specialist in management and policy studies, finds it "very curious" that "in spite of the great success of the current period in terms of technological development, economic growth, and the spread of affluence . . . it is easy to find many expressions of pessimism."[1] Another observer, John Maddox, complains that the public is being assailed by "prophecies of calamity."[2] Political scientist Harvey Simmons adds: "It is as if society was on the verge of, or perhaps even in the first phase of, some kind of vast social or cultural revolution whose exact nature has not yet been understood but of which people see premonitions all around them."[3] In growing numbers, authors have succumbed to the compulsion to deal with decline. All recognize the malaise of the contemporary United States, or more generally, Western socioeconomic organization, and they sound its death knell. However, there is sharp disagreement concerning diagnosis, prognosis, and treatment of the illness. Some authors believe suitable policies or adjustments can save the system, although in drastically altered form; others see the condition as beyond repair. Whether by steady evolution or violent upheaval a new socioeconomic system will replace the existing one. The coming system, or the mode of its birth, is viewed with alarm, or resignation, and by a few, even with hopeful anticipation.

It is my intent to place the perennial but elusive question of socioeconomic decline or atrophy within a general analytical and historical framework. I see decline as an intrinsic process growing directly out of affluence. John Stuart Mill[4] and John Maynard Keynes,[5] writing nearly a century apart, both believed that economic growth would lead to a utopian finale in which individuals would cultivate the art of life. However, I shall suggest that dystopia will be the more likely outcome of economic abundance and the search for the "finer things."

In a nutshell, *altruism,* or the "taste" for helping others, is a member of the family of "higher needs" described by the psychologist Abraham H. Maslow. *Affluence* in turn calls forth a vastly increased demand for altruism, which is more and more often being supplied by the state. Unfortunately, the massive and persistent programs produced by the state are on balance perverse or counterproductive. When the hoped-for reform produces the opposite effect, the stage is set for decline or "general crisis" or *retro-*

development. Thus, the highest stage of capitalism is not imperialism, as Lenin thought, but altruism!

Interestingly, it is in both the most backward and the most advanced societies that the temptation is strongest for the government to intervene in economy and society. The motives, however, are very different. Douglas C. North and Robert Paul Thomas in *The Rise of the Western World* have shown how, during the early modern period, the young states in France and Spain enforced and perpetuated monopoly rights in order to raise much-needed tax revenue. The creation of inefficient property rights in turn retarded economic growth. On the other hand, beginning in the seventeenth century we observe many examples of a largely perverse reliance on state planning and management to force industrialization: Prussia under Frederick the Great, Russia under both Czarist and Soviet rulers, the People's Republic of China, and indeed most of the Third World. "The heart of this choice," explains David S. Landes in *The Unbound Prometheus,* "is ambition, a hunger for growth (which is assumed to mean industrialization) and the fruits of growth that chafes at delay, has no patience for the working of the free market, and sees in authority a means of forcing the gates of time." [6] Alternatively, a government may intervene, as in nineteenth-century France in order to recapture the (imagined or real) glories of preindustrial society. Beyond this point attention will be directed to societies that achieved affluence only to destroy it in the name of humanity rather than to those more numerous ones in which nationalistic or revenue or prestige-seeking rulers arrested the ascent to affluence.

The essential theory is developed in part I. R. H. Coase has recently reminded economists that modern utility theory "which analyzes the effect of human preferences on economic behavior . . . tells us little about the purposes which impel people to action." He regards sociobiology as a discipline that can contribute to the formulation of a theory relating preferences to certain basic needs—that is, to human nature.[7] To this end, chapter 1 takes the first step of demonstrating the reality of a specific altruistic need or desire by examining the supportive positions taken, not only by sociobiologists, but by philosophers, ethologists, comparative psychologists, and social scientists. Of special significance, however, is the key point made by sociobiologists such as David P. Barash and George Edgin Pugh that *by-product altruism*—altruism directed at genetic strangers—becomes consistent with the biological theory of *kin selection* when proper account is taken of the difficulties of designing an altruistic response that would be triggered only by closely related individuals. Next, I take up political altruism—the advantages to donors of channeling a major portion of altruistic contributions through the state instead of relying solely on private wealth.

In chapter 2, I set forth Maslow's view (which I share) that human beings have basic needs over and above the physiological and that these needs are not merely cultural artifacts or otherwise idiosyncratic. The "demand" for altruism is then integrated into modern microeconomics frameworks inspired by Maslow's works on "growth actualization" and by those of the economist Gary S. Becker on "social interactions." This involves viewing people as rational altruistic individuals choosing, subject to a budget constraint, between "others' necessaries" and "own amenities." The theoretical analysis leads to two major conclusions. First, as societies become more affluent they will not only demand more altruism ("others' necessaries") but will also substitute political for private altruism. Second, the level of real income (or amenity consumption) at which a society becomes affluent and markedly increases its spending on altruism as well as other higher needs is not fixed, but instead varies inversely with the relative price of amenity. Since technological progress has operated to reduce the relative prices of amenities over time, it follows that the wealthier Greek or Roman of antiquity, while "poor" in amenities, might be as much or even more interested in making altruistic donations than an affluent American. The theoretical analysis is supported by a variety of evidence: anthropological observation of a change in the character of giving from Neolithic to post-Neolithic societies, statistical evidence relating philanthropic contributions to donor income, and psychological survey research findings regarding "Post-Materialistic" values.

John Stuart Mill was merely indulging a Victorian brand of

snobbery in his remark that "notwithstanding some incipient signs of a better tendency" among Americans of his day, "the life of the whole of one sex is devoted to dollar hunting, and of the other to breeding dollar-hunters." But he was much more right than he knew in saying that American life "is not the kind of social perfection which philanthropists to come will feel any very eager desire to assist in realizing." [8] Indeed the central problem of the affluent United States is the *kind* of philanthropy it practices: the well-to-do desire to improve society, but the humanitarian reforms they find plausible and "purchase" result in social disruptions. I expand on this theme in chapter 3, with special attention to the perverse consequences of much governmental social and economic intervention. I construct a theory linking humanitarian reforms and social disruptions by combining the insights of Jay W. Forrester and Joseph A. Schumpeter. Chapter 4 views politicians and intellectuals as profit-making producers and distributors of plausible but perverse reforms to a market in which the consumers are rationally ignorant affluent-altruists.

In part II, the hypothesis linking affluence with perverse altruism is confronted by the experience of wealthier societies of the past including the Roman Empire (chapter 5), Sung China (chapter 6), and classical Athens (chapter 7). Within such diverse societies it would be difficult to attribute demands for ameliorative social reforms to one or another variable peculiar to the contemporary United States or West. The historical evidence, especially the Roman, suggests that affluent societies increasingly introduce humanitarian but perverse reforms that tend to atrophy the economy and thereby undermine both affluence and altruism. Chapter 8 begins by comprehending the process of socioeconomic decline in terms of retro-development, the latter being a dynamic feedback process leading typically to a reversion to a (relatively) stationary low-level economy and, as Cipolla puts it, to a "loss of pre-eminence." [9] This process, however, should in the limit be understood to include the destruction of the powerful state apparatus that had originally strangled affluence in the name of altruism. Economic history takes on a cyclical aspect. Living standards rise and fall. Such a perspective stands opposed to notions of unilineal self-generating stages of economic evolution or unique, irreversible take-offs into sustained growth.

Part III consists of three chapters. Chapter 9 deals with the construction of the British welfare state from 1870 to 1914. Chapter 10 takes up the question of whether Sweden's affluent economy, long held out by welfareists as proof that genuine social reform will not collapse a market economy, has already entered into sharp decline. In chapter 11, I speculate on whether the United States will decline. Will the United States, drained by Great Society spending programs and reaping the perverse fruits, be transformed into an altruistic despotism controlled by the dominant mass media and the most prestigious universities? Or is the United States merely experiencing the birth pangs of a more intensively planned society? I think not. True planning, as well as the market, are viewed by the affluents as betrayals of the poor or the unemployed, or as racist, sexist, fascist, antienvironment, and so forth. Further, in spite of the brave talk there is very little evidence that government has consistently applied even the relatively simple lessons of Keynesian economics, much less cost-benefit and systems analysis. At the present time, social engineering, not planning, looms on the horizon. The former is best viewed as an attempt to altruistically remodel society in terms of quantified but fundamentally superficial plans.

Furthermore, I do not believe that a new ruling class consisting of apolitical or neutral technocrats is in the offing. Such experts are in no position to revolt against the affluents. To win the struggle for the souls of the well-to-do, and with this power and wealth, the technocrats must abandon science in favor of "social justice," "tough new energy policies," and the like.

The United States may yet discover ways to escape decline, but unfortunately retro-development is much more than just another scary futuristic scenario. Undoubtedly there are countertrends that will slow or even reverse the process for given periods of time. But the primary evolutionary tendency in affluent societies is for decline to occur, and it is difficult to visualize the kinds of conscious, feasible policies that might "permanently" reverse this trend.

Finally, I am not hopeful that disaster can be averted by a "constitutional revolution" that would alter the incentive structure of government bureaucrats and place constitutional restrictions on the budgetary and tax powers of legislative bodies. Poggi's line that separates the state from society comes from the societal side.[10] The bureaucrats are not pushing themselves into the autonomous social realm: the "affluents" are pulling them over the line.

PART I

ALTRUISM, AFFLUENCE, AND THE PERVERSITY OF SOCIAL AMELIORATION

CHAPTER 1

THE ALTRUISTIC DESIRE AND POLITICAL ALTRUISM

We must renounce the theory which accounts for every moral sentiment by the principle of self-love.

—David Hume

Benevolence is the heart of man, and rightness his road.

—Mencius

Self-sacrifice is no less primordial than self-preservation.

—Herbert Spencer

Recently economists have shown increased interest in integrating so-called higher or spiritual desires or "innate social values" in an economic framework. Economic nationalism or the desire to have national property controlled by one's national group,[1] the desire to participate in public decision making,[2] and the quest for personal liberation or differentiation [3] are but three examples. Here, we shall study the desire to employ public power to help one's fellow man—that is, political altruism or ameliorative social reform.

David Hume, the eighteenth-century philosopher, maintained that "benevolence" is a basic human instinct (or primary drive).

3

He spoke of such a "principle in our nature as humanity or a concern for others." [4] Similar views were expressed by Adam Smith.[5] Rousseau was certain of a "force of natural compassion" that even "the greatest depravity of morals has as yet hardly been able to destroy" and "by moderating the violence of love of self in each individual, contributes to the preservation of the whole species." [6] Herbert Spencer, the much-maligned giant of sociology, added in 1901: "From the dawn of life egoism has been dependent upon altruism as altruism has been dependent upon egoism, and in the course of evolution the reciprocal services of the two have been increasing." [7] Such assertions, of course, receive introspective support, but they are also consistent with the work of modern ethologists who study whole patterns of animal behavior, comparative psychologists, and sociobiologists. Both the ethologists and the sociobiologists, the latter actually working with models postulating an "altruist gene," [8] believe that natural selection favors a certain amount of behavior having beneficial consequences for a recipient even at some disadvantage to the donor. Examples of the beneficial behavior include: reproductive restraints (e.g., eusociality), sharing of food, territory, and nests; alarm calls by social insects, birds, and mammals at the approach of predators; suicidal behavior of social insects; and defense of apparently unrelated chicks by penguins.[9]

Tullock, among others, has, however, shown in a paper entitled "Altruism, Malice, and Public Goods" that the standard biological theory of altruism needs to be modified when it goes beyond the kin-selection mechanism, which favors altruism among close relatives, to group selection. Much altruistic behavior among humans in present-day Western society is, after all, directed at genetic strangers. However, *given the existence of an adaptive altruist gene, helping behavior, very much like sexual copulation, becomes "sweet" even when it is divorced from the attempt to increase one's genetic representation in succeeding generations.*[10] Humans adopt children and even find their protective instincts triggered by cute puppies. As Pugh points out, such *by-product* altruism illustrates the "difficulty of designing real-world behavioral mechanisms that cannot be triggered by more distantly related individuals." [11,12] It may also reflect the primeval conditions in which the altruist gene evolved, for as Dawkins notes, in nature it is not usual for parents to find a stranger in their nest, and consequently nature has not bothered to make the gene more selective.[13]

The comparative psychologists suspect the existence of a "certain innate disposition toward the acquisition of altruistic behavior . . . as evidenced, for example, in reactions to distress in others." [14] Certainly Aronfreed's survey of experimental data concerning the sharing and aiding behavior of both children and adults is not inconsistent with an altruistic need.[15]

Many economists also accept the idea of a "taste" for altruism. On the assumption that individuals receive pleasure from distributing their wealth to others, they have dealt with charitable donations and philanthropic grants,[16] as well as with "corporate altruism." [17] Economists who have investigated events following natural and other external disasters have shown that prices do not rise as much as they ought to in order to equate demand and supply and that charity by residents of the disaster area increases. Douty has rationalized such behavior in terms of an emergent-altruism, whereas Collard sees it as an elemental desire to restore the social fabric. Formal economic models have begun increasingly to incorporate altruism (and other forms of interdependent preferences).[18] Much of this work is summarized, refined, and improved upon by Collard in his 1978 study, *Altruism and the Economy.*

But why political altruism? Obviously altruistic donors can and do privately reward selected recipients. Nevertheless, there are real advantages to channeling a major portion of these contributions through the state. First, in large, mobile, and complex societies, needy individuals and worthy causes cannot be identified and compared, nor can resource transfers be administered without consuming more of these scarce resources. (As in other kinds of activity, such costs can be reduced by specialization.) Consequently, individuals seeking to maximize their altruistic output are increasingly turning from almsgiving in the classic sense to aiding the needy indirectly by donating to philanthropic organizations.[19] Indirect charity also obviates the need for a painful exposure to the needy, as graphically depicted in 1526 by the scholar Juan Luis Vives in a influential pamphlet advocating a new system of public charity: "Suppose there is at some church or other a high festival drawing great crowds: one has to make one's way into the building between two lines of diseases, vomitings, ulcers, or other afflictions disgusting even to speak of. This is the one same route for boys, girls, old men, pregnant women. Do you think they can all be so made of iron that they would not be disturbed, fasting as they are, at the sight?" [20]

The modern state (one of society's many organizations) employs policemen, clerks, accountants, lawyers, public health experts, and so on, and maintains extensive income tax and other records to carry out its primal functions. Quite possibly there are strong technical complementarities (i.e., mutually reinforcing increases in input productivities and cost reductions) between these primal functions and philanthropic activity. This line of explanation appears to be consistent with historical evidence.

In sixteenth-century England as a result of complete separation of charity from police power, "The honest poor were punished and sometimes fed; the vagabond was fed and sometimes punished." [21] Meanwhile, "in the cities of the Low Countries professional beggars circulated among the various charitable institutions obtaining a pittance from several of them at once, to the detriment of other paupers whose fate was particularly appalling." [22] Not surprisingly, during the sixteenth century, a period of significant population growth and mobility, Europe was swept by a welfare-reform movement. The central idea of the various Poor Laws was to organize and centralize charity under civil, not clerical authorities by registering and aiding the old, sick, and incompetent while simultaneously employing the poor-relief police to ban and punish begging.[23]

Just as passenger conveyors are also efficient conveyors of mail and just as universities efficiently produce research as a by-product of teaching (or is it the other way around?), so the state, with its resources to investigate and punish, is a relatively efficient producer of altruistic output. Thus, a portion of its tax receipts are really voluntary charitable contributions.

Support for this proposition regarding voluntary giving to the state comes from disparate sources. In the ancient world there were no organized charities comparable with those of today in the

United States. In classical Greece the publicly administered funds devoted in whole or part to benevolent purposes were derived in part from private gifts.[24] A similar situation existed in sixteenth-century England.[25] The charitable nature of poor relief by the English state of that era is clearly revealed by the refusal of its legislators to make contributions compulsory until nearly the end of Elizabeth's reign. Until the Acts of 1572, 1576, and especially 1598, the Elizabethans relied with notable success upon statutes that facilitated bequests and enjoined the duty of charity upon all. More than £1.5 million in charitable bequests were made from the end of the fifteenth century until Elizabeth's last years.[26] Moreover, as late as the middle of the next century, voluntary contributions to parish churchwardens were still being turned over to town mayors.[27] In 1693, King William III named a week during which the overseers in London were to "collect the benevolences of charitable people at their dwellings." [28] Much later, in Edwardian times the British Unemployed Workman Act during its first year relied on a special charitable fund amounting to £153,000, which was raised in response to a public appeal by Queen Alexandra.[29] Only a few years ago headlines were made by voluntary private contributions to New York City during its budget crisis.

Consider a second explanation of political altruism. One derives personal benefits of two sorts from one's altruistic contributions: a somewhat better world for oneself and others to live in and a sense of satisfaction from having helped to bring it about. With respect to the latter pleasure, note the first-century C.E. Roman philosopher Seneca's definition of *beneficium* as a "benevolent action which gives pleasure and finds pleasure in so doing" and his dictum that "the reward of all the virtues is inherent in themselves." [30,31] But simultaneously, the altruist produces a public good—a better world for *other* people to live in. This "third-party" benefit must be added to the altruist's private benefit to find the full social benefit. Since, however, marginal social benefits exceed marginal private benefits, voluntary altruistic contributions will fall short of the socially optimal level. In response to this "market failure" situation the prospective donors may agree (at least implicitly) to allow the state to compel *all* to pay taxes in order to move altruistic production closer to its optimal level.[32]

Goldfarb provides not only the mathematics of the "voluntary coercion" argument but the common sense. Assume that the satisfaction of a rich person depends on the satisfaction of the poor, but not on the satisfaction of other rich people. A rich person derives satisfaction from contributing $1 to charity;

> but the loss of $1 grieves him. If . . . the government . . . taxes him (and every other rich man) $1 and gives the total collected to the poor his grief is the same as in the charity case, but his satisfaction is much larger. . . . Thus, he might be unwilling to donate the $1 to charity (the satisfaction being less than the grief), but very willing to vote for the $1 tax (the satisfaction is bigger than in the charity case, and therefore can be greater than the grief).[33]

Support for this model of income transfers is provided by statistical tests carried out by Larry L. Orr with respect to Aid for Dependent Children (AFDC). Orr observed an inverse relationship between the ratio of total AFDC recipients to state population and the average state monthly payment per AFDC recipient.[34]

The earlier argument regarding technical complementarities suggests that the political process and the state are efficient instruments (relative to the market) for forming and enforcing what Goldfarb calls a "charity contract" whose essential content is, "I will contribute $1 if all . . . the other rich people do." [35] None of this, of course, determines the form taken by charity—that is, *aid in kind* versus *aid in cash.* Here we confront a raging debate with theoretical, empirical, and ideological overtones (see appendix 1). The main conclusion is that when both costs and benefits are taken into account the result may contradict the conventional wisdom: in-kind aid can be efficient, whereas a "simplified" system of cash assistance can waste resources.

Finally let us turn to "Robin Hood" altruism. For a definition, we need look no further than to legal philosopher Ronald Dworkin, who provided his no doubt approving readers in the *New York Review of Books* with an admirable slogan: "A more equal society is a better society even if its citizens prefer inequality." On the other hand, Hirschleifer has branded the phenomenon as "moralistic aggression." An emotion of "justice," perhaps genetically evolved, leads third parties to serve as additional enforcers in suppressing antisocial behavior. Sometimes, as in intervention against the neighborhood bully, such suppression is useful. But the present focus is on donors who in order to increase their own altruistic consumption of distributive justice contribute resources to organizations that employ force to transfer income from unwilling selfish or cheating persons to victims and to those in need. Force is, after all, the main business of the state! Contributions take the form of labor, money, and votes to politicians and parties who promise to carry out the desired income transfers upon taking office. Some "Robin Hood" altruists, however, seek to escape from paying their full share of the ultimate cost of a reform because it exceeds their benefit. Here we confront the "limousine liberal," who supports such causes as busing for racial integration and constructing low-income housing projects in more affluent neighborhoods—but not for his own children and not in his own neighborhood. Obviously, "Robin Hood" altruism and "limousine liberalism" are partial, selective, and hypocritical; but they are also genuine to the extent that reform passage costs (in both time and cash), and tax costs are voluntarily borne by the donor.[36]

Note that aid to the poor as a political right and as charity are not mutually exclusive. Taxes paid in response to conditions of technical complementarity or excess of social over private benefits are in fact charity. The government operates as a United Fund. Even "Robin Hood" altruism has its charitable dimension.[37] Of course while the three sources of political altruism and the independent political power of the poor (with their below average voting participation rate) are conceptually distinct, their relative influence in the growth of the welfare state is difficult to disentangle empirically. Nevertheless, it is most important to realize that altruism need not be very widespread in order for it to have a significant redistribution impact. This emerges in rather dramatic form from a simplified model of representative democracy constructed by Hochman and Rodgers. *Given an optimal spatial distribution* and, for example, *that 12 percent of the voters are poor (recipients), only 24 percent of the voters need to be benevolent donors in order to secure passage of a redistribution bill.*[38]

That the demand for private and political altruism would be extremely strong in periods of emergency and suffering such as the beginnings of the sharp economic reorientation in the West in the sixteenth century and the unprecedented world economic crisis of the 1930s is of course easily understood as an aspect of emergent altruism. As Barkun suggests, economic depression is a form of disaster and can accordingly produce the intense psychological and social responses, the mysterious chemistry, usually associated with natural catastrophes.[39] When the Social Security Act of 1935 provided an automatic, continuously available source of unemployment insurance, aid for dependent children, and old age pensions, it responded in a direct manner to obvious problems of the day. Prior to the act, private intrafamily transfers were the main source of emergency support. But as Daniel Orr notes, reliance on intrafamily transfers became "a remote possibility in light of the way that personal wealth was affected by the failure of financial markets and catastrophic unemployment during the early 1930's." [40] With passage of the Social Security Act, the political base for social reform understandably evaporated and the era of New Deal social activism ground to a halt.[41]

It is not only more challenging but also more important to explain what happens to the demand for altruism during periods of unprecedented prosperity and well-being, such as that experienced in the United States since World War II ended. During the same 1952 to 1972 period in which its per capita income in constant dollars increased by 70 percent and the percentage of families with money income less than $5,000 fell from 36.8 to 16.6 percent of its population the nation sought "to eliminate the paradox of poverty in the midst of plenty." This, indeed, became official policy when the landmark Economic Opportunity Act was passed in 1964. In 1891 Herbert Spencer took note of the "curious" way in which "the more things improve the louder become the exclamations about their badness." [42] Unsurprisingly, then, the true paradox here is the sharpened interest in poverty during an era of sharply rising incomes and despite the absence of pressing demands or powerful lobbying groups among the poor themselves! In this connection, Lawrence M. Friedman makes the very important point that the war against poverty or, more generally, the war against social problems, reflected a general demand that existed quite apart from the specific demands of organized groups; the wars did *not* boil up out of demands of special-interest groups such as the poor.[43]

From 1950 to 1970 private philanthropic payments by donors (living donors, charitable bequests, corporate contributions, foundation grants, etc.) increased more than fourfold, from $4.5 to $19.3 billion. By 1975 the total had risen to $26.9 billion.[44] And this increase fails to take into account the estimated value of volunteer labor services that amounted to between 20 and 40 percent of cash donations in 1964–65.[45] Over the 1950–70 period, government "social welfare" expenditures (including education, income maintenance, health, etc.) rose more than sixfold, from $23.5 to $145.9 billion, and, as a percentage of gross national product, from 8.9 to 15.3.[46] By 1975 the percentage had risen to 19.1. During the latter half of the period (1960–70), income maintenance expenditures grew at the unprecedented annual rate of 11.3 percent in 1929 constant dollars.[47] Some perspective is obtained by noting that in the mid-1970s social welfare expenditures were growing twice as fast as gross national product and that in 1975 "social welfare" accounted for 56.0 percent of total government expenditure, more than three times as much as national defense! Finally, government "transfer payments" (social security, public assistance, interest on public debt, etc.) rose from less than 20 percent of government spending in 1952 to 37 percent of the total in 1977; calculated in constant-price dollars, the 1977 figure is almost 44 percent.[48]

Unfortunately, it is difficult to accurately gauge trends in redistribution of income to the poor. One rough but nevertheless revealing indicator is obtained by examining trends in the federal government's expenditures on income transfers through income-conditioned programs. The latter, whose benefits accrue primarily to the poor, include the federal component of Aid for Dependent Children (AFDC); Supplemental Security Income (SSI); medicaid; food stamps; and assorted antipoverty efforts in the areas of manpower, housing, and education. From 1968 to 1975 federal expenditures nearly doubled in real terms (1973 constant-price dollars) from $15.5 to over $29 billion! [49] The increase in expenditures is reflected in the number of persons receiving benefits: from 9 to 16 million for cash public assistance; from 11.5 to 25 million for medicaid; from 2.5 to 19 million for food stamps.[50]

Moreover, during the same 1965–75 period federal expenditures for "social insurance" rose nearly 75 percent in constant-price dollars, mainly on Old Age, Survivors, Disability Insurance (OASDI) and Unemployment Insurance (UI), both of which include significant redistributive components. Taking together the major welfare and insurance programs, federal expenditures rose from 4 to 7 percent of gross national product in 1975.[51] Using family income data altered to include the recipient value of in-kind transfers, Haveman cites studies indicating that from 1965 to 1975 the incidence of officially defined poverty has been "markedly reduced" to "fewer than 5 percent of all household units."[52] Paglin, on the other hand, cashes out housing, nutrition, and medical in-kind programs at market value and concludes that from 1959 to 1975 the poverty rate dropped from 17.6 to 3.6 percent of the population. In terms of absolute numbers the drop is from 31.9 million poor to 7.8 million, or 75 percent. When various statistical anomalies are taken into account, the number of poor in 1975 is 6.3 million persons, and the poverty rate is only 3 percent.[53] But Browning points out that such studies "have considered only about half of all in-kind transfers, and therefore substantially understate their actual impact." He estimates that "the average poor family in 1973 had an income 30 percent *above* its poverty line" and adds that in 1972 the net income of the lowest fifth of the income distribution was $76 billion with about two thirds of this or $50 billion in the form of cash transfers, education benefits, and other in-kind benefits.[54] Lynn presents data on changes in the "poverty gap"—that is, the total number of dollars required to bring every low-income family up to a minimum decency level such as the SSA "official" poverty lines. In millions of 1972 dollars the official census poverty gap was $11,845 in 1968 and $12,032 in 1972, or roughly constant. However, the picture changes dramatically when the official census poverty gap is revised to take into account the rapidly growing in-kind benefits, income misreporting, and redefinition of the accounting units: for 1968 the gap is $8,330, and it drops sharply to $5,353 in 1972. The revised gap is 70.3 percent of the official gap in 1968, but owing largely to the growth of in-kind benefits it is only 44.5 percent in 1972.[55]

The above data are incomplete with respect to several rapidly growing types of government expenditure and also fail to take account of private philanthropic transfers to the poor, and of the leveling due to the rapid growth of social security wealth.

For example, Aaron notes that "Between 1970 and 1975, social security wealth increased almost sevenfold, rising from 29 percent of net worth to 94 percent. . . . In short, a form of wealth distributed far more evenly than other assets. . . . has been growing . . . rapidly. . . . The result has been an equalization of lifetime capacity to consume that is unrecognized in any official statistics."[56] As for private philanthropy, in 1965, 7 percent of such payments went to "human resources" (welfare), and about 25 percent went to this category plus "health." Very rough calculations by Weisbrod and Long indicate that in 1965, 20 percent of volunteer labor time went to "social welfare" and 37 percent went to "social welfare" plus "health."[57]

With respect to government, the first omission is of expenditures arising from attempts to restructure social institutions to benefit the poor by means of minimum wage laws, equal opportunity laws and regulations, community action agencies, legal services, busing schoolchildren for racial integration, and more. The federal government budgeted $513 million for "civil rights enforcement" in fiscal year 1978. This figure will continue to rise in the near future. Second, the poor are concentrated in urban centers, where they receive significant benefits from government expenditures for police and environmental protection. Obviously, Browning's estimate of a 6 percent of gross national product transfer to the poor in 1973[58] is a very conservative one, but whatever the exact figure, there is no doubt that redistribution to the poor has increased sharply from 1950 to the present.

As already noted, much altruistic production by government is not reflected in "transfers" and "social welfare." An upper-limit view on government altruistic expenditures is provided by the growth of the "welfare state," that is, of government expenditures for domestic programs. Freeman observes:

> It required 163 years, from 1789 to 1952, for government expenditures for domestic programs to reach $34 billion; in the succeeding 20 years they virtually exploded from $34 to $257 billion. . . . An over sevenfold growth in domestic programs signifies a decisive change in the role and nature of domestic government in the United States.[59]

Of course, the expenditure change since 1952 is overstated because of inflation, but Freeman's overall conclusion is well taken. From 1950 until 1970 governmental spending (except for defense and defense-related sums) rose from 16.2 to 25.4 percent of gross national product. "Civilian" spending grew at an annual rate in 1929 constant-price dollars of 6.6 percent from 1960 to 1970.[60]

To conclude our survey of the growth of altruism in the United States, we shall examine the dramatic growth in federal regulation. From 1970 to 1977 the number of major federal regulatory agencies rose from twenty to twenty-seven, and the total annual budget jumped from $1.6 to $8.2 billion.[61] It is most important to realize that the expansion of regulatory activity has occurred primarily in the areas of health, safety, consumer protection, affirmative action, and the environment. The new regulatory agencies such as Equal Employment Opportunity Commission (EEOC, 1964), Environmental Protection Agency (EPA, 1970), Consumer Product Safety Commission (CPSC, 1972), and Occupational Safety and Health Administration (OSHA, 1977), which are concerned with serving the "public interest" and solving social problems, now overshadow older agencies like the Interstate Commerce Commission (ICC, 1887), Federal Trade Commission (FTC, 1914), Federal Communications Commission (FCC, 1934), and Civil Aeronautics Board (CAB, 1938). The latter agencies were originally intended to restore competition or to regulate natural monopolies, but over the course of time they became responsive primarily to the special interests of the regulated industries.[62] In recent years older agencies such as the Food and Drug Administration (FDA, 1931) have gained new force. An overall perspective is provided by Lilley and Miller who have grouped regulatory agencies into "old-style economic regulators" that typically focus on "markets, rates, and the obligation to serve" and "new-style social regulators" that focus on "the conditions under which goods and services are produced and the physical characteristics of products." From 1970 to 1975 "new-style" expenditures rose by $2,802 million to a total of $4,251 million while "old style" spending rose by $262 million to a total of only $428 million.[63]

Altruistic production, however, is not always commensurate with altruistic public expenditure. Other barometers of the growth of regulatory activity are available. From 1970 to 1975 the number of pages published annually in the *Federal Register* rose from 20,000 to over 60,200, or 201 percent! Also over this period the number of pages in the *Code of Federal Regulations* grew 33 percent, from 54,000 to 72,000.[64] For the federal government as a whole, the number of administrative law judges who preside over regulatory hearings has increased from 196 in 1946 to 1,100 in 1977.[65] Moreover, little data exist regarding the *private* expenditures called forth by regulation. It has been estimated that the regulations of EPA will cost the economy an additional $40 billion per year by 1984.[66] One firm, E.I. Du Pont de Nemours & Company spends $5 million annually to file 15,000 federally mandated reports.[67] Another, Dow Chemical, U.S.A., estimates that federal regulations cost it $147 million in 1975, of which more than one third is "excessive by the standards of good business practice." Dow's expenditure jumped to over $186 million in 1977.[68] The Federal Communications Commission imposes reporting requirements that consume an estimated 30 million employee-hours per year, and it costs business about 250 million hours to comply with only three of the Internal Revenue's Service's reporting requirements.[69] Private firms overall have been estimated to spend between $25 and $32 billion a year filling out federal forms and questionnaires.[70] According to a *New York Times* report, "Government regulation is perhaps the biggest growth industry in Washington, spawning the opening of scores of new law firms devoted mainly to handling matters posed by the flurry of new directives" while established firms with "headquarters in other cities have opened branch offices . . . to help clients with regulatory difficulties." [71] *Newsday* adds that "with new education laws, regulations, and court decisions . . . the role of school attorney has evolved from that of an occasional adviser to the pivotal position of constant consultant." [72]

Robert DeFina of Washington University places the question of the private costs of federal regulatory activity in a general conceptual framework.

> A rational approach to the problem of determining this effect entails a "fiscal farsightedness," since every dollar spent in the administrative operation of a regulatory program has a multiplier effect in the private sector, in the sense that regulations require expenditures for compliance. This final burden takes the form of both direct outlays by business and resulting higher prices to consumers for products produced by these businesses.

DeFina refers to a recent study in which several federal regulations and regulatory commissions were examined with respect to cost estimates (but not cost effectivenss). For the several categories investigated, DeFina estimates total regulatory costs of $65.5 billion in 1976. This estimate includes $3.2 billion in federal "administrative costs" plus $62.3 billion in private sector "compliance costs." Finally, in view of sharp increases in federal regulatory budgets since 1976, DeFina finds "it is clear that this figure of $65.5 billion is an underestimate of the present situation." [73] For one of the areas not covered by DeFina, Housing and Urban Development, a recent study by the Rutgers University Center for Urban Policy Research estimates that government delays and regulations add 1 to 2 percent per month to the price of a new house. In addition, a federal task force has concluded that federal, state, and local government regulation are prime factors in escalating housing prices.[74]

CHAPTER 2

ALTRUISM IN THE AFFLUENT SOCIETY

It is quite true that man lives by bread alone—when there is no bread.

—Abraham H. Maslow

Life involves, before anything else, eating and drinking, a habitation and clothing. The first historical act is thus the production of the means to satisfy these needs. . . . But as soon as a need is satisfied new needs are made.

—Karl Marx and Friedrich Engels

The values of Western publics have been shifting from an overwhelming emphasis on material well-being and physical security toward greater emphasis on the quality of life.

—Ronald Inglehart

Diverse social scientists and social critics have in one way or another asserted a positive effect of income levels on manifestations of altruism. On one side are the "sociological" formulations of Veblen, Schumpeter, Spencer, Sumner, Kristol, and Nisbet. On the other are the "microeconomics" formulations of Schultz, Fabricant, Allvine and Tarpley, Banfield, and Buchanan. (The positions of these scholars are summarized in appendix 3.) Here, we

17

shall expand on these insights and place the question of the relationship between altruism and income in a more general and systematic framework. In sections 1 and 2 the desire for altruism is placed in consumer-choice frameworks inspired by the psychological literature of the "growth actualization" school. Appendix 4 applies Becker's economic theory of "social interactions." In both cases careful attention is given to the theoretical implications for the income elasticity of demand (i.e., the percentage change in altruism resulting from a 1 percent change in income). Section 3 reviews behavioral evidence relating to the income elasticity. The impact of income on the structure of demand—political versus private altruism—is analyzed in section 4. Section 5 closes the chapter with a discussion of other politically significant higher desires.

(1) GROWTH ACTUALIZATION THEORY

The best-known exponent of the growth actualization school is Abraham Maslow. Briefly, this view of personality is that human beings have basic inborn needs over and above the physiological. These needs must be satisfied if an individual is to enjoy "mental health." Further, the basic needs are arranged in a "hierarchy of relative prepotency"; only after a more basic or "lower" need is satisfied does the next, or "higher need, become a motivator. Recognizing that most individuals are at the same time partially satisfied in all their basic needs and partially unsatisfied in all their basic needs," Maslow denies that a need "must be satisfied 100 percent before the next emerges." However, Maslow seems to slide into conceptual difficulties when somewhat later he states that "a satisfied need is not a motivator." [1]

The five basic need areas or motivators identified by Maslow are (in order of decreasing strength): physiological, safety, belongingness and love, esteem, and self-actualization or self-fulfillment.[2] Obviously these areas are vague and ambiguous. Where does physiological need end and the desire for comfort or amenity begin? Is there really a difference between love and esteem? Exactly what does Maslow mean when he describes self-actualization as a desire "to become everything that one is capable of becoming"? [3] In spite of these problems, it is eminently plausible and consistent with Maslow's analysis to expect that individuals typically will turn as their purchasing power increases from the satisfaction of lower, more material, more urgent needs, to higher but less urgent spiritual needs.

Indeed, this expectation is broadly confirmed by a survey study of values administered in April 1968 by the National Opinion Research Center (NORC) to a sample of American adults. It was found that *a comfortable life* ("a prosperous life") was valued more highly by the poor than by the rich, whereas a *sense of accomplishment* was ranked more highly by the rich than by the the poor (see table 1).

The working hypothesis of this study is that altruism is one of the higher desires. Indeed, this is in accordance with Maslow's vision of the "self-actualizing" individual who rises above the distinction between selfishness and unselfishness and derives as much pleasure from the pleasure and self-actualization of *others* as from his own! [4] For Maslow, then, self-fulfillment involves altruism. The hypothesis also receives introspective support and seems consistent with the Freudian view of a "turn from egoism to altruism" in the development of young children which the psychiatrist Rochlin describes as involving a modification of the "center of interest in the self into a gratifying investment in another, in a cause, or in an ideal." [5]

Empirical support for the place of altruism in the Maslovian need hierarchy has been provided by anthropological research, voting studies, public opinion survey data, and econometric studies. According to Ronald Cohen, anthropologists have observed a change in the character of giving from Neolithic societies (less wealthy in terms of per capita consumption) to more wealthy post-Neolithic societies: "Whereas giving is reciprocal among hunters, it is both reciprocal and progressively more redistributive among post-hunters who farm, keep cattle, or both." [6] Cohen also draws the conclusion from his own field experience and the ethnographic literature that affective responses such as empathy and sympathy are more pronounced in (wealthier) Western societies than in other (less affluent) societies.[7]

TABLE 1
Median Rankings [a] of Values in the 1968 National
Opinion Research Center Survey of American Adults
for Groups Varying in Income (Sample Size, N = 1,325)

Value	Under $2,000 (N = 139)	$2,000 –3,999 (N = 239)	$4,000 –5,999 (N = 217)	$6,000 –7,999 (N = 249)	$8,000 –9,999 (N = 178)	$10,000 –14,999 (N = 208)	$15,000 and over (N = 95)
A comfortable life	7.2	8.5	8.4	8.1	10.0	11.0	13.4
An exciting life	15.3	15.4	15.6	15.4	15.4	15.2	14.3
A sense of accomplishment	10.4	10.3	9.1	9.4	8.4	7.6	6.1
A world at peace	2.7	3.1	3.2	3.4	3.9	3.8	3.5
A world of beauty	13.6	12.7	13.5	14.0	13.8	13.7	12.6
Equality	7.0	8.5	8.3	9.0	7.8	9.7	7.5
Family security	5.6	4.6	3.6	3.2	3.2	3.6	4.1
Freedom	6.8	5.2	5.2	5.4	5.9	5.9	5.0
Happiness	7.7	8.0	7.1	6.9	7.6	8.1	9.2
Inner harmony	11.6	10.9	10.8	10.5	10.2	9.9	9.2
Mature love	14.4	14.0	12.3	12.2	10.8	11.5	11.8
National security	8.9	9.5	9.7	9.5	9.3	9.4	11.3
Pleasure	13.6	14.5	14.7	14.7	15.1	15.0	15.2
Salvation	6.6	7.3	9.4	8.4	8.6	10.1	13.3
Self-respect	7.9	7.2	7.6	8.4	7.9	7.2	7.8

Value	Under $2,000 (N = 139)	$2,000 -3,999 (N = 239)	$4,000 -5,999 (N = 217)	$6,000 -7,999 (N = 249)	$8,000 -9,999 (N = 178)	$10,000 -14,999 (N = 208)	$15,000 and over (N = 95)
Social recognition	13.6	13.9	14.8	14.6	14.2	15.1	14.6
True friendship	7.9	8.5	9.2	9.9	10.1	9.7	9.4
Wisdom	8.7	8.5	8.8	7.0	8.1	7.4	5.6

Source: Rokeach, p. 60.

[a] The median of the rankings assigned to each of the 18 listed values by the individuals in the specified income group.

The previously cited 1968 NORC survey of American values reveals, not surprisingly, that *equality* (brotherhood, equal opportunity for all) receives its highest ranking in the under $2,000 income group. More interestingly, the ranking of *equality* tends to decline to a minimum in the $10,000 to $14,999 income group and to rise perceptibly in the $15,000 and over income group (see table 1). Economists Hochman and Rodgers have manipulated survey data in order to focus more directly upon the income distribution preferences of the *nonrecipients* of welfare spending (an income of $7,000 being taken as the breakpoint). They examined voter responses to questions in several California polls in 1970 and estimated that at least 50 percent of the middle and upper classes were benevolent. The latter estimate was obtained by subtracting from the percentage responding that "welfare is a moral imperative," the percentage responding that "welfare prevents crime." This second percentage was taken to reflect self-interest. Obviously, this procedure is very rough, but it is of interest to note that " 'net' benevolence thus measured, varies directly with income." The computed frequencies rose from 39 percent in the $7,000 to $10,000 income class to 56 percent in the more than $20,000 income class.[8]

Additional evidence of an ecological nature, suggesting that the demand for altruism increases with income (i.e., that it is a superior good), is provided in a study of voting behavior carried out by Wilson and Banfield. They observed a positive relationship be-

tween median family income in a political ward (taken to represent property tax payments) and the percentage yes vote on such
expenditure measures as "County Hospital," "Tuberculosis Hospital," and "Welfare Levy" in Cleveland and its suburbs. This
positive relationship, it should be remembered, exists even though
higher-income individuals bear the property tax while the benefits
are reaped primarily by indigents.

Ronald Inglehart, in his study *The Silent Revolution,* examined
1972–73 public opinion survey data for the United States and ten
Western European nations. He classified those individuals stressing "maintaining order in the nation" and "fighting rising prices"
as "Materialist," while those stressing "giving the people more to
say in important political decisions" and "protecting freedom of
speech" were classified as "Post-Materialist." Inglehart found that
wealthier countries tend to have relatively high proportions of
individuals stressing higher-order or Post-Materialist values.[9] In
addition, 1973 surveys included data on family income which
showed "a weak but consistent relationship with value type: those
with higher incomes are more likely to be Post-Materialists. There
is an average difference of about 10 percentage points between
the lowest income group and the highest."[10] Truly, as pollster
Louis Harris observes, "America is Karl Marx upside down": on
the issues of the 1960s and 1970s (e.g., consumerism, pollution,
women's liberation, race, abortion, and communism), "the under
$5,000 income group could be found consistently to be on the side
of resisting change, while . . . in the $15,000 and over income,
people were tuned in to change."[11]

With such a variety of supporting evidence, the next step is to
place Maslow's analysis within the framework provided by modern consumption theory. The nonspecialist reader is invited to
skip the indifference curve analysis: the main conclusions are
summarized and extended at the end of section 2.

(2) MICROECONOMICS OF GROWTH ACTUALIZATION

To facilitate the exposition, all other higher needs are ignored
and the consumer is viewed as a rational altruist choosing, subject
to a budget constraint, only between "others' necessaries" *(N)* and

"own amenities" *(A)*. It is assumed that the relative prices of goods included within N do not change with respect to each other, so that they may be combined in a single good. Similarly, all amenities are lumped in A. This permits us to carry on the analysis with the two-dimensional figure 1.

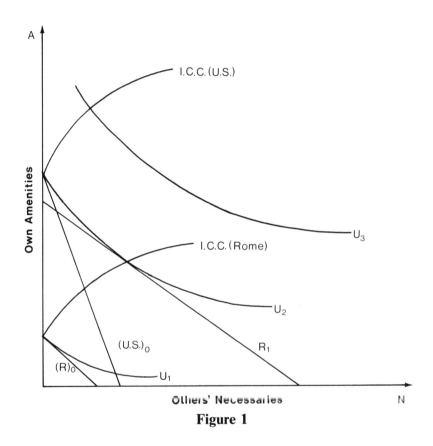

Figure 1

U_1, U_2, and U_3 are indifference curves; $(R)_0$ and $(R)_1$ are (parallel) Roman budget lines; $(U.S.)_0$ is a United States budget line; $(U.S.)_0$ is steeper than $(R)_0$ to reflect the lower relative price of A in the United States; *I.C.C. (R)* and *I.C.C. (U.S.)* are the respective income consumption curves.

Over an initial range of income the U.S. consumer (having satisfied the "own necessaries" desire), would spend all or virtually all of his or her income on A, but relative prices of N to A constant, when income had risen sufficiently both the absolute level of N and the ratio of N to A would begin to rise. That is, the income elasticity of demand for "others' necessaries" is positive and exceeds that for "own amenities" (see figure 1). In short, the modern technologically equipped household becomes less insistent about its need for additional amenities. It is not required to delve into the consumer's state of mind, but Maslow's motivating needs might be identified as those with the highest income elasticity.

Relative prices of N to A do differ from one society to another. Even today's poor American has easy access to amenities (personal transportation, temperature control, entertainment, plumbing, etc.) outside the reach of the wealthiest individuals of past centuries. Technological progress has decreased the relative price of "amenity," and economic theory predicts that any given level of real income (utility) would therefore be "produced" in a more amenity-intensive manner.[12]

To take account of discrepancies in the ratio of N to A it is not necessary to resort to taste (or cultural) differences or to ad hoc consumption theories stressing relative incomes or rates of change in income as opposed to absolute income. As the figure suggests, the American and the Roman simply move along different income consumption curves.

Summarizing: (1) altruism represented by "others' necessaries" is viewed in the growth actualization framework as a higher desire; (2) as money income increases the quantity of altruism demanded increases both absolutely and relative to lower desires represented by "own amenities"; (3) since technological change has lowered the relative price of amenities, the modern consumer chooses to purchase more "own amenities" relative to "others' necessaries" than would, say, a Roman consumer enjoying the same level of real income (i.e., satisfaction).

The above conclusions are consistent with the observations of economic historians. Cipolla, for example, concludes from his examination of sixteenth- and seventeenth-century budget data, "even when it had overtones of extravagance" the consumption of the rich "never showed much variety. The . . . state of the arts did not offer the consumer the great variety of products and services which characterize industrial societies."[13] Zimmern reminds his modern reader that the ancient Greeks were "civilized without being comfortable"; they "sat at the table of life without expecting any dessert," and because of this they "saw more of the use and beauty and goodness of the few things which were vouchsafed them—their minds, their bodies, and nature outside and around them." [14] The rich Greek or Roman of antiquity, being necessarily "poor" in amenities by present standards, chose his consumption bundle accordingly. He was as much or more concerned with spiritual desires, with questions of human character and duty, than is the affluent American.[15]

Of course the indifference curve analysis has ignored the possibility that preferences, or what economists call utility functions, have changed. One great mind, David Hume, would have upheld the assumption of constant preferences: "Would you know the sentiments . . . of the Greeks and Romans? Study well the actions of the French and English. . . . Mankind are . . . much the same in all times and places." [16]

(3) DEMAND FOR ALTRUISM: CHARITABLE GIVING

Does the evidence for donations lend support to the preceding argument? [17]

Philanthropic contributions by living donors increased by more than 3.5 times from 1950 to 1970. Do contributions rise with income? What about the percentage contributed? Individual income tax return data for 1970 showing philanthropic contributions as a percent of adjusted gross income (AGI) are shown in table 2. The pattern is U-shaped: the percentage donated declines up to an income of $10,000 to $25,000 and rises thereafter. The initial range of the curve is, however, suspect for several reasons. Most important, small givers contribute mainly to religious organizations, whereas large givers contribute mainly to educational institutions and hospitals.[18] However, as Schwartz suggests, many religious contributions are not philanthrophy but "literal service charges imposed by one's church." [19] Most obvious in this regard are contributions that in reality are payments for attendance in parochial schools. Second, the lower-income group includes a larger fraction of older persons and of others whose income is understated because it is tax exempt.

TABLE 2
PHILANTHROPIC CONTRIBUTIONS [a] AS PERCENT OF ADJUSTED GROSS INCOME [b] IN
INDIVIDUAL INCOME TAX RETURNS WITH ITEMIZED DEDUCTIONS (UNITED STATES, 1970). [c]

Income (thousands of $)	Contribution (%)	Income (thousands of $)	Contribution (%)
1–2	6.1	25–50	2.6
2–3	5.4	50–100	3.3
3–5	4.3	100–500	5.7
5–10	3.0	500 +	13.3
10–25	2.4		

SOURCE: Goode, Table A-9, p. 307.

[a] Gifts (cash and property but not personal services) by private donors to U.S. organizations: religious, charitable, scientific, literary, educational, veterans, governmental, hospitals, etc.

[b] Adjusted gross income is income net of business costs, but before personal exemptions.

[c] In 1970 about nine tenths of estimated total contributions were claimed as itemized deductions. The upper limit on deductions is in general 50 percent of adjusted gross income. In 1970 about 43 percent of all taxpayers employed the standard deductions option.

Another troublesome problem is that the true cost or "price" of contributions (relative to the price of own consumption) falls as income rises. This happens, of course, because the tax rate rises with income (see table 3). The picture of the impact of income on contributions can be clarified by considering the income parameter derived from an explicit statistical model.

Even a casual examination of such evidence reveals that the parameter estimates are subject to a wide range of uncertainty.[20] However, for several reasons Feldstein's results are probably the most reliable and may be summarized as follows:

1. Income level and charitable giving vary directly.
2. The impact of income on giving sharpens as income rises. The income elasticity is 0.7 in the $4,000 to $10,000 class and 1.4 in the over $100,000 class.
3. When (as is appropriate) religious contributions are excluded, the estimated impact of income increases. In a majority of cases the income elasticities exceed unity, and

in one instance the elasticity is 1.9. That is, the percentage increase in contributions is nearly 2 times the percentage increase in income.[21]

TABLE 3
EFFECTIVE INCOME TAX RATES ON INDIVIDUAL INCOME (UNITED STATES, 1970).

Income (thousands of $)	Actual Tax Rate	Income (thousands of $)	Actual Tax Rate
2–3	1.4	15–20	12.4
3–4	3.4	20–25	14.2
4–5	5.0	25–50	17.4
5–6	6.3	50–100	25.2
6–7	7.2	100–150	29.6
7–8	7.9	150–200	30.2
8–9	8.6	200–500	30.4
9–10	9.3	500–1,000	30.7
10–15	10.3	1,000+	31.4

SOURCE: Goode, Table A-11, p. 309.

Let us take a brief look at corporate giving, which tripled between 1950 and 1970. Obviously the profit motive is quite important here,[22] but it is still of some interest to glance at the relationship between giving and corporate income. Nelson, utilizing aggregate annual data for 1936 to 1963 and taking account of the "price" of contributions (complement of the tax rate), found that a 1.0 percent increase in corporate net income after taxes led to a 1.05 percent increase in contributions.

It is difficult to determine the proportion of government expenditure belonging in the philanthropic category. We are reminded by Tullock that a sizable fraction of "social welfare" expenditures ends up as transfers back and forth within middle-income groups rather than to persons below some "poverty line." [23] Indeed Browning estimates that less than half the expenditures are transferred to those in the poorest quarter of the population.[24] It does not follow, however, that transfers within the middle class (or, more generally, within any income class) necessarily reflect "selfish" as opposed to generous motivations. First, allowance must be made for the nontrivial administrative and psychological costs of distinguishing between deserving (i.e., poor) and nondeserving recipients. More basically, the gift (via government) by a healthy, childless, nonveteran, middle-class person to a hospital, school, or veteran is no less generous because the recipient is another middle-class person. In all such cases there is no quid pro quo other than the satisfaction one human being derives from helping another fulfill certain valued needs. After all, the word "philanthropy" literally means love of mankind. The point is that "recipients of 'welfare' need not be poor, only eligible." [25]

But what lies behind this eligibility? A number of psychological studies suggest that individuals are more likely to help others who are similar to themselves.[26] Such findings are in turn consistent with a variety of evidence.

From a global perspective, the American poor are themselves middle class. Nevertheless, Americans are decidedly more generous with native poor. Feelings of sympathy do not stop at a country's borders, but generally speaking they become considerably less intense. Another example is provided by the so-called Puritan ethic. Middle-class donors have always been suspicious of "idlers" or the "improvident" poor and have sought to favor the "honest" or "deserving" poor, with whom they can more readily identify.[27] Animal field studies also reveal that altruism is more common among closely related than among distantly related individuals.

Conceivably, human as well as the animal behavior may be manifestations of kin selection, one of the most cogent explanations of the biology of altruism: the selection value of altruism increases as the proportion of genes is common between donor and recipient increases.[28] Is socioeconomic similarity (like physical similarity) a function of genetic relatedness? It is much more reasonable to assume that we are dealing here with by-product altruism. For example, our sympathy for the hunted baby harp seals, suggests psychologist Willard Gaylin, "arises from an aesthetic bias that is very much related to the natural tendency to care for the young and to visualize any young in terms of *our* young." [29] From the perspective of by-product altruism, benevolence directed at similar but genetically distinct individuals becomes a special kind of "local" public good. Communities, after all, need not be spatial.

The existence of a progressive income tax can be taken as a piece of evidence that is consistent with the hypothesis that the demand for altruism is income elastic.[30] Note further that in an August 1972 Harris Survey, 73 percent of the $15,000 and over income group favored "tax reform" with the rich paying more, in comparison to a quite similar percentage of 76 for the presumed beneficiaries in the under $5,000 income group. A final piece of evidence is provided by a statistical analysis carried out by Larry L. Orr that shows a strong direct relationship between state per capita income and average state monthly AFDC payments. A $1.00 increase in real state per capita income raises real AFDC payments for a family of four by about $0.43 in 1963–67 and by $0.64 in 1968–72.[31]

Clearly, a variety of factors other than income growth have contributed to the explosive growth of "social welfare" expenditures or, more generally, of the welfare state. These include a rise in the relative price of government services coupled with an inelastic demand; imitation of trends elsewhere in the world (e.g., Sweden and the Soviet Union); an increased desire to be insured against the consequences of becoming ill, poor, and so on; [32] demographic changes; the political power of rent-seeking vested interest groups (including both benevolent and nonbenevolent bureaucrats); the rise in the relative importance of taxes on human versus nonhuman capital in government budgetary revenues; [33] and philosophical changes in general.

So the linkage of income growth and altruism is only part of a complex story, but how important a part? From 1950 to 1970 current-dollar "social welfare" or welfare state expenditures grew 6 to 7 times while gross national product in current dollars increased about 2.7 times. A unitary income elasticity of demand for altruism would, therefore, "explain" about 40 to 45 percent of expenditure growth. If, taking an upper-limit view, the income elasticity were as high as 2, 80 to 90 percent would be accounted for.[34]

(4) DEMAND STRUCTURE: POLITICAL VS. PRIVATE ALTRUISM

It seems reasonable to assume that increases in the production of aid for one's fellow would be the outcome of increases in both political and private altruism. However the "market failure" and (perhaps) the "technical complementarity" arguments of chapter 1 suggest that in affluent societies, taxes will be substituted for private charity as the preferred means of income redistribution. The underlying reasoning for the prediction derived from market failure is provided by Goldfarb:

> the more rich people there are, the larger will be the transfer to the poor which results from a $1 tax on each rich person. Thus, in a society with . . . "few" rich people [the rich] will not view taxes as having a large advantage over charity, whereas in a society with . . . "many" rich . . . there would be a bigger advantage to taxes over charity.[35]

Briefly, as the proportion of rich persons to a (constant) total population increases, so does their psychic income return from a given tax scheme; hence, the ratio of political to private charity rises. The implications of technical complementarity are not nearly so clear-cut but may be in the same direction. More affluent societies will tend simultaneously to be more complex societies (e.g., urbanization, specialization). It does not seem unreasonable to expect that increased societal complexity would in turn increase the efficiency of the state relative to private philanthropic organizations in the production of altruistic goods.

For a private good, each individual gets his own amount. But in the case of public goods individuals have available to them the total amount of the good. Weisbrod's theory of the provision of public goods by voluntary (nonprofit) organizations also seems to predict that affluent societies will substitute political for private altruism. First, Weisbrod notes that the government may not provide a public good even though many citizens desire it.[36] In this event, frustrated demanders will be forced to turn away from more efficient production by the state and resort to production by voluntary organizations. However, Weisbrod does not really explain why the frustrated demanders would not secure state provision by giving their gifts directly to the state as was done in classical Greece and sixteenth-century England. Weisbrod's argument holds only if some sort of "friction" or state supply lag is introduced or, alternatively, if the majority (or the rulers) are actually opposed—that is, if the community is heterogeneous in tastes, interests, or the amount of information.[37] Under such circumstances it is reasonable to join Weisbrod in expecting the voluntary sector to precede the government sector in the provision of public goods. Weisbrod concludes that later on "perhaps in response to economic development [which can be equated with affluence], the number of positive demanders might increase and so the government would become a provider of the good involved." [38,39]

To summarize: *the arguments presented in this chapter suggest not only that affluent societies will desire more altruism but will also substitute political for private altruism.* The evidence in the United States is consistent with these predictions. From 1950 to 1970 per capita income in constant dollars increased roughly 70 percent. In 1950 the ratio of government "social welfare" expenditures to private (noncorporate) "philanthropy payments" was 5 as compared with more than 7 in 1970. For the more inclusive "government expenditures on domestic programs" the corresponding ratios rise from 6 to more than 13. Both private and political altruism are increasing strongly in absolute terms (see chapter 1), but more and more, government production dwarfs private production. The British experience appears to have been quite similar. During the period after World War I, if not earlier, British philanthropy evolved into the "junior partner in the welfare firm." [40] While full documentation would require a significant research effort, it seems quite possible that the above comparisons actually underestimate the sharpness of the trend in the substitution of political for private altruism.

Whatever its validity for other types of government expenditure, Adolph Wagner's famous law predicting a rising share as income rises [41] *may very well hold for altruism.*

(5) OTHER POLITICALLY RELEVANT HIGHER DESIRES

Turning briefly to a different desire, Monsen and Downs, economists, speak of a "Law of Consumer Differentiation," which "involves an income elastic desire to express individuality within some larger group." This is exemplified in the affluent United States in the revolt by middle-class youth against middle-class "materialism," which has taken such forms as the "use of drugs, new sex customs, and shabby dress." [42] Kahn and Wiener add "strange and exotic" political ideologies and religions and a "cult of aestheticism: for the upper middle-class adults." [43,44] The economic historian Cipolla, observing historical "empires," concludes that once the privileged group has satisfied its "elementary and normal needs" there is a "natural tendency . . . to move towards excesses and to strive for abnormal sensations and unnatural experiences." [45] For Fairlie's *Spoiled Child of the Western World* the true meaning of "liberation" is a "rebellion of the self . . . against a lack of opportunity for self-realization which is perceived as being in great part the result of the learned attitudes and behavior of the individual." [46] Kahn and Wiener suggest the paradox that the affluent society may "decrease the individual's economic frustrations but increase his aggression against the society," which in turn leads to alienation.[47] Obviously, the desires for personal liberation, differentiation, and novelty need not be fulfilled in a pathological or politically significant manner, but such patterns appear to loom large in determining the course of history. Extreme impatience with the failure to fulfill such desires may result in profound social problems.

Finally, in support of a desire for wisdom there is introspective evidence, the observations of psychologists such as Maslow [48] and the speculations of Kahn and Wiener regarding the affluent society of the year 2000:

We can imagine a situation in which, say, 70 to 80 percent of people become gentlemen and put a great deal of effort into various types of self-development. . . . one could imagine, for example, a very serious emphasis on sports, on competitive "partner" games (chess, bridge), on music, art, languages, or serious travel, or on the study of science, philosophy, and so on. The crucial point here is that a large majority of the population may feel it important to develop skills, activities, and knowledge to meet very high minimum absolute standards, and a large minority more or less compete to be an elite of elites.[49]

More concretely, the 1968 NORC survey of American values reveals that affluent individuals rank *wisdom* more highly than poorer ones (see table 1). I suspect that the desire for wisdom is the highest desire and that its fulfillment may ultimately serve to rescue human society from the cycle of decline triggered by affluence and acting through perverse social reforms.

CHAPTER 3

PERVERSITY OF POLITICAL ALTRUISM

A prosperous society will decay as soon as evil ceases.
                              —Bernard de Mandeville (1724)

Behavior patterns that may have been adaptive under biological conditions are inappropriate and even dangerous under the cultural innovations of today.
                              —David P. Barash

The typical citizen drops down to a lower level of mental performance as soon as he enters the political field.
                              —Joseph A. Schumpeter

Banfield has noted with some apprehension that in our affluent society "large numbers of persons are being rapidly assimilated to the upper classes and are coming to have incomes—time as well as money—that permit them to indulge their taste for 'service' and doing good in political action." [1] Banfield's apprehension is based on his belief, which I share, that the political expression of this taste for "doing good" or "reforming" is perverse. I do not wish to imply that altruism in general is perverse; that would be nonsense. Altruistic codes and conduct not only play an important role in nonmarket resource allocations but also contribute to the

34

smooth functioning of markets by taking the place of law and regulation and by reducing the costs of information, contract making, and enforcement.[2] Phelps eloquently summarizes the latter aspect.

> The adherence to certain altruistic precepts and traditions by the participants in commercial markets makes a crucial contribution to the national income and thus, very likely, to Bentham-Bergson economic welfare. The price system would work less well, and would be less widely applied, were it not that the economic agents—portrayed by the Walrasian model of the price system as flint-hearted maximizers—in fact display a decent regard for the interests of those with whom they exchange and for society as a whole.[3]

Clearly, some altruism is better than none. But how much is enough?

I believe that altruistic behavior becomes counterproductive in an affluent society whose real income has attained a level that markedly increases the demand for altruism. The problem is not simply one of private altruism (good) versus political altruism (evil). Of course it is true that (largely) in response to the economic forces discussed in section 4 of chapter 2, individuals as they become richer increasingly desire to substitute political for private altruism. But altruism becomes dangerous because of the range of policy options available, the kinds of options selected, and above all the massive scale and persistence with which the attempt to improve society is carried through.

An amusing and revealing example is provided by the situation in Milford, Illinois. There, the baby-sitters who operate informal day-care centers in their homes are quitting rather than submitting to a state licensing law that would require investigations and unscheduled visits. Naturally the loss of their baby-sitters has greatly upset the working women, who wonder why their choice is being taken away. The answer is provided by the state licensing coordinator: "If we protect the users of other services, why shouldn't we protect the user of day-care services?" [4]

More generally it appears obvious to the well-to-do Establishment that reforms of the market system ranging from laws mandating minimum wages, maximum housing rents and natural gas prices, and minute details of business management, to those requiring the outlawing of pay toilets (New York State) [5] will help the poor, the disadvantaged, and the gullible (or vulnerable) individual while discomforting only his or her exploiters; that is, employers, slumlords, retailers, and manufacturers. Such beliefs are on a par with the "simple folk image of the flat earth with the sun and heavenly bodies pursuing their courses across the dome of the sky." [6]

The welfare system, too, is considered by this same Establishment as a means of equalizing income distribution instead of helping those *temporarily* in need together with the disabled, aged, orphaned, and widowed, that is, the "deserving" poor of all societies. Applauded by the Establishment are court orders and Department of Justice consent decrees forcing employers to ignore considerations of genuine productivity potential in favoring hiring according to racial, ethnic, or sexual criteria. Hailed as a milestone in human progress is also the 1975 Supreme Court decision *(Goss* v. *Lopez)* to grant "due process" to public school children (suspension or expulsion only after the close equivalent of a criminal trial). In another triumph in the "war against unjust accusation" the federal courts have ruled that dangerous and destructive tenants in housing projects can be evicted only after a long process that includes an evidentiary hearing, at which the victims of violence must testify. Busing schoolchildren for the purpose of racial integration, building low-income housing developments in the suburbs, privacy laws,[7] rehabilitating criminals and reforming prisons, or softening the rigors of military life and diluting military codes all find justification in terms of some humanitarian argument.

In all these and many more instances the Establishment altruists failed to draw a connection between the policies they desire and newly emerging social phenomena they deplore, including mass unemployment of ghetto youth, deterioration and abandonment of buildings and even entire city sections, energy "shortages," breakup of families, a public school system devoured by discipline problems and "race riots," terror in housing projects, permanent wards of the state, soaring crime rates and brutalization of the aged, urban bankruptcy, and ineffective and extravagant armed services. The resentments engendered by the perverse policies are mainly redirected against various target groups in the population such as "middle-class racists," teachers, oil companies, "slumlords." One reform follows another, calling forth yet another "overload" on government in the name of altruism.

Why does the affluent Establishment that seeks to do good support dangerous or even disastrous reforms? Is there a social mechanism linking altruistic reforms with social disasters? The remainder of this chapter is devoted to answering these questions. First, however, the concept of "perversity" should be made more complete.

An altruistic donation (act, reform, policy) is judged perverse if, after taking account of his or her direct psychic income from having made the donation, the donor suffers net harm. Obviously, this is a "consumer"-oriented definition: an altruistic policy yielding net benefits to the recipients while causing net harm to the donors is "perverse." On the other hand, altruistic reforms causing the recipients to suffer net harm (a minimum wage law?) would very likely (but not inevitably) cause net harm to the donors as well, and thus qualify as "perverse" reforms. A clear example is provided by a marginal tax rate sufficiently high to so reduce labor supply (and production) that the amount transferred to recipients is reduced.

(1) REASONS FOR PERVERSITY: RATIONAL IGNORANCE

One explanation advanced is that the political altruism of the well-to-do rests on flimsy foundations, that is, that their convictions are only skin deep. What they are really searching for, according to DeMuth, are "opportunities for dramatic self-expression." This desire manifests itself in adopting moralistic and abstract attitudes that mostly do not correspond to the practical approach, which, as DeMuth points out, "requires attention to the base as well as the noble in human affairs." [8] Schumpeter goes even further. He maintains that the basic cause is sheer *ignorance*. Even if alternative social policies could be experimented with, according to Schumpeter, the results would still be quite difficult to interpret. In the absence of hard data and the underutilization of those available, it is therefore easy for politicians to take credit, for example, "for vanquishing polluters while making no disclosure to the public of how much the cleanliness will cost them." [9] James Wilson shrewdly observes that although they form the "audience" for reforms intended to aid the urban poor, the affluents really fail to see the show. Because many of them have moved out of cities, they have little direct experience with the results of the programs they sponsor. By increasingly performing for the audience rather than for their constituency, urban politicians have "nationalized" the urban crisis and, thereby, intensified it. Undoubtedly the most satisfying scene is the slumlord being run out of town. How is the suburban audience to know that city-employed bureaucrats are inadequate as replacements for these hard-core tenement owners? [10]

Moreover, the applicable social science theories are often quite sophisticated. The case for capitalism, Schumpeter explains, "could never be made simple. People would have to be possessed of an insight and a power of analysis which are altogether beyond them."[11] The heirs of capitalist development are outraged by the existence of poverty without having the slightest understanding of why they are rich! How many of them have grasped Hayek's crucial point that:

> The frequent recurrence of . . . undeserved strokes of misfortune affecting some group is . . . an inseparable part of the steering mechanism of the market: it is the manner in which the cybernetic principle of negative feedback operates to maintain the order of the market. It is only through such changes which indicate that some activities ought to be reduced, that the efforts of all can be continuously adjusted to a greater variety of facts than can be known to any one person or agency, and that utilization of dispersed knowledge is achieved on which the well-being of the Great Society rests.[12]

Charles L. Schultze, chairman of President Carter's Council of Economic Advisers, is convinced that "no one but economists (and not all of them)" really understand how markets operate. "Somehow the cars get into the showrooms and the loaves of bread onto the grocery shelves, but the whole thing is like an oft-repeated highwire act: we don't really understand how it's possible, but it's been done so often we are no longer surprised." [13] A good analogy.

But people understand far less than they are capable of. The more complete explanation is hinted at in Schumpeter's observation that "without the initiative that comes from immediate responsibility, ignorance will persist in the face of masses of evidence." [14] Given the difficulties of understanding social science theories and, of equal importance, the negligible influence *one* individual can exert on social policy, even the most altruistic person would likely conclude that the cost exceeded the expected return in social improvement. *Altruism in no way excludes rational calculation, and under the circumstances it is irrational to delve beneath what is "obvious" or "common sense."* Milton Friedman's rule that "it is against the private interest to vote in the public interest" [15] obviously applies. The altruist's lack of diligence in learning more about the social problems he or she wishes to solve is an aspect of *rational ignorance*. While the nonaltruist may be as ignorant as the altruist, his ignorance is nonoperational since he is not seeking to reform society.

Individuals do try to reduce the cost of decision making. One rational response to the high ratio of information cost to return is the tendency of each individual to let his or her personal experience serve as a rule of thumb in evaluating remote situations with the natural result that alien interests, traditions, and the likes are often discarded as unreal.[16] Obviously, such myopia can be disastrous.

The question remains: Why should the "obvious" or "common-sense" or personal experience be consistently perverse with respect to current public policy questions?

(2) REASONS FOR PERVERSITY: COUNTERINTUITIVE
COMPLEX SYSTEMS

Jay W. Forrester has suggested that complex systems are "counterintuitive": "Choosing an ineffective or detrimental policy for coping with a complex system is not a matter of random chance. The intuitive processes will select the wrong solution much more often than not." [17]

Let us proceed to develop the line of reasoning that underlies this uncomfortable assertion. Intuitive responses have usually been developed in the context of "first-order, negative-feedback loops." We can see them, for example, when hands too close to the stove get burned, hands too far away become cold. The effect of distance from the stove is not only direct but rapid.[18] To this it may be added that altruistic responses to strangers are learned or evaluated in the context of the possibilities of privation, danger, or physical diasters. (Indeed, altruistic responses in such circumstances may have been genetically selected over the course of prehuman and human evolutionary development; see chapter 1.) Accordingly, Barton notes:

> The suffering . . . has simple and understandable causes, and the remedies lie ready at hand. If people are injured, take them to a doctor, if they are homeless, shelter them; if they are hungry, feed them, if they are trapped in wreckage, free them.[19]

Being predisposed or having learned to look close to the symptoms for the solution of a problem, we approach complex systems in this way. But the cause that seems so plausible is, in this alien context, only a coincident occurrence. The cause itself is a mere resultant. The policies designed to cope with the plausible cause will instead have detrimental "side effects" that may easily worsen the problem. The cogency of Forrester's position is easily demonstrated by reviewing a number of major social reforms.

If we wish to achieve an objective X, it is quite "natural" for us to specify the required behavior in law. Yet consider a relatively simple economic reform, a minimum wage law: the wage rate is not the only "state variable" determining income; furthermore, its effect on the employment rate (the other state variable) lags behind. A recent statistical study by Mincer demonstrates the following conclusions regarding the employment effects of minimum wage legislation: (1) labor moves out of the covered sector into the uncovered sector, reducing wages in the latter; (2) people leave the labor force; (3) labor becomes unemployed; (4) for a 1 percent increase in the (relative) minimum wage rate, the employment rate (ratio of employment to population) declines by the following percentages—0.20 white teens, 0.46 nonwhite teens, 0.18 white males (20–24), 0.35 nonwhite males (20–24).[20] Teenagers and blacks taken as *groups* are almost certainly made worse off by increases in the level or coverage of minimum wage laws. However, public welfare programs partially compensate and possibly, in some instances, more than compensate for income losses due to disemployment.[21] In addition to becoming unemployed or receiving lower wages in the uncovered sector, they also tend to be shunted into part-time jobs that provide little meaningful on-the-job training.

Perhaps somewhat optimistically, Gramlich has found that adult women may derive a net benefit from minimum wage laws. Another "unforeseen" and as yet unmeasured consequence of minimum wage laws is a deterioration in working conditions. As Alchian explains, displaced employees will offer to forsake some of such things as coffee breaks, vacations, cleanliness, a more leisurely pace, and the like, in order to be paid the higher legally required minimum wage rate.[22]

Browning has stressed the crucial role of voter ignorance in explaining the perennial appeal of minimum wage laws.

Ignorance of the unemployment effects is probably important, but it is not the sole factor. More important is the fact that the average person who is not directly affected by the law is unaware of the indirect cost he bears in the form of a lower wage rate and/or higher product price. If this is the case, or if he believes that employers do bear the cost in the form of reduced profits, he could be expected to favor a minimum wage law over a cash transfer under which he must pay part of the cost in the form of harsher taxes.[23]

Note with respect of Browning's final point that to the extent the voter believes the cost of the minimum wage law is absorbed by the employer he is a "Robin Hood" altruist or "moralistic aggressor" (see chapter 1).

Consider the following "mystery": between 1952 and 1972, a period of general prosperity, the number of Aid to Families with Dependent Children recipients increased by 456 percent while the under 18 population rose by 41 percent; in 89 percent of the cases the father was 'absent from home.' Freeman explains that because "the average monthly benefit of AFDC families more than doubled, $82 to $191, a 133 percent increase during a period when consumer prices rose 58 percent," therefore it is not surprising that AFDC has "replaced employment as the normal source of sustenance for over three million women and men." [24] AFDC, which was regarded at its creation in 1935 as a source of income in emergency situations, evolved into a variety of guaranteed income paid to over 90 percent of all households eligible for benefits.

Nor is it surprising, since the increasingly attractive benefits were not available to male-headed families, that AFDC contributed significantly to the destabilization of family structure. Levitan and Taggart refer to a cross-sectional study of 1970 data for 44 metropolitan areas that found that for a 1 percent increase in the AFDC stipend the proportion of nonwhite women heading families rose by roughly 0.2 percent.[25] The latter authors also estimate, probably conservatively, that 40 percent of the increase in nonwhite mothers on AFDC might be attributed to a rise in the propensity to head families with children.[26] Thus, it would appear that millions were being spent on a program that was intended to preserve a family setting for children but that actually encouraged marital dissolution.[27]

Small wonder also that the number of welfare recipients in New York City more than doubled between 1966 and 1971 when the monthly allowance, including that of rent, for a family of four increased by 73 percent.[28] The city's standard benefits (AFDC, medicaid, food stamps, and free school lunches) amounted to substantially more than could be earned in many low-skilled jobs: $5,500 tax free or the equivalent of gross annual pay of $7,000.[29] This, it may be added, fails to take account of the subsidies provided by New York's large public hospital and housing systems and other public services.

More generally, the existing econometric studies agree that income maintenance plans reduce work incentives: fewer hours are worked, or individuals withdraw entirely from the labor force.[30] However, the magnitude of the impact is not certain.[31] Recently, however, the Rand Corporation released an adjusted analysis of 1,300 New Jersey and Pennsylvania families that had participated from 1967 to 1970 in an experimental program to determine effects of a negative income tax (N.I.T.). John Cogan found that *white male* heads of households on the average *worked five to seven hours less a week* if they received the payments! "This represents a large and statistically significant labor supply withdrawal particularly so because male heads of households are considered the group least likely to respond to the work-discouraging elements of N.I.T." The findings—unadjusted for biases—of the Seattle and Denver guaranteed income experiments, which included 5,000 families, were that an income guarantee of $3,750 in 1974 and a marginal tax rate of 70 percent would have the following *national* effects: "husbands would reduce their work effort 11.2 percent, wives by 32.2 percent, and female heads of families by 9.4 percent." [32] Anderson, A Senior Fellow of Stanford University's Hoover Institution, roughly adjusted the Seattle-Denver findings for several rather important biases and reached this conclusion: "The amount of work reduction ranges from a low of 22 percent to a high of 69 percent for husbands, from 35 percent to 75 percent for wives, from 46 percent to 75 percent for dependents, and from 19 percent to 71 percent for female heads." [33]

Next, "to estimate the *total amount of work reduction* that would be brought about by a guaranteed income," Anderson weighted the above estimates by the relative importance of the four categories of workers in the total low-income work force. The result is striking:

If it happened that all the bias estimates . . . were accurate, we could expect that the institution of a guaranteed income in the United States would cause—in round numbers—a minimum of a 30 percent reduction in the work effort of low-income workers. We could also expect that there would be a reasonably good chance that the amount of work reduction could be as high as 50 percent. And there would be the remote possibility that it could exceed 70 percent.[34]

Welfare payments make poverty less harsh to bear, but as van den Haag nicely puts it, "once poverty becomes a marketable service, its supply rises as does the price it brings . . . relative to other services." [35] Childbearing, marital or family disruption, drug addiction, sickness, or selectivity thus easily reduce one's employability without one's necessarily resorting to false or illegal methods. This application of the law of supply illumines a variety of current issues including the ongoing crisis in the Social Security System, excessive and escalating medical care costs, and the lengthy average duration of unemployment. I take these up in turn.

Recently benefit payments have exceeded tax receipts, leading to a precipitous dwindling of Social Security Administration trust funds. This led Congress in 1977 to pass a massive increase in social security payroll taxes: the tax rose in 1978 and each year thereafter until 1990 unless inflation halts. A major contributing factor has been the spectacular growth of the disability insurance program. Outlays have been rising at an average annual rate of 21 percent for five years while it is estimated that the number of recipients will rise from 4.8 to 10 million by the year 2000.[36] Originally the program had provided for monthly cash pensions to severely disabled workers at age 50 so that they would not have to wait for an old age pension at 65. First the minimum age provision was dropped, and in 1958 dependents became eligible to collect. Perhaps more significantly the benefit structure was made more and more generous. In 1977 a young married worker with a child could get as much as $1,051 a month tax free plus medicare (in 1979 the corresponding figure dropped to $904). In 1976 a House subcommittee estimated that some young disabled workers could receive benefits up to 38 percent higher than their after-tax earnings prior to disability! Thus, during a period in which it has become easier and more worthwhile to claim benefits, the number of recipients has risen to 4.8 million instead of the "mere" 1 million predicted in 1956. To be eligible a worker must suffer a

> physical impairment . . . of such severity that he is not only unable to do his previous work, but cannot considering his age, education, and work experience engage in any kind of substantial work which exists in the national economy, regardless of whether such work exists in the immediate area in which he lives, or whether a specific job vacancy exists for him or whether he would be hired if he applied for work.

But what is meant by the capacity to do "substantial work"? How would a social security official measure it? Surely it is not surprising that larger pensions coupled with the lack of objective criteria for determining eligibility have caused an increase in the "supply" of severely disabled persons.[37]

Feldstein presents arguments and evidence suggesting that the primary effect of our system of unemployment insurance is not to lower unemployment by raising aggregate demand for goods and services but to create unemployment by impairing the incentives of both workers and employers. Most obviously, the system reduces the cost of increasing the period of unemployment for those who are already unemployed. Feldstein calculated that (contrary to popular belief) "unemployment insurance currently replaces *two-thirds* or more of lost net income," and he presents a detailed example in which an individual who "stays unemployed for 11 weeks instead of 10, . . . loses an additional $120 in gross earnings but only $15.50 in net income. The reward for working is less than $0.50 per hour. The implied tax rate is 87 percent." [38] Moreover, this $15.50 in income would at least partially be offset by work-related expenses. Under the circumstances, why not spend the extra week looking for a slightly better job, or working around the house, or simply taking a vacation! Such responses are rational from the unemployed individual's point of view but are inefficient for the economy as a whole because the production value of the "lost week" exceeds the benefits of the unemployed individual. A study cited by Feldstein suggests that currently the lost productive time may amount to 540,000 man-years annually. In addition, Feldstein believes that the present system "provides both employers and employees with the incentive to organize production in such a way that increases the level of unemployment by making casual jobs too common." [39]

Federal medicare and medicaid programs, which reimburse hospitals individually on the basis of the costs each has incurred, promote the escalation of medical costs. Here the side effect is the positive incentive for each hospital to add high-cost technology and services.[40] Medicaid itself was something of a legislative accident. Apparently to meet the charge that medicare served the medical needs of the nonaged poor, a $15 billion medicaid program was appended late in the day and without any debate to the 1965 medicare legislation.[41] At the time Medicaid was virtually ignored, but once in place it became increasingly generous and mushroomed into an enormous program in terms of both expenditures and numbers of recipients.[42] Soon HEW Secretary Califano was saying that without "cost-restraints" (i.e., direct regulation of the practices of individual hospitals and even medical practitioners), "federal spending . . . would climb between 1978 and 1982, to $66 billion." [43]

One plan [44] would limit revenue increases for acute-care hospitals to about 9 percent per year excepting only wages of nonsupervisory personnel. The controls would be administered by medicare, medicaid, state agencies, and private insurers. Also a national ceiling would be placed on capital expenditures at about half the $5 billion spent for this purpose in 1976. The ceiling would be distributed among the states according to population factors, construction costs, and the "need" for expansion and modernization. Administration of capital expenditures would be placed in the hands of local health-systems agencies. It can, of course, be predicted that the implementation of such plans will encourage the use of labor-intensive techniques while control over capital expenditures will operate to inhibit the use of beneficial new medical technology. As a stopgap, Califano announced new HEW regulations limiting medicare payments for the twelve most commonly done laboratory tests and for medical equipment bought or rented by patients "to the lowest price that is widely available for the same quality in a particular community," instead of paying on the basis of average charges or even higher ones as was done previously.[45]

Additional examples of "making problems worse by making them more profitable." [46] are not difficult to find. It may come as a shock to the consumerist movement, but Peltzman concludes that one result of his econometric study of automobile safety regulation is that it "has not affected the highway death rate." [47] Is it possible that drivers have offset the technological improvements by taking greater accident risks? The latter, remember, would include driving a greater number of miles. As Alchian notes, individuals prefer a "balanced package, so they will trade off some of the greater safety for a less attentive, easier, more extensive driving." [48] Similarly, prison reformers might be disturbed by findings that rehabilitating criminals in order to lower the rate of recidivism may end up increasing it because of the improvement in the quality of prison life. Thus a *New York Times* story [49] reveals that "despite" having "one of the most progressive and humane" prison systems, the Swedish rate of return "is over 70 percent—as high as anywhere in the world." All prisoners are given individual rooms that resemble university student quarters. (The word "cell" is frowned upon.) Prisoners serving less than a year are sent to institutions without walls or fences where they may hold civilian jobs, sometimes at the going wage rate. One open institution "offers" sauna baths, swimming, skiing, and a golf driving range. The closed prisons are relatively relaxed and provide for conjugal visits at least once a week and three-day furloughs for all but a few high-risk prisoners. "Mr." Björklund, an eight- or -nine-time loser, who is head of the Central Organization for Prisoners, states that "the living conditions in our prisons are quite acceptable and certainly no deterrent to crime." (Is his honesty the best policy for criminals?) All this has led Sweden's chief prosecutor to moan that "Our philosophy of rehabilitation has been shipwrecked." [50]

Urban policy provides many additional examples of the perverse side effects of humanitarian reforms. Conventional urban tax policies and administrative regulations penalize the most pro-

ductive while attracting to the cities the least productive. As Forrester concludes, the result is to "produce economic decline and
trap in poverty the very people they are designed to serve." [51]

Turning to rent controls, New York City represents the most
infamous example, but controls are also operating in about 175
New Jersey cities; Boston and three other Massachusetts cities;
the District of Columbia; and various cities in Alaska, Maine,
Virginia, Maryland, and Connecticut. As if to illustrate San-
tayana's warning that "those who cannot remember the past are
condemned to repeat it," political pressure for new rent controls is
endemic.[52] The "past" in this case is distressingly consistent. An
apartment specialist with the National Association of Home
Builders (NAHB) claims that in Washington, D.C., rent controls
have not only caused a decline in maintenance but an unwillingness to start or finance new projects due to the fear that controls
will spread.[53] No matter, Lehman College of CUNY Distinguished Professor of Economics Robert Lekachman explains rent
control by asserting that "the construction industry has lamenta-
bly failed to provide anything like the needed quantities of low
and moderate housing." [54] Despite Lekachman, the attempt "to
provide occupancy rights against harsh evictions" nevertheless
produces housing shortages and deteriorating or abandoned housing. President Carter was afforded a rubble-strewn demonstration
of this during his "sudden and dramatic trip" to the South Bronx
where he found the "devastation that has taken place" to be "very
sobering." [55] Predictably, the president said that the federal government should do something to help, but that "something" did
not include the suggestion that rent controls be abolished.[56]

The ironies of housing policy do not end with rent control. The
impact of a merciful social policy toward *rent evasion* must also be
considered. Roger Starr, former head of New York City's Housing
and Development Administration, has told this story.

> To begin with, courts have increasingly found themselves re-
> luctant actually to order evictions from rented homes,
> even for such summary delinquencies as the failure to pay
> rent. . . .[57] HUD itself issued draft eviction regulations in the
> late spring of 1976. They stipulated that those enjoying

federal housing benefits could not be evicted for nonpayment of rent without a full evidentiary hearing.[58]

The Department of Housing and Urban Development's requirement of an evidentiary hearing is no small matter, since instead of a summary proceeding in which the tenant must produce rent receipts or canceled checks, the landlord must prepare a case and produce witnesses while coping with the inevitable delays in court and requests for adjournments. In addition, in order to uphold the dignity of the welfare recipient the federal government penalizes states that try to protect the owner by issuing two-party rent checks. If checks payable jointly to landlord and tenant exceed 10 percent of the total checks issued, the excess may be deducted from the total federal grants coming to a state.[59] Starr concludes that "more tender attitudes toward rent delinquency" have discouraged new ownership of and investment in housing with a consequent reduction in the supply of housing. This reduction involves not only private but public (i.e., governmental) investors who "hesitate to commit resources to an increasingly hazardous enterprise." [60]

In the name of equality of educational opportunity, particularly to benefit black students, HEW and the courts have mandated citywide busing to racially integrate the schools in such cities as Detroit, Dayton, Denver, Boston, Memphis, San Francisco, Dallas, Indianapolis, and Los Angeles. The result has been a rapid exodus of white children from city schools. James S. Coleman has summarized some of the salient facts.

In Boston, there was a loss of about 4 percent per year of white students before partial desegregation occurred in 1974. In 1974, there was a loss of 16 percent; and in 1975, when Phase II went into effect . . . there was a still further loss of 19 percent. . . . In Denver the white student population was almost stable before desegregation, averaging a one percent loss per year. After partial desegregation in 1970, the white student loss was 7 percent per year for the next six years, leaving only 64 percent as many whites in the Denver schools in 1975 as in 1969. In Dallas, the loss of white students . . .

was less than 2 percent per year until partial desegregation in 1971; since then, the loss has been about 9 percent a year, again leaving only 64 percent as many whites in the schools in 1975 as in 1970.[61]

In 1975 when a policy was initiated to bus children from Louisville into its suburbs in Jefferson County there was an exodus into nearby Bullitt County, outside the court's jurisdiction.[62] Orfield in a Brookings Institution study claims that busing across suburban boundary lines is the only approach that will work in the "long run" for big cities. He fails to warn us, however, that in an even longer run the bus may have to be replaced by the transport jet or ocean liner. In any event, in 1978 the voters of Cleveland responded to federal court-ordered busing by voting down the school tax, which plunged the school system into chaos.[63]

But who exactly is leaving? Coleman points out that "it is those with higher income and education who leave cities in which busing is instituted, and *not* those who are more prejudiced." [64] Thus, contrary to its purported goals, busing may actually operate to intensify racist sentiment in the cities.[65] In another ironic twist, the New York City Board of Education responded to HEW charges of illegal segregation in classrooms by blaming federally mandated programs: about 90 percent of the segregated classes were ordered by a federal court decree requiring bilingual classes for Hispanic children who wanted them as well as Title I remedial classes, which are federally financed under HEW's authority.[66]

A flight from the cities has also been encouraged by federal efforts on behalf of persons accused or convicted of crimes. Federal policies, as Coleman notes, "are largely directed toward insuring that the have-nots receive equal protection from the law." He continues that they generally involve (as in the famous *Miranda* case) "intervention on behalf of a defendant who appears helpless with few resources monetary or otherwise." [67] The lengths to which this is being carried is illustrated by a federal judge in Connecticut who ordered the early release of a convicted bank robber because the prisoner's constitutional rights had been violated while he was in prison.[68] Earlier in Alabama after Judge Frank M. Johnson's sweeping remedial order of January 1976 to correct such violations as overcrowding, filth, inadequate food and medical care, the state, unable (or unwilling) to bear the cost of eliminating the deficiencies, "released 2,000 of 5,400 prisoners on parole, to work release programs, and to halfway houses." [69] The Supreme Court's Arkansas prisons decision (June 1978) will inevitably lead prisons to disgorge additional predators upon the hapless public. Meanwhile, U.S. District Court Judge William Wayne Justice, a self-described "populist," has ordered the Justice Department to join a suit against the Texas Department of Corrections. The latter's defense counsel contends that compliance with Justice Department guidelines would mean that all fifteen units of the prison system would have to be replaced at a cost of possibly $1 billion.[70] When the crime rate rises, as it must in response to declining deterrence, the law-abiding citizens who can afford to flee from the concentrations of have-nots into the suburbs or even rural areas.[71]

Is it only a coincidence that the almost forgotten scourge of protectionism has enjoyed a massive revival in the very industries who receive the greatest impact from altruistic government regulation? The textile industry estimates it will have to spend $6 billion over the next five years to comply with two OSHA regulations intended to reduce noise and dust in the mills. Meanwhile, the U.S. has participated in negotiations with the developing countries to extend a worldwide pact on textiles called the Multifiber Agreement to include new understandings calling for further constraints on imports into industrial countries.[72] The steel industry has been forced to spend $3 billion to control air and water pollution and will, very probably, have to spend an additional $5.5 billion in the next six to eight years to comply with EPA directives.[73] The industry also groans under the burden of 5,600 regulations from twenty-seven different agencies, with OSHA alone accounting for 4,000 rules.[74] The Carter administration has sought to help domestic producers amid well-publicized charges of "dumping" on the parts of foreign steel producers. (But an FTC study found little dumping by foreign producers and concluded that the Japanese were doing well in the American market because their production costs were relatively low.) [75] Carter's plan has been to reduce steel imports by means of a system of

mandatory trigger or reference prices for from forty to sixty prin-
cipal categories of imported steel. These trigger prices, calculated
with the aid of Japanese cost data, would be set close to domestic
price levels. The FTC staff report cited above calls this a "per-
nicious" form of trade restriction that will cost American consumers more than $1 billion annually. The loss to consumers may
be even greater in the long run. *Regulation* [76] points out that the
reference price system will lead to an intensification of foreign
competition for "indirect steel exports," including ships and automobiles. In the not very distant future then, the government may
find itself amid renewed cries of dumping, imposing import restrictions on products in which steel is an important component.

Admittedly the air and water are purer and the factories are
more pleasant, at least usually. However, suspicion is mounting
that air pollution regulations contributed to five grain elevator
fires that killed sixty-two persons in the winter of 1978. Apparently rules imposed by the states in response to EPA directives for
a reduction in elevator dust vented outside the structures ended
up increasing the amount of dust inside the elevators. This increase, in turn, raised the risk of explosion. According to *Business
Week*,[77] OSHA, which is responsible for safety in the workplace,
"failed to see what was happening and to impose rules to prevent
it." But does the average American really come out ahead? More
specifically, as Allvine and Tarpley [78] point out, the stringent environmental standards of the 1980s calling for the steel industry to
remove the last 5 or 10 percent of its pollution may be more costly
than the entire first 90 percent. Surely, it is justified to wonder
whether such a massive commitment of resources and sacrifice of
alternative goods is justified by the incremental benefits of a
cleaner environment. In this connection it is most important to
note that improvements in air and water quality are due mainly to
rather simple changes rather than to the expensive and bureau-
cracy-ridden federal-state discharge regulation controls. Edwin S.
Mills [79] points out that improvement in water quality has been
due largely to local sewage plant construction. This is in effect an
improvement in the public provision of indirect-discharge services, whereas air quality improvement is due mostly to the substitution of clean for dirty fuels.

As a final example let us recall the celebrated natural gas short-age of the winter of 1976–77 with its 65 degree homes and en-forced factory closings. It is well to note that beginning in the 1950s the Federal Power Commission, in order to keep down prices to consumers, effectively enforced a price ceiling on natural gas sold to interstate pipeline companies. The shortage of natural gas assumed monumental proportions when such variables as higher oil prices and a cold winter significantly increased the de-mand, but the shortage itself was caused by the FPC's decision to hold prices below the market-clearing level.[80] Field price regula-tion discouraged the development of new gas production technol-ogy and inhibited the search for new gas reserves. Indeed, U.S. production of natural gas stagnated at the start of the 1970s and began to decline in 1972. Smaller gas supplies in turn increased the demand for substitutes such as oil and electricity, so that these prices tended to rise. Consequently the latter, more numerous group of consumers were made worse off by natural gas price controls.[81] The controls also encouraged the "leakage" of natural gas to unregulated industrial or intrastate consumers, who paid three to four times the permitted interstate price.[82] Excess de-mand for gas at the regulated price created a nonprice rationing dilemma in the Northeast. Since industrial use of gas as a boiler fuel was considered "inferior," industry was encouraged to relo-cate to gas-producing states (the Sunbelt states) where gas was available to firms willing to pay the prevailing market price.

The central conclusion of a sophisticated econometric study by Breyer and MacAvoy is that:

new reserve supplies might have been three times greater, and immediate production twice as great, if there had been no field price regulation. The higher market-clearing prices would have brought forth additional discovered reserves more than twice the entire amount of additions to interstate inventory over the 1961–1968 period.[83]

But the evidence that natural gas supplies would be quite price responsive was ignored if not suppressed. The conflict and confu-sion go on, and at this writing it remains to be seen whether the

Natural Gas Policy Act passed late in 1978 will allow us to "come out of the cold." Moreover, if price controls on gasoline are not lifted gasoline shortages will become a permanent fact of life.

(3) CONCLUSIONS

The arguments and illustrations regarding the perversity of altruistic social reform must now be generalized and extended. An excellent beginning is provided by F. A. Hayek in his *The Mirage of Social Justice.*

> There can be little doubt that the moral feelings which express themselves in the demand for "social justice" derive from an attitude which in more primitive conditions the individual developed towards fellow members of the small group to which he belonged. Towards the personally known member of one's own group it may well have been a recognized duty to assist him and to adjust one's actions to his needs. This is made possible by the knowledge of his person and his circumstances. The situation is wholly different in the Great or Open Society. Here the products and services of each benefit mostly persons he does not know. The greater productivity of such a society rests on a division of labor extending far beyond the range any one person can survey.[84]

Thus, in complex societies there are always "hidden causes" whose impacts are counter to the desires of the rationally ignorant, intuitive reformer. "Suppressing one symptom only causes trouble to burst forth at another point." [85] In short, *when confronted by a counterintuitive social system the rationally ignorant affluent-altruist will overestimate benefits and underestimate his personal cost.*

In his book on *Second-Order Consequences* Raymond Bauer observes that "if even only a few innovations have serious wide-ranging consequences, society may be drastically changed." [86] Further, since the process by which presumed solutions may actually worsen a problem is not understood, Forrester predicts "downward spirals" in which the bad medicine is intensified so that matters become still worse.[87] Kahn and Wiener describe the possible sequence of events as follows:

1. A series of relatively small changes are proposed.
2. In each case the changed situation is preferable . . . to the old situation.
3. The changes are cumulative.
4. Once the series of changes has been made people think of the new situation as undesirable or disastrous. . . .
5. Yet it is now impossible to reverse the sequence because of irrevocable changes, too great an investment, or changed values.[88]

Thus it would seem the problems attacked by political altruists in an affluent society reach a point or a technique is employed (at the secondary or tertiary reform level if not at the primary) at which the overall effect becomes perverse. This undoubtedly is the road along which the United States has been speeding, but the data are not available to gauge exactly the distance traveled or the possibility of a U turn.[89]

CHAPTER 4

PUBLIC POLICY ENTREPRENEURS AND INTELLECTUALS

The strong hostility of most intellectuals toward Madison Avenue is possibly due to the rivalry between the two groups.
—George J. Stigler

On learning of Samuel Johnson's remark that patriotism is the last refuge of the scoundrel, Roscoe Conkling, a New York politician widely acquainted with scoundrels, remarked that Dr. Johnson had overlooked the possibilities of the word "reform."
—James Q. Wilson

Government itself has become the most affluent institution of the affluent society.
—Richard Rose and Guy Peters

Under the circumstances described in chapter 3 it is only natural that various sorts of public policy entrepreneurs will supply altruistic social programs that are subsumable to the conventional wisdom of the obvious (or "folk science" or "pop Marxism"). "Liberal" politicians who seek to stay in office or to join foundations or university faculties never tire of proclaiming the need to "reorder national priorities." The strong demand for altruistic po-

56

litical reforms invitingly opens doors of political action to the group of wealthy public-service-oriented families Karl calls the "philanthropic elite." The Kennedys, Rockefellers, Roosevelts, and Stevensons are among those belonging to this group. Conservative politicians hope to capitalize on the anger of the less affluent lower middle class ("middle Americans"), but to do so they must first avoid the fatal scorn of the well-to-do. This is accomplished by urging such panaceas as "revenue sharing" and by rebuking such strawmen as civil servants and labor unions. And then there are the intellectuals:—the "new class" that has assumed prominence in the so-called postindustrial society.

These "powers of the spoken and written word" [1] or "knowledge workers" are not satisfied simply to interpret social phenomena; they also attempt to *influence* and *transform* them." [2] Some of them may be "theologically oriented" converts to a "socialist myth of redemption" [3] who as victims of "educated incapacity" [4] flee from reality,[5] and as a result become alienated [6] in a capitalist society. Under the freedom of choice that capitalism permits, it is quite possible, as Shils [7] maintains, that "the diverse paths of intellectual creativity, as well as an inevitable tendency toward negativism, impel a partial rejection of the prevailing system of cultural values."

On the other hand, in complex societies the "prevailing system of cultural values" is not all that monolithic, and none of this necessarily "impels" intellectuals to express their tension by advocating altruistic political reforms. In fact, they have done so rarely. Such intellectuals might prefer to confine themselves to criticism of intellectual authority or of the sociocultural sphere. They may even participate in the political arena by advocating the cancellation of altruistic reforms or the introduction of non- or anti-altruistic reforms (e.g., intellectual supporters of Hitlerism and Stalinism). Although Eisenstadt [8] does not overlook the standard treatment of intellectuals as critics and "would-be guardians of a society's 'conscience'—but only when that conscience was thought to be opposed to the established order," he stresses the historical importance of intellectuals as "creators and carriers of tradition." Tussman [9] adds that a specialized kind of intellectual, the artist, is almost invariably cast "in the role of rebel as if he is doomed by his insight to be against his society." But "art has a celebratory as well as an oppositionist function," and for each "Aristophanes leading a great prolonged Bronx cheer from the gallery" there is an "Aeschylus celebrating Athens and the Law, the taming of the Furies."

Of equal or even greater importance is the (whispered) fact that the typical intellectual is a good businessman. As Alan A. Walters [10] notes, "to do well and good at the same time is an achievement." Intellectuals in the Middle Ages concerned themselves with justifying rule by tradition and later on by "divine right," or by the "people." They have flattered and pleased princes and wealthy patrons, serviced a new urban bourgeoisie in the Renaissance or a military-industrial complex in the United States of the 1950s, and asserted that dialectical materialism or inheritance of acquired characteristics constitute true science. Capetian monarchs of the thirteenth century "neither founded nor permitted to be founded any new universities" that might compete with Paris and subsequently found that "each time its opinion was sought the university produced the answer the king wanted." [11] Von Martin [12] noted that every "ruling class" needs and will pay for its retainers. The new urban bourgeois of the Renaissance applauded the new humanist intellectuals' achievement- and activity-oriented themes. In their turn the latter "welcomed the new patronage not only for economic reasons but also for the sake of their own social position, and thus the interests of both parties concerned were served." The "modern intellectual" is an "individualist entrepreneur."

At present is it not the social scientists, physicists, humanists, and journalists who devise and applaud the "progressive" and anticapitalist rhetoric and reforms found so convincing and satisfying by the humanitarian well-to-do who carry off most of the grants, government positions, readers, distinguished professorships, and the like? [13] Numerous faculty surveys leave not the slightest doubt that the most liberal academics are to be found in the most prestigious universities. Do these findings reflect, as Lipset [14] seems to assume, the intrinsic superiority of liberals with respect to research interest and intellectual creativity? Or do they expose that our "upper-tier" bastions of academic freedom employ political or profit (i.e., fund-raising) criteria in determining which members of the professoriate will be recruited, endowed with research funds and contracts, tenured, and promoted? [15]

As usual, Milton Friedman [16] states the position of these intellectuals with great clarity:

> The socialists and interventionists . . . who have been the intellectual architects of our suicidal course, will suffer no severe personal injury—at least in the near future—if they fail to recognize the error of their ways. On the contrary, many of them would lose if they did so. They have found a profitable market for their views and might be hard put to develop an equally salable new product.

Those intellectuals who cry that the emperor is naked and the reforms harmful are vulnerable and can expect only the calumniations of their fellows: "cynic," "racist," "conservative," and most crushing of all, "spokesman of the Establishment." Thus, SUNY Distinguished Professor Lewis Coser [17] in his discussion of "neoconservatives like Banfield" wonders in print "will it offend the academic proprieties if I say that a man who can write in this way somehow lacks an elemental sense of common humanity." Thus, when sociobiologist Edward O. Wilson, his ankle in a cast, was introduced at the American Association for the Advancement of Science in Washington, "a group of demonstrators poured water over his head and chanted slogans linking his ideas with racism, sexism, and other evils." [18] Under such barrages it is difficult to remain loyal to scientific values. "Why," asks James Buchanan,[19] are many economists "so reluctant to apply straightforward economic theory to the central policy issues? Why have so many . . . chosen, instead, to launch into the never-never land of abstruse mathematics on the one hand and the tedious detail of empirical rigor on the other?" Buchanan's plausible hypothesis is that "they can, in this way, join their fellow intellectuals in quasi-serious policy dialogue without jeopardizing their 'progressive' role."

Even during the Joe McCarthy period (1950–54), suggest Lipset and Dobson,[20] academic careers were jeopardized more by public support of McCarthy than by bitter opposition to him. On the other hand, the CIA's personnel director claims that there is evidence that faculty who acknowledge informal contacts with the CIA, "despite recognized standing in their fields of expertise have been subjected to professional disabilities, including denial of tenure and dismissal from their positions." [21] Can we expect prompt corrective actions to be taken by the ACLU and AAUP? [22] But then as Harvard sociologist Nathan Keyfitz [23] warns: "excessive insistence on the privileges of tenure in the United States today . . . could protect the *(conservative or apolitical)* occupants of tenured slots against the entry of non-tenured faculty who might be subversive [italics mine]." Keyfitz's idea that academic freedom should protect only "radical" social and economic ideas is only too common on the university campus.[24]

The victory in the intellectual war over socioeconomic phenomena, and hence its spoils, goes to the "progressives," not because they are more clever or even more ruthless, but for a more fundamental reason elaborated at length in chapter 3: people do not understand the operation of societies in general and markets in particular. As Milton Friedman [25] has had occasion to learn, it is much harder to get across the idea of solving problems via markets than "the notion that particular people are pulling levers and doing things to you" or that society should "pass a law and appoint a Minister." Why, then, resort to convoluted explanations? For example, that for intellectuals "unlike other groups" the "antagonism" to the system "does not appear to be reduced by success and the rewards it brings." [26] If the demand persists, why should the supply be expected to dry up? [27] Lipset and Dobson [28] state in this context that the "adversary culture" finds support "among the educated wealthy, where it has taken the form of 'radical-chic,' an involvement usually on the fund-raising level, with participation in well-publicized social events for causes identified with the most exploited elements in society."

Sixteen years before Galbraith wrote in his *The Affluent Society* about "contrived private wants" and the need for expansion of the public sector at the expense of private consumption ("social balance") he had been anticipated and refuted by Schumpeter:

> The ways in which issues and the popular will on any public issue are being manufactured is exactly analogous to the ways of commercial advertising.[29]

But

> the general hostile atmosphere which surrounds the capitalist engine . . . is the really significant phenomenon. . . . It is the raw material for the intellectual group to work on. . . . The role of the intellectual group consists primarily in stimulating, energizing, verbalizing, and organizing this material.[30]

One must admire untiring supersalesman Galbraith, who even now amid the shambles his recommendations have helped to cause has the chutzpah to lobby for more of the same! For example, in a letter he urged President Carter to abandon plans for a tax cut in 1978 because "the effect of tax cutting is to expand the purchases of consumer goods by the relatively affluent two thirds of our population." This, he continued, we cannot afford to do "at a time when our cities and their services are in desperate need, when urban services in the ghettos are appalling, when educational, recreational and other public budgets have been severely curtailed, when streets are unsafe and filthy, when health and welfare reform are being postponed at least partly because of their cost." [31]

Boulding [32] points out that there was "no real grass roots demand for social security." Instead it was "sold" to politicians by a group of "able and socially minded intellectuals." Levine [33] cites the importance of Michael Harrington's book, *The Other America* (1962), and Dwight Macdonald's 1963 article in the *New Yorker* in the development of the War on Poverty. Nevertheless, despite Schumpeter's insight and an unprecedented rate of social innovation we continue to read laments such as Mesthene's:

there exist only relatively inadequate institutional mechanisms devoted to exploring technological possibilities for new
socially desirable public goods. . . .[34]

and

public institutions do not have means equivalent to advertising and market research to inform the public about new possibilities and to test the potential demand for them.[35]

The facts are otherwise. Officials of the Office of Management and
Budget and the Civil Service Commission report that the federal
government alone spends at least $1 billion but perhaps as much
as $1.5 billion annually to advertise its programs. (It is not clear
whether these estimates include the imputed value of donated
media space and time.) Top press officers earn as much as
$50,000, and some hold the Madison Avenue-sounding title of
"Assistant Secretary in the Cabinet." Virtually every federal
agency has its own public relations crew busily involved in "self-
promotion." [36] And Demsetz [37] adds that they are immune from
antifraud laws!

Briefly summing up: The well-to-do *need* to improve society.
However, lacking sufficient incentives to become properly informed (the rational ignorance problem), the reforms they find
plausible and can afford to "buy" result in social disruptions. The
plausible but perverse reforms are in turn produced by a "new
class" of political entrepreneurs including politicians and intellectuals. On the one side L. M. Friedman [38] notes that there is a
"general demand from the inarticulate public for movement,
change, and progress and, on the other, a substantial corps of
'professional reformers'" often "inside government or shuttling
between government and the academy." Inevitably, as Tom Bethell [39] aptly puts it, the "bucket of wealth . . . slops all over the
turf" of the reformer "enroute to the poor."

PART II

HISTORICAL EVIDENCE ON DECLINE OF AFFLUENT SOCIETIES

CHAPTER 5

DECLINE OF ROME

If a man were called to fix the period in the history of the world during which the condition of the human race was most happy and prosperous, he would, without hesitation name that which elapsed from the Death of Domitian to the accession of Commodus [C.E. 96–180]

—Edward Gibbon (1776)

Following the fate of nearly all the states of the world . . . from poverty to riches, and from riches to corruption.

—Montesquieu

The problem remains. Why was the victorious advance of capitalism stopped?

—M. Rostovtzeff

During the Pax Romana the empire enjoyed during the first two centuries of the common era a prosperity that was unprecedented, not only from the perspective of the past, but indeed until recent times.[1] Rome itself became wealthier than any city that had existed. Fresh water was supplied by a system of aqueducts not surpassed until the nineteenth century, and many, if not most, homes had main service pipes that were equipped with cisterns and taps. Augustus (27 B.C.E.–14 C.E.) and Tiberius (14–37 C.E.) pursued a policy of free trade,[2] and Walbank [3] considers the prosperity of the early empire a "triumph for the principles of economic *laissez-faire.*" During the early Imperial period technical progress [4] was considerable in many trades (e.g., the construction of oil and wine presses) and even spectacular in the case of glass production. Not only were rotary motion technologies widely adopted, but Roman engineers increased significantly the power of watermills whose epitome was reached near Arles in Provence in the form of an industrial complex producing flour for 80,000 people. Kiechle [5] concludes that during the late Republican and early Imperial periods "developments in several cases almost reached the limit set to technical progress before the rise of modern science."

The empire's prosperity was by no means skin deep; it permeated the entire peninsula and the provinces (Egypt, the East, Gaul, Spain, and Africa) and involved the rapid growth of a relatively large middle class. Stobart [6] reports that for the first time "the inscriptions show us a happy and industrious class of artisans and humble tradesmen, grading down through the freedmen to the slaves, many of whom now lived and worked under quite tolerable conditions." Fragmentary but useful quantitative material on wages and living costs are available for Egypt under Roman rule during the second century C.E. These data, summarized by Colin Clark,[7] suggest that the full-time earnings of a skilled worker amounted to 1,200 drachmai per year (4 drachmai per day and 300 working days). At the same time, the estimated minimum cost of living for a family of four was at most 520 drachmai per year (130 drachmai per adult). Thus, about 60 percent of potential earnings remained after deducting minimum expenditures. The corresponding residual for an unskilled household is roughly 50 percent.[8] According to Heichelheim,[9] "during the period from the first century to the time of Marcus Aurelius real wages increased in Egypt and even elsewhere," but Palestinian real wages were "far superior" to those paid in heavily populated Egypt.

The second century was also the time of the famous line of "Good Emperors"–Nerva through Marcus Aurelius (96–180).[10] In apparent sincerity these rulers adopted the Stoic doctrine of the brotherhood and equality of men. Toynbee [11] credits the "miracle of converting the Roman Wolf into a Platonic watch-dog" to Greek philosophy—indeed a miracle, since the personalized mythology of the Romans saw them as descendants of Romulus, the child of a seduced vestal virgin, slayer of his brother Remus, and despoiler of the Sabine women. Legal reforms gradually eliminated the difference in legal status between Roman citizen and Roman subject. With the support of the affluents, the emperors rejected the earlier role of "night watchman" and attempted conscientiously to serve the interests of the population. Legislation sought to aid the weak against the strong, the poor against the rich.[12] According to MacMullen,[13] "anyone who compares imperial edicts of the earlier Principate with those of the third century must be struck by the rising note of moral didacticism."

H. Bolkestein [14] suggests that as early as the first century wealthy Romans began to exhibit a tendency to give to the poor without expecting an equivalent return. The latter inference regarding motives is based primarily on the fact that the wealthy increased the lavishness of their gifts in the face of the common people's declining influence in elections to high public offices. The motives of the Severi (193–235), who consolidated their rule after a period of civil strife, were suspect, but the humane policy toward the poorer classes was continued and indeed strengthened in the third century. Under the tyrant Caracalla (211) full citizenship was all the same conferred on the free citizens of all the provinces. The Severi, with the aid of the great jurists Papinian, Ulpian, and Paulus, may be said to have completed the structure of the Roman welfare state. Of this period Ernest Renan [15] wrote that:

> Everybody's condition improved . . . to bring relief to those who suffer became the universal concern. The cruel Roman aristocracy was being replaced by a provincial aristocracy of honest people who wanted to do good. . . . People became kind, gentle, patient, human. As always happens, socialist ideas taking advantage of this broadmindedness, made their appearance.

Here are some concrete illustrations. In support of public health and higher education Vespasian (74) granted doctors and teachers exemptions from taxation. Fiscal immunity for doctors was placed on a larger scale by Hadrian, and it is usually assumed that free treatment of the poor was expected. Nerva and Trajan initiated a truly major social reform. Treasury funds amounting to more than twice the annual revenues of the state were used to make low-interest loans (5 percent instead of the usual 12) on Italian farm mortgages. The annual interest payments were to be distributed to needy parents for raising their children. The scheme began with forty Italian cities and 5,000 children and was commemorated on Trajan's coins and his Arch at Beneventum.[16] More generally, Trajan's (98–117) favorite slogan was *felicitas temporum* ("the happiness of the age"), and his favorite theme the Imperial cornucopia pouring out corn, oil, and wine upon a grateful world. Later emperors extended the "alimentary" program (it was restored after a lapse by Septimus Severus), which was finally terminated by Diocletian. Loans were also advanced to aid young married couples to get established. Legal limits were placed upon discretionary powers of government officials, including the duration of protective custody. Westermann [17] refers to a variety of evidence suggesting that the public attitude toward slaves changed markedly during the first two centuries of the Empire in the direction of an increased recognition of their humanity, although Hicks [18] suggests that this change reflected the rising value of labor (i.e., of real wages). Thus, for example, Petronius had one of his characters, the freedman Trimalchio, suggest that slaves were nurtured upon the same milk as the free. During the reign of Hadrian (117–138) decrees improved the legal status of slaves (mistreated slaves were given the right to demand to be put up for sale, and many could contract marriages and raise families), widows, and orphans. The favorite theme on this emperor's coins showed Hadrian lifting a weeping woman from the ground, and among his favorite slogans was *liberalitas*, which related to the cancellation of unpaid taxes. "Especially in the case of Hadrian," Mazzolani [19] adds, "there is a clear intention on the part of the emperor to show open approval of the levelling ideas of the political philosophers of his day, as preached by the orators in court, by religious speakers at street-corners, and by artists in marble." He sought to be recognized by the title Restitutor Orbis Terrarum ("benefactor of the whole world").

Urban life was generously enhanced by the treasuries of Hadrian, Antonius Pius, and Marcus Aurelius.

> Water systems and aqueducts, sewers, temples, free public baths, city-halls and other public buildings, schools, roads, harbors, market places, shady porticoes, theaters, and gymnasia were erected from state funds by imperial architects all the way from London to Baghdad, from the Alps to Sahara.[20]

Under Alexander Severus the state subsidized additional urban projects including the lighting of Rome's baths so that they might remain open in the evening. Hadrian began to "civilize" the army by allowing military camps to become cities and towns, and Septimus Severus not only permitted soldiers to marry but actually granted a variety of privileges in order to make the army a more attractive career.

The Hadrianic decrees that sought to keep local prices down reflect well the economic thinking of the time. He sought to accomplish this by limiting the export of olive oil from Athens and by fulminating against "middlemen," who, for example, made the price of fish prohibitive for poor people: "The whole amount of the fish had to be sold either by the fishermen themselves or by those who first purchased the fish from them." [21] A tablet found in southern Portugal contains Hadrian's decrees "regulating the life of a mining village, laying down rules for the local shoemaker and barber, and arranging for the boilers in the public bath." [22] Emperor Claudius (41–54) forbade eating houses to sell cooked meat or warm water; Antonius Pius sought to strengthen guilds [23] by limiting membership and by the imposition of an age test and physical examination. Later a man was even forbidden to join more than one guild. More basically, in the attempt to provide a stable food supply for the large cities, the state made shambles of the economy. First rulers took the initiative of organizing and regulating production via privileged corporations and then, unsatisfied with the result, went on to fix maximum prices in order to limit "price fluctuations." [24]

Maximum prices surely contributed to the drastic decline in Italian and Greek production of wheat and to the resulting famines and disorders. Farmers now found it more profitable to produce olive oil or wine. Domitian (92) tried to curtail the latter response by outlawing the planting of new wines (a policy not officially terminated until 280), which in turn probably contributed to the observed expansion of pasturage and even land abandonment.[25] The contraction of cultivated area *(agri deserti)* in the later empire gave rise to a theory of soil exhaustion. But Jones [26] rejects this theory and asserts, instead, "only land of marginal quality . . . fell out of cultivation." This occurred in response to a high rate of taxation "crudely assessed on simple categories— olives, vineyard, arable, pasture—without distinction of quality and sometimes on area alone."

And then there was the state's dole to the "proletariat" of Rome (all free Romans neither senators nor knights).[27] In passing, let us here point to the familiar note sounded by the use of the term "client" to describe those receiving the dole from wealthy Roman patrons. The state dole began with a monthly distribution of free grain, but by the time of Marcus Aurelius there were generous daily distributions of bread, olive oil, and pork, to say nothing of gifts by the emperors of money, wine, and games, and the state's sale of various foodstuffs at bargain prices to all consumers, regardless of wealth. In the third century, wine, salt, and even tunics and handkerchiefs were distributed, and the dole was extended to Alexandria and other Egyptian cities. It has been estimated that in the second century some 400,000 of Rome's total citizen population of probably no more than 1 million were eligible to receive free corn. Carcopino [28] adds that Romans finally enjoyed at least one day of holiday for each day of work! How could programs of this magnitude not have caused a massive deterioration in work incentives? Characteristically the Roman literature even includes stories of rich men who freed their slaves in order to make them eligible to receive the dole.[29]

The second and third centuries saw a growing and deepening urban crisis.[30] Large sums were spent by municipalities to keep down the price of bread and other commodities, and the Roman dole was widely emulated. Such policies, in addition to local government support for public education, physical training, public entertainment, and religious observances as well as the previously mentioned Imperial public works projects, contributed to a deterioration of work incentives and to a flight by peasants, among others, into the cities. This in turn led to a persistent "shortage" of farm labor, which Bernardi [31] correlates with the rising relative prices of agricultural goods in the second half of the second century. The demands on municipal budgets were thereby increased, further intensifying the crisis. Ever more municipalities found themselves heavily indebted and unable to fulfill their tax obligations to the emperor. Local governors asked for and received the cancellation of arrears and tax reductions, but the ultimate price was the loss of the city-state's autonomy. Hadrian, for example, granted tax waivers amounting to nearly one fourth of the annual expenses of his state. In a spirit of "paternal benevolence" the emperors who had "bailed out" a city (e.g., Marcus Aurelius) wished to permanently improve its financial status and thus appointed curators and correctors to manage or advise local authorities on such matters. By the time of Alexander Severus (222–235) these "temporary" commissioners had become permanent and, in fact, had supplanted the local authorities in many municipalities.

In 301 Diocletian issued an edict of prices and wages that was engraved on stone tablets and set up in marketplaces throughout the empire.[32] This edict, which set a maximum price for every commodity and service ("from partridges to pocket handkerchiefs"), made no distinction between retail and wholesale prices and no allowance for season, local differences in conditions, or transportation costs. Death was the legal penalty for violation, not only for the seller or withholder of goods, but for the customer who paid an illegally high price. Diocletian's introduction to the edict is extremely revealing and quite consistent with the linkage between altruism and ignorance. He begins by declaring that uncontrolled economic activity is a "religion of the godless" and then explains:

it seems good to us . . . who are the fathers of the people, that justice intervene to settle matters impartially, in order that which, long hoped for, humanity itself could not bring about may be secured for the common government of all by the remedies which our care affords. . . . Who is of so hardened a heart and so untouched by a feeling for humanity that he can be unaware . . . that in the sale of wares which are exchanged in the market . . . an exorbitant tendency in prices has spread to such an extent that the unbridled desire of plundering is held in check neither by abundance nor by seasons of plenty.[33]

Finley [34] refers to the "realism" of Diocletian: "He simply did not like what was happening in this sphere." [35] But Frank [36] quotes a contemporary writer, who states that "Businessmen closed shop . . . many articles of commerce disappeared . . . and food riots at once resulted." Much blood was shed and many died. Quite naturally the edict was difficult to enforce, and finally it was revoked by Constantine.

Of more lasting significance for the economic health of the empire, Diocletian and his successors began to enforce the old *centesimae usarae,* or legal maximum interest rate of 12 percent.[37] In the context of the currency debasement and consequent rampant inflation of the times the destructive effects of the curtailment of loanable funds upon economic efficiency must have been greatly magnified.[38] Constantine compounded the damage by introducing a maximum interest rate on loans in kind (e.g., on seed loans to farmers). The entire economic life of the towns was more and more regulated by the bureaucracy.

The purchase and preparation of all raw materials by the craftsmen, together with the fixing of prices for all articles coming into the town, came under what amounted to constant supervision . . . together with the determination of prices for the sale and export of goods produced within the city's boundaries. Intermediate trade (carrying trade or commission agency) was entirely restricted on moral grounds.[39]

Indeed, by the fourth century there had been a vast increase in the size and activity of the Roman Imperial bureaucracy.[40] This growth operated to smother the modest economic recovery following the political and military turmoil of the third century. The middle and upper classes were victimized by heavy Imperial taxation and by a now regularized and legalized system of "liturgies" that involved compulsory service and responsibility for the poor.[41]

In the interests of this system, Imperial edicts sought to restrict severely geographic, occupational, and social mobility. The effects were reinforced by tariff rates on goods passing from one district of the empire to another, which had risen from at most 5 percent to 12.5 to 25 percent.[42] "A world of free, private economic activity had given place to one of rigid state control." [43] Late antiquity exhibited as well distinct signs of technical stagnation.

In the evolution of compulsory services an important step was taken in the reign of Alexander Severus (230). The *collegia*, or guilds, in the various trades and crafts were given legal monopolies and were required to perform services previously furnished by the state (e.g., free distribution of grain). The returns to guild members, special privileges officially termed *solacium*, or "consolation," including exemption from taxes, corvées, and municipal charges were apparently insufficient. This led to the passage of laws that prohibited withdrawal of capital, required compulsory enrollment of men of means and lifetime membership (270), declared that a member's property is guild property (369), attached sons to the guild, and finally made even sons-in-law liable to the performance of guild duties.[44]

Even temporary breaks in service came to be equated with military desertion, and beginning in the fourth century shippers were placed under obligation to carry grain at rates fixed by the state. With Constantine (332) attachment to the soil also became hereditary. The resort to serfdom is best interpreted as an effort to lower the cost of collecting taxes in an economy in which this cost had risen sharply because of the ruination of the market sector [45] by perverse reforms. Nor was the rich and varied religious life of the empire immune to totalitarian controls: in the fourth century the state adopted Christianity and enforced religious uniformity.[46]

The *curiales* (property-owning urban middle-class members of municipal senates) were, at the end of the second century, made responsible with their own property for public duties including the collection and return of taxes to the emperor.[47] Membership in the *curiales* too became hereditary:

No one could leave his native place except on pain of discharging the liturgies of his former as well as of his new homes. . . . Property of *curiales* could not be sold without the consent of the governor or of the curia. The purchaser of such an estate assumed the civic responsibilities attached to it.[48]

But the policy of sharply raising taxes [49] while real incomes had fallen because of the strangulation of the market sector contributed to the decay and ruin of the urban bourgeoisie and artisans. Ultimately the hated and bankrupt *curiales,* like the "slumlords" of New York City, "often preferred to abandon their property and take refuge in flight . . . many cities . . . degenerated into villages or were completely abandoned." [50] Abbott [51] adds that "some enlisted in the army or even fled into the desert" and in the fourth century, "service in the common council was even made a penalty imposed upon criminals." Much like the trek of businesses, sports franchises, from cities to suburbs, and so on, Roman merchants sought to evade special taxes and duties by leaving the great centers of commerce for remote places.[52] From the end of the third century onward the empire's cities were clearly contracting in both area and population.

During the fifth century, not only did state factories become important, but the emperor had to create special officials to purchase and transport the goods previously provided by private merchants.[53] Brigandage, however, became a growth industry. In order to discourage the competition offered to the state by private protection forces, edicts of 397 and 399 forbade men trained in the gladiatorial schools to enter private service.[54] In 388 Theodosius prohibited ordinary citizens from carrying arms.[55] Meanwhile to escape the tax-gathering *curiales* the small farmers fled to join the brigands, or to live as refugees among the barbarians, or typically traded their land or freedom for the protection offered by wealthy landlords known as the "potentates." [56] The latter, ensconced in their villas, evaded or were immune from taxation. This immunity contributed to urban decay by encouraging the villas to manufacture goods previously purchased in the cities.

The taxes for abandoned land were in turn collectively imposed on local landowners, leading to new abandonments.[57] High marginal tax rates for ground planted with grapevines induced farmers to destroy the cultures. The state, determined to collect the taxes, responded in 381 by establishing the death penalty and confiscation of property for such destruction.[58]

Needless to say, economic life had been immobilized by the destruction of incentives, and there was no return to the affluence of the second century. The decline in urban life was reflected in a decreased volume of trade that led to smaller and less specialized firms. The crafts, for example, once more became integrated with retail trade. "Le grand commerce" across the Mediterranean never ceased, but no longer did it flourish. Rostovtzeff [59] considered "the salient feature of the economic life of the late Roman empire to be gradual impoverishment." The state treasury fell into a pitiable condition: "The military problem of the Late Empire can be reduced to a financial problem." [60] "Even the naturally rich portions of the Western Empire fell into such a state of poverty that they could no longer pay for their defense." [61] Bernardi [62] adds that the negative consequences of the fiscal crisis extended to services other than defense against barbarians and brigands, including "provisioning of the great cities, gratuitous distributions to the urban plebs, transportation, maintenance of roads, public games, etc." From riches to altruism to decline and alienation from the state. Ultimately the West was submerged in total disaster by small bands of barbaric tribesmen.[63] The great humanitarian movement of the earlier empire became a dim memory only vaguely reflected in the evolving Christian tradition.[64]

CHAPTER 6

DECLINE OF SUNG CHINA

The intriguing question is why this precocious economic and industrial expansion in Sung China, [960 C.E.–1279 C.E.] did not lead to developments similar to the later and more famous Industrial Revolution of nineteenth century Europe.

—Robert Hartwell

Chinese society has been called "bureaucratic feudalism," and that may go a long way to explain why the Chinese, in spite of their brilliant successes in earlier science and technology, were not able, as their colleagues in Europe were, to break through the bonds of medieval ideas, and advance to what we call modern science and technology. I think one of the great reasons is that China was fundamentally an irrigation-agricultural civilization, as contrasted with the pastoral-navigational civilization of Europe; with the consequent prevention of the merchants' rise to power.

—Joseph Needham

The Sung dynasty (960 C.E.–1279 C.E.) began after a successful military coup. Despite many disturbing gaps and ambiguities, the evidence on decline is very suggestive. During the eighth through twelfth centuries and especially beginning in the tenth century,

China enjoyed rapid economic growth and, ultimately, unprecedented prosperity.[1] Elvin describes a "medieval economic revolution" that was sparked by revolutions in agriculture, water transport, money and credit, and industrial technology.

The key agricultural developments taking place in the south were mastery of wet-field rice cultivation techniques and in the early eleventh century the introduction of early ripening Champa rice. The latter made it possible to grow two crops on the same land in one year. Other noteworthy innovations were substitution of wheat for millet cultivation in the north (made possible by better milling machinery), more extensive use of various fertilizers, the introduction of drought-resistant seed strains, and advances in hydraulic techniques symbolized by "the dam, the sluice-gate, the noria (peripheral pot-wheel), and the treadle water-pump." [2] Ways were found to pass through or around previously unpassable difficult places on the rivers such as the Yangtze gorges. The commercial revolution was facilitated by the increased use of paper money. With respect to industry, Hartwell [3] speaks of an "eleventh century revolution in the . . . use of iron and coal which closely paralleled the history . . . of Great Britain from 1540–1640." Elvin [4] adds that China created "the world's earliest mechanized industry." For example, the reciprocating steam engine, which attained its definitive form in 1800 in Europe, "consisted essentially of two structural patterns which had been working widely and effectively in China about 1200." [5] The Sung period can also be credited with the canal lock gate and empirical knowledge of deficiency diseases.

By the eleventh century industrial and agricultural specialization within and among regions had created a Chinese economy more complex than any of earlier times. Quantitative evidence regarding the distribution of the rapidly growing income is unavailable, but Hucker [6] states that "for the first time in Chinese history a genuinely national urban class was emerging" and also that "the bourgeoisie became a substantial segment of the population," perhaps even "a more substantial segment than at any other time in Chinese history prior to the twentieth century." Shiba [7] describes the "collapse" of the "older system of closed-off officially-controlled city markets" together with atrophy of legal restrictions that "confined merchants and artisans . . . to specified quarters." Even the peasantry, according to Elvin,[8] was transformed by increased contact with the market into a "class of adaptable, rational profit oriented petty entrepreneurs." Moreover, despite the professed disdain and distrust of the merchant class, "the Sung dynasty provided the first abundant set of records showing officials in business. Many used assumed names or hired managers to run both regular and contraband trades." [9] Indirect evidence of widely diffused prosperity is also provided by reports of rather rapid population growth during this period. To summarize: incomes increased in response to relaxation of the traditional taboo on the overt pursuit of profit.

The glorious Sung economic revolution was matched by a cultural revolution described by Goodrich:[10]

> great compendiums of history, works on natural science, and political economy, of a character and quality such as neither China nor the West, except for a short period in Greece had ever dreamed of.

> the greatest . . . Chinese paintings that are now extant.

> gardens, once enjoyed only by princes became the fashion for the well-to-do.

> ceramic tradition . . . was developed to a point which some authorities believe has never been surpassed.

> private education flourished . . . promising students were admitted even though unable to pay the fees.

> collecting archeological objects became fashionable in the eleventh century, when many tombs were opened.

In addition, the period was the high point of traditional Chinese medicine.

But north China was lost to nomads (Chin) in 1126, and the Mongols conquered the entire country in 1279. The period of

Mongol rule (1279–1368) is considered by many Chinese to be the bleakest in their history. Hucker [11] believes that in "considerable measure" the victory of the new northerners can be attributed "to a decline in military spirit in Sung times." Lo [12] adds that the nomadic incursions came at a time when China was racked by civil strife. In a nutshell:

> A vital early Sung society had stressed individuality. . . . Eventually . . . this dynamism was eroded and the struggle for new achievements gave way to a determination to hold on to and enjoy what had already been won. Selfishness and corruption among the bureaucrats, stagnation in the society; this was the China that fell to the Mongols in 1279.[13]

An added dimension of insight is provided by Elvin's [14] observation that the Chinese society that had "advanced to the threshold of a systematic investigation of nature" became "inward-looking." Beginning in the fourteenth century, science was increasingly "short-circuited by a reliance on introspection and intuition." The Chinese economy between 1300 and 1500 fell into a deep decline. Hucker,[15] questioning why the medieval economic revolution did not continue and why traditional China failed to generate its own industrial revolution, observes that such problems have "bedeviled specialists for generations." Elvin [16] considers the causes to be "still largely inexplicable." One answer may well be the role played by ameliorative social reforms,[17] which we shall discuss here.

There is no doubt that Confucian writers of late T'ang and Sung times displayed a novel and strong humanitarian reformist drive. This exerted great influence on emperors and government officials, who themselves were usually Confucian scholars. The famous motto of the early Sung political reformer Fan Chung-yeh is revealing: "The true scholar should be first in worrying about the world's troubles and last in the enjoyment of its pleasures." [18] In the Sung dynasty's second century, reform programs grew more sweeping. Each "crisis" was met by a "barrage of planning and new law. Individualism and commercial activity ceased to be viewed pragmatically and, increasingly, fell into ideological disfavor." [19] The scholar-officials criticized the merchants' alleged attempts to make profits by "cornering markets," because this was at the expense of the poor. The most famous and important reformer was Wang An-shih, who introduced spectacular, but somewhat obscure, changes while serving from 1069 to 1073 as chief councilor to the Northern Sung emperor, Shen Tsung. Before turning to the details of the reforms they should be placed in proper historical perspective. Liu and Golas [20] point out that "Wang was only the most notable representative of a dynamic reform strain existing for some time in neo-Confucianism . . . the motivation for . . . reform grew weaker after Wang but it by no means disappeared."

An accurate analysis of Wang's "New Laws" or "New Policies" is difficult because many specialists have apparently been more concerned with Wang's sincerity and the ideological implications of his activities than with the reforms themselves. Eberhard [21] suggested that the young emperor turned against "a policy of *laissez-faire* in trade" and turned to Wang's group, which in turn carried out a number of reforms directed against the "monopolistic merchants." Marxist-oriented scholars (in this as in other cases), at a loss to explain altruistic reforms carried out by the "ruling class," picture Wang as representing the interests of "small landowners" or, alternatively, as striving in the interests of the rulers to prevent social revolution. I will do my best to interpret the sketchy evidence.

In 1069 Wang introduced the Farming Loans or "green sprouts program" in which the state made low-interest loans to needy farmers. Instead of the prevailing market rate of 60 to 70 percent, the state charged between 20 and 30 percent. The state loans were made twice a year: the first at planting time and the second in the spring when the rice sprouts were green. Repayment was to take place at harvest time, but in the event of a bad harvest the farmer might be granted a one-year delay. According to Lee,[22] the officials who administered the program "demanded that the rich should stand surety for the poor," with the result that when poor farmers deserted their land "the rich surety who had to pay his unfortunate neighbors' debts soon found himself as poor as they." The Tax Transport and Distribution System was introduced briefly in 1069 and in broader terms in 1072. Regional officials were authorized "to purchase goods in the cheapest market with economy of transportation in mind; or to sell goods under comparably profitable circumstances." [23] Severe problems apparently arose because the government set maximum prices on its purchases. Balazs [24] points out that the state

> granted in A.D. 1073, a kind of "privilege" according to which merchants were to pay a monthly fee for exemption from this obligation and the government was to pay the market price for the goods. Twelve years later, however, the state returned to the former system.

Under the State Trade System of 1072 "trade bureaus" purchased goods from small businessmen and offered them low-interest loans. Apparently the purpose was to halt "hoarding" of goods and "cornering" of markets by large merchants who owned warehouses. An imperial edict of 1074 reports that "business was at a standstill and people were thrown out of their jobs." [25]

Wang resigned in 1074, was taken back in 1075, and resigned permanently in 1076. However, his reforms were continued until the emperor's death in 1085. In 1093, under Emperor Che Tsung, "most of the New Policies were revived and several were extended in application to additional geographic regions." [26] This "post-reform phase" lasted until just before the conquest of north China by nomads in 1126. Additionally, in 1098 an edict was issued calling for the establishment of relief homes all over the empire. In 1102 and 1104 medical relief institutions and public cemeteries were created. From 1159 on the government sold grain from state granaries at bargain prices. During the Southern Sung era the relief roles and the amounts dispersed greatly increased. Moreover, Hsu [27] reports that such items were dispensed as "banquets, mosquito nets, burial sacrifices, and the hiring of wet-nurses and maid-servants." But Eberhard [28] cautions: "All these data . . . should be treated with care: we really do not know how often free medicines were distributed, how many state hospitals there were, how they functioned and who was actually accepted as a patient."

Around the time of Emperor Hsiao Tsung (1163–1189) an edict

required larger landholders to sell from their stocks of grains at below market clearing prices for public relief. Lee [29] notes, "the ranks of the hungry increased faster than the means devised for their relief." Official reports now mentioned that in the southeastern area, the most fertile in China, land was being deserted, savings vanishing, land yields declining (a 50 percent drop in one area), and famines were becoming more frequent and widespread. In an attempt to remedy this condition Emperor Hsiao Tsung issued a decree to open the fields "which had been enclosed by the rich in order to monopolize the water supply." [30] This no doubt intensified the agricultural crisis, since sophisticated rice growing is retarded by the absence of well-defined private property rights. In the absence of such rights, farmers lack incentives to undertake the arduous effort of first building and then maintaining irrigation ditches and rice beds in a proper state of repair.[31] Not surprisingly, reports began to pour in of families deserting their farms in increasing numbers.

By the end of the Sung period the state was resorting to thinly disguised expropriations. In the 1260s Chief Councilor Chia Ssu-tao instituted the public field laws that set a maximum limit on the size of landed properties. Excess holdings were "purchased" by the state and rented out as public lands. The resulting income was used to meet the requirements of the army. Finally a brigand- and famine-ridden country fell to the Mongols. K'o concludes that Chinese capitalism could not survive the Sung state's widespread interference in the economy. Hucker [32] is willing to entertain the possibility that the decline was due to "smothering governmental control of large-scale business."

CHAPTER 7

PROSPERITY AND ALTRUISM IN CLASSICAL ATHENS

For a man grows eager to work when he sees another, a richer man, who bestirs himself to plough and plant and put his oikos in good order; and neighbor vies with neighbor as he hastens eagerly after wealth. This strife is beneficial for men.

—Hesiod (700 B.C.E.)

We need not import modern entrepreneurial theory into ancient Hellas, but . . . men of the era did desire to gain the fruits of economic progress and . . . their very interest did help promote the development of a more complicated economic structure than the world had ever seen.

—Chester Starr

The statesman who accustoms a citizen to the idea that he is entitled to a dole regardless of necessity and without making any return therefore must expect the citizens' demands will speedily become such that he who attempts to satisfy them will undertake a task like that of the Danaids.

—A. M. Andreades

Athens was an affluent society during the half century beginning with the victory of the Greeks over Persia in 480–479 B.C.E.

and ending with the onset of the Peloponnesian War in 431.[1] Emerging from the Dark Ages (1100–900) and taking advantage of the general progress of the Mediterranean world, the entire Greek economy had been "rocketing" since the sixth century in what Starr[2] calls "the most remarkable example of structural alteration and economic growth in western history." This age of expansion was characterized by the growth of manufacturing and overseas trade within the Aegean and between the Aegean and the Near East. With respect to technological change it was a period of very significant progress: goldsmiths made use of granulation techniques; the working of iron became common; molds for making clay figurines were introduced; stone was used in major buildings. Viljoen[3] mentions the invention of several laborsaving devices, such as wood-turning lathes, windlasses, pulleys, and cranes. True, much of this technological upsurge was based on Eastern knowledge, but as Starr[4] points out, "Greek craftsmen *did* go beyond their Near Eastern sources in matters of techniques," and "even elaborations and improvements play a very large role in the increase of productivity, perhaps as great in the end as major breakthroughs."

The Athenian situation was unique in several respects. First in 483 silver veins of unprecedented richness were discovered in Laurion. Then Athens benefited from the "tribute" paid by its allies in the Delian League against Persia (478). Finally, over the course of thirty years Athens managed to convert the league into an empire. Consequently during the Age of Pericles Athens reaped substantial monopolistic returns from its imperial position. The Athenians' most tangible benefit was, of course, the annual tribute that may have amounted to 60 percent of total state revenues in 430.[5] But in about 420 an Athenian aristocrat described the broader returns to control of the sea: "One city yields timber to her, another iron, a third bronze, a fourth linen yarn, a fifth wax, and so on. Moreover, Athens prevents her rivals from transporting to other countries than Attica by the threat of driving them from the sea altogether."[6]

Given the paucity of data, it is not surprising that the degree of affluence is subject to uncertainty and dispute among economic historians. The strongest quantitative evidence for affluence is

Glotz's. Noting that Athenian citizens had long been grouped into classes based on fixed minimum-income levels, Glotz examined trends in the proportion of Thetes, the lowest class. He estimated that from 480 to 431 the Thetes declined from two thirds to less than half of all citizens. But Glotz's [7] conclusion that a "prodigious increase in wealth raised a great number of Athenians in the class scale" is weakened by his admission that inflation had operated to "lower the real value of the fixed minimum rates of the classes." On the other hand, this conclusion is supported by French's [8] statement that unlike earlier times, in the imperial period the upper economic strata "included many whose possessions did not derive from land but from commerce and industry, and many of whom were not even citizens."

Glotz also analyzed wage rate and consumer good price data from the time of Pericles. He found that an ordinary laborer with a wife and two children could have earned enough to subsist "without even being compelled to work on every working day." [9] About 40 percent of wages for a 300-day year remain after the deduction of minimum expenditures for food, clothing, and shelter. Heichelheim,[10] while noting the approximate nature of this estimate, points to the implication that "even the slave laborers of the time of Pericles could have a higher standard of living than free city servants and qualified free laborers, during the whole of the later history of Greece and Rome"! However, although French [11] considers it "likely" that the richest members of the community "were in 430 B.C. better off than the richest members in 500," he is unwilling "on the basis of the available evidence" to assert that "there was a substantial rise in the material living standards of the Athenian community as a whole." Specifically, in comparing sixth- and fifth-century Athens, French is "struck" by the absence of "positive evidence for any real increase in creature comforts such as one cannot help noting between the standards of the early Roman republican and early Roman imperial period." My own impression is that Glotz's calculations probably overestimate Athenian affluence but are far more convincing than French's assertions and comparisons. The latter, by the way, ignore significant improvements in the ease and aesthetics of Athenian life. Moreover, even French [12] notes that in Periclean Athens the influx of cheap alien domestic (slave) labor led to the "reasonable expectation of every free-born family, even though their means be slender, to own at least one servant" who released the housewife from the "heavy and degrading chores of the daily round" and, more generally, provided the owners the "inestimable blessing of unenforced leisure."

Athenian affluence increased the demand for and consumption of aesthetic values: the time of Pericles was Athens' period of unprecedented cultural efflorescence. The demand for political participation also increased. Let us examine the role of the Athenian polis in the economy.[13] It is known that "by 500 the rural world consisted of many small and middling farmers who were subject mainly to the constraints of the market place." [14] With the exception of grain imports Athens did not indulge in the massive interferences with free market determination of prices, wages, and interest rates [15] so familiar in the histories of Imperial Rome and Sung China. Neither did the state establish monopolies of raw materials or of manufactures (the latter were developments of the later Hellenistic Age). The polis even farmed out its tax collections and contracted for the construction of public works. Heichelheim [16] summarizes well the stance of the Athenian polis with respect to market forces.

> The ruling polis classes had practically never an interest in having their state interfere, with aims directed at economic planning. . . . Our period was an intensive and wealth promoting time of almost free economic advance . . . which was only to be surpassed by the comparable development in Europe during the centuries of the Renaissance and by the industrial revolutions of the 18th and 19th centuries.

What happened to the demand for altruism? Several pieces of evidence suggest a marked increase, reflected almost exclusively in a sharp upturn in social welfare expenditures.[17] To begin with, note the liturgies (literally, "folk works") of the well-to-do. These voluntary contributions to the state served to finance a number of enterprises, including grain and flour provisioning of the polis, choirs in the plays, gymnasium festivals, religious processions, and so forth. The state's distribution of sacrificed meat supplemented the mainly vegetarian diet of poorer Athenians and possibly provided them with a substantial meat dinner about once a week. From time to time there were also windfall distributions of money and grain. Even the state's payments for various services masked social welfare expenditures. Apparently, pay given to soldiers and sailors was quite generous in comparison with civilian wages. Then there were the *misthophoria*—payments for political participation. In the time of Pericles the generous payments to the 500 councilors were supplemented by payments to jurors of the *heliaia* and all the lower courts. This pay was increased sharply by the "demagogue" Cleon in 425. Out of 6,000 jurors on the register (chosen by lot from among the applicants) about 3,000, or 7.5 percent of all citizens, sat every day. According to Aristotle the juries for public cases typically numbered 500. It is difficult to believe that huge juries served the interests of judicial efficiency or, alternatively, were required in order to fulfill an increased desire for political participation. French's [18] explanation makes more sense: the payments represented a "very convenient channel for the distribution of welfare payments." Similarly, citing Aristotle, Bonner [19] concludes that the idea "was first suggested by Aristides, the founder of the Athenian empire, as a means of distributing the profits of imperialism to the lower classes." In the fifth century these payments were collected primarily by town-dwelling older citizens (jurors had to be over thirty years of age) and the temporarily unemployed.[20] Taking together, the jurors and the military, about half of the Athenian citizens were on the state's payroll at one time or another.

Surely, as French [21] notes, the effect of such payments was "to take off the sharpest edge of citizen poverty," but did they also, as Heichelheim [22] claims, provide "a middle class living to numerous citizens"? Jones rejects the latter possibility (at least with respect to *misthophoria).* He presents evidence that the payment to jurors was only half that of a laborer. But even if the remuneration rate is relatively small, it must not be forgotten that the work of the juror was much easier and more pleasant than the laborer's.

In concluding this discussion of social welfare, some quantitative perspective is provided by Andreades' data. In 420, payments for political participation and for the "cult budget" together made up 23 percent of all state expenditures. With the addition of public assistance payments, the total rises to 31 percent.

The final defeat of Athens at the hands of Sparta in 404 brought affluence to an end.[23] The income of the Athenian state dropped from 1,000 talents in 430 to as low as 130 talents in 355. French believes the damage to the rural stock of Attica lowered its farm income for at least half a century.[24] Athenian living standards were also substantially reduced because of its loss of imperial position and by impediments to the normal flow of commerce caused by the unsettled political conditions of the time. Heichelheim concludes from an analysis of wage and price data that in the fourth century at most one third of a laborer's wage remained for nonessential expenses as compared with about a half in the fifth century. Emigration reduced the citizen population of Athens from 40,000 to 21,000. The proportion of the poorest class (Thetes) rose to 57 percent of citizens. Emigration, together with an increased demand for Greek goods in the time of Alexander, produced a period of prosperity lasting from the late fourth into the early third century. But by 275 an "economic revolution" in trade and methods of production pushed Athens back on the path of relative economic decline.

During the depression of the fourth century payment to jurors became a form of unemployment insurance.[25] It seems reasonable to assume that the depression also played a role in the adoption of two new welfare measures: the extension of the payment for political participation to include attendance at the general assembly, which met some forty days a year; and a more radical departure, the *theoricon*. The latter began as a monetary dole given to Athenian citizens, apparently in connection with their attendance at the official theater festivals. Later it merged with the daily dole *(diobelia)* to the indigent. Judging from the complaints in the literature and the reported class conflicts a point was reached at which the well-to-do were no longer willing to pay the bills. The liturgies ceased to be voluntary contributions and took on the characteristics of confiscations. The *theoric* funds were not only increased but were also viewed to be sacred and above criticism. The earlier intense search for wealth, shared not only by the upper classes but by humble craftsmen, more and more was replaced by "the Platonic and Aristotelian disdain for 'profit' or for the sordid aspects of making money *(chrematistke)*."[26] The Greek affluents, like their modern counterparts, turned away from economic development and innovation and instead embraced justice and the quality of life. The desire for empirical knowledge, which reached its height with the Pythagoreans of the fifth century, more and more came to be replaced by an emphasis on "pure reason," which found its culmination in the teleology of Plato.

At least two eminent historians are of the opinion that the accumulated weight of the various social welfare expenditures beginning in the affluent Periclean Age finally smothered the Athenian economy. Ehrenberg[27] suggests that:

> the whole system finally broke down through the decline of taxable values and the limitation of consumption, through the excessive demand for pay for citizens and foreign soldiers, the understandable reluctance, as well as actual impoverishment, of a considerable section of the well-to-do.

For the moral drawn by Andreades, the reader is referred to the chapter headnote.

CHAPTER 8

DECLINE AND REVIVAL OF THE MARKET

There is a tradition among historians that charity is a virtue of the highly civilized. The student of ancient lands is in difficulties if he tries to proceed on that theory.

—Tenney Frank

Capitalism shaped whole periods of Antiquity, and indeed precisely those periods we call "golden ages." . . . *Bureaucracy stifled private enterprise in Antiquity.*

—Max Weber

From the social and economic point of view, we mean by decline the gradual relapse of the ancient world to very primitive forms of economic life, into an almost pure "house-economy."

—M. Rostovtzeff

If, as I have argued, affluent societies increasingly introduce ameliorative social reforms that, given the rational ignorance of the reformers and the counterintuitive nature of society, are likely to have perverse effects, must this kind of utilization of the political system then have as its ultimate outcome the shackling of the economy and the elimination of both affluence and altruism?

Those who have reflected on the Roman experience have reached divergent answers. According to Walbank,[1] the evolution of the "semiplanned economy" was primarily a necessary response to the (unexplained) "failure" of private enterprise. Petit [2] seems to suspect that governmental nonintervention in the economy, a "policy too long maintained, was responsible for the evolution of the late Empire towards totalitarianism, and . . . technological stagnation." But other scholars explicitly place the blame on ameliorative social reform. In Hayek's [3] view, the economic conditions of the late empire were the result of the egalitarian social policy introduced in the second century. Jacques Pirenne,[4] in turn, reaches the conclusion that "egalitarianism, an offshoot of humanitarianism" ended "in the enslavement of the citizens to the advantage of the omnipotent state." As Rostovtzeff saw it, the overdose of planning and bureaucracy played a key role in preventing "ancient capitalism" from flowering into modern capitalism. A recent writer, Paul Johnson,[5] believes that "The Graeco-Roman world-civilization disappeared because it had lost the political and economic freedoms, personified in its urban middle class on which it had been built."

Max Weber seemed to be of more than one mind. On one hand he refers to monopolies, state workshops, compulsory guild organizations, liturgies, and the like as a "net of obligations" within which the Roman state "throttled capitalism slowly but surely":

> For otherwise how can we explain the fact that capitalism did not flourish either in the first two centuries of the Empire nor in the fourth century, both periods of relative peace and order without parallel in the whole classical age of antiquity. . . . The great merchants of the Early Empire, whose trading ventures extended to Scandinavia, disappeared. . . . Even as early as the reign of Marcus Aurelius, the economy had become stagnant and the tax burden on the lower classes was very heavy.[6]

But Weber also stated that "ancient capitalism was based on politics, on the exploitation for private profit of the political conquests of the imperialist city-state and when this source of profit disappeared capital formation ceased." Thus:

by protecting subjects and by establishing peace the Roman Empire condemned ancient capitalism to death. The supply of slaves dwindled, and gone were all those opportunities for profit which the wars of *polis* with *polis* had created; gone too were the trade monopolies held by individual city-states, and above all, gone were the profits of plundering the public domains and the subject peoples. These changes together meant that ancient capitalism lost the sources from which it had drawn nourishment.[7]

Weber failed to reconcile these two explanatory themes of excessive regulation and decline of opportunities for exploitation.[8]

Starr,[9] observing the "corrupt, brutal regimentation of the late Empire," notes "that the rulers arrived at this situation in their efforts to maintain the framework of ancient civilization." This to him was the "bitterest of irony." Bernardi's recapitulation captures much of the problem and deserves quotation at length.

The prevalence of the idea of the Welfare State little by little imposed upon the State great charges and tasks, that were out of proportion to the possibilities of its income. . . . From this situation the State saved itself, first at the expense of the old urban nobility, whose wealth was confiscated—a sacrifice imposed upon them by rival groups forming in the army and bureaucracy—then with the revenue drawn from both the small and the large property. . . . A dangerous vicious circle comes into action. Increased state expenditures on the army, the bureaucracy, in the welfare state commitments brought about a continual unbearable tax pressure . . . the tendency to evasion . . . on the part of high officials and large landowners, was increased. . . . This vicious circle could lead to only one result, that which clearly shows itself in the course of the fifth century. The bankruptcy of the enormous State at the same time as small privileged groups, while they evade taxation, heap up riches and create around their villas economic and social microcosms, completely cut off from the central authority. It was the end of the Roman world. It was the beginning of the Middle Ages.[10]

Our age, Bark [11] reminds us, thinks of "revolutions" as progressive not retrogressive. yet "retrogressive revolution" is "precisely what was taking place in Western, and for a time in Eastern, Roman, society in the fourth and fifth centuries." Nor, as the historical part of this study demonstrates, is the evidence connecting altruistic reform and the decline of affluent societies confined entirely to Rome.

The entire process is best comprehended by Sirkin's visualization of retro-development: a dynamic feedback process leading to reversion to a stationary low-level economy. To accomplish this, the process needs to be modified in the context of the theoretical analysis of affluence-altruism and of the historical experience of the Roman Empire (especially in the West) and Sung China. But apparently not Athens, which in spite of marked similarities still appears to stand outside the process. Athenian prosperity was undermined by military defeat at the hands of Sparta and its allies rather than by the social welfare expenditures. On the other hand, the evidence does make one wonder whether the fourth-century recovery would have been more vigorous had the fifth-century expenditures never been made. *The profits of empire vanished but not the expectations they had engendered, so the "rich" were taxed to finance the state payments and doles to which the "impoverished masses" had become accustomed.*

The chain of events that is predicted by the "low-level equilibrium model" is as follows: affluence induces altruistic reforms; lower-class impatience with the rate of progress triggers social strife;[12] simultaneously, the precedents set by the reforms unleash powerful demands for new reforms ("rent-seeking") to benefit new groups (occupational, sectional, ethnic, etc.); continued deterioration of economic and political performance due to the reforms themselves and "overcrowding" of government trigger further "disaggregation of interests" and new civil strife with a possible accompanying invitation to aggressive, predatory behavior by internal adventurers [13] and by foreign states;[14] "emergency" measures subjecting individuals to various forms of compulsion by the state lead to further declines in output and economic efficiency;[15] temporary compulsive measures are extended until they become permanent; repetition of feedbacks until equilibrium with a simple low-level economy and society that is tradition-, localistic-, and other-world oriented.[16]

Hayek [17] has placed great stress on the third element in the retro-development chain, involving the precedents set by altruistic reforms:

> a government dependent on public opinion, and particularly a democracy, will not be able to confine itself to attempts to supplement the market in the mitigation of the lot of the poorest. . . . By the measures it takes it will produce opinions and set standards which will force it to continue on the course on which it has embarked.

In a political "vicious circle" each reform sets the stage for new reforms in the interests of justice and fairness or to aid those regarded as lacking political influence. The state comes to be viewed as a "grab-bag" or, as Poggi [18] aptly puts it, a "colony" and the slogan of the day becomes: "If everyone else is getting theirs, why shouldn't we?" Naturally, rent-seeking activity leads to diminishing distributive returns: as they age government expenditure programs move toward distributional neutrality.[19] In the final analysis, the main result of rent-seeking activity is to undermine further—that is, beyond the damage done by the altruistic reforms themselves—society's reliance on the efficient allocation of scarce resources via the market mechanism.[20]

For example, Krauss [21] links the upsurge of U.S. international trade protectionism in the 1970s with the general growth of welfare state social policies: "The welfare state promises economic security. Adjustment implies change. Therefore, it is virtually a syllogism that the growth of interventionist government would imply an increased demand for protection." Trade and other forms of protectionism are, in turn, linked to retro-development: "If the very protectionist policies required to obtain economic security induce stagnation in the process, we have what a good Marxist might call the inner contradictions of the welfare state."

Moving to another example, Esman [22] considers the question of why the "prosperous and peaceful" period since World War II has witnessed "the escalation of grievances and demands expressed and politicized in ethnic terms." He cites as one explanation the growth of the welfare state that simultaneously raises expectations and stimulates sectional and ethnic grievances. The relatively poorer groups complain that not enough is being done to help them, while the relatively richer groups complain that their hard-earned prosperity is being drained. One striking outcome of this sort of struggle is "creeping minoritization"—that is, the gradual expansion of the federal government's definition of a "minority" to include poor whites, veterans, and even women (actually a majority).[23]

It is worthwhile to pause briefly to compare this explanation of decline with the one offered by W. W. Rostow in *How It All Began.* Rostow begins by suggesting that "modern society has experienced "two centuries of self-sustained growth that began in the late eighteenth century." "Why," he asks, "did not traditional societies generate self-sustained growth?" [24] Before turning to Rostow's answer it seems reasonable to ask: "How long must an economy grow before Rostow will classify the growth as 'self-sustained'?" Rostow [25] concedes that several premodern societies enjoyed "periods" of economic expansion and prosperity that "sooner or later" gave way to decline. In fact, the periods of expansion in the Roman Empire and Sung China are comparable in duration to the modern expansion. So perhaps the answer to Rostow's question is: "They did!" However, for Rostow the upswings in premodern societies only resemble "pre-industrial modernization," whereas decline is triggered, not by perverse reforms, but by the absence of a regular flow of technological innovations.

The traditional societies did not generate inventions and innovations as a regular flow into the economy. Therefore, they ultimately strained and broke against a technological ceiling that set limits on the inputs of men and resources governments could generate for war, or on the population that the land could support.[26]

I find this explanation to be unsatisfying for two reasons. First, Rostow admits that there was "some" invention and innovation in the premodern world, notably in food growing and textiles, "but they occurred slowly and sporadically." [27] I submit that this characterization is not factual and certainly does not apply to Sung China. Neither does it appear to correspond to the experience of Greece during its age of expansion from 800 to 500 B.C.E. Starr [28] warns that modern treatments of ancient technology have tended to "concentrate on the lack of *continued* technological improvement to such a degree that the innovations in the age of expansion almost disappear from sight." As for Rome, Kiechle [29] insists that technical progress was "considerable" during the late Republican and early Imperial periods but stagnated beginning in the second century C.E. Second, Rostow's [30] explanation for the alleged absence of a regular flow of technological innovation in premodern societies appears to be tautological: "Their cultures and religions did not set for the rulers the objective of regular growth." This situation is contrasted with later times in which "regularly increasing output emerged in men's minds as a realistic option." (Why was this option not realistic in earlier times?) However, the rulers played a central role in encouraging invention and innovation. (Was this role really unique?) [31] *For Rostow, traditionalism and an antigrowth mentality are fixed components of the basic personality of premodern societies but are absent in modern society. In the present analysis such character traits emerged in premodern societies during the process of retro-development and may now be emerging in modern society.*

Retro-development is both the end and the beginning of the story. North and Thomas have offered strong support for the Smith-Mill thesis that economic growth and, finally, affluence are not possible in the absence of efficient economic organization. If individuals are to be encouraged to undertake socially desirable activities, the private costs must not exceed the private benefits. *Reforms that massively undermine incentives cause retro-development, but, in good dialectical fashion, the retro-development process includes the destruction of the very state apparatus that strangled affluence in the name of altruism.* Once again efficient organization is possible. Here, perhaps, is the long sought for explanation of "self-sustained" economic growth. Indeed, this is precisely the lesson taught by Baechler's [32] maxim: "The first condition for the maximization of economic efficiency is the liberation of civil society with respect to the state." In the expanding interstices of the "primitive" economic system individuals increasingly are able to indulge their "natural propensity to truck, barter, and exchange"—that is, to mutually interact spontaneously and to undertake wealth-augmenting activities. Increasing output and the pursuit of riches becomes once again a realistic option. Stagnation gives way to innovation. Hesitantly at first but then more and more swiftly the economy travels the fabled "yellow-brick road" to affluence. The initial stages of the growth process are described by North and Thomas in the *Rise of the Western World* and by Rostow in his insightful, fact-filled chapter on "The Politics of Modernization." [33]

PART III

OMENS AND PROPHECIES

CHAPTER 9

BRITAIN AS THE WAVE OF OUR FUTURE

Around and after 1870 British wealth was the envy of the world; the rest of the world came . . . to learn [Britain's] technology.
—Sidney Pollard and David W. Crossley

What luxury it is to do good!
—Richard Potter (father of Beatrice Webb)

In our days of active philanthropy, hosts of people eager to achieve benefits for their less fortunate fellows by what seem the shortest methods, are busily occupied in developing administrative arrangements of a kind proper to a lower type society, are bringing about retrogression while aiming at progression.
—Herbert Spencer (1884)

Do current British economic problems [1] provide one more omen of the ultimate consequences of welfareism? This is the theme of a collection of essays compiled by R. Emmett Tyrell, Jr., called *The Future That Doesn't Work: Social Democracy's Failures in Britain.* "The United Kingdom has become the latest version of the Sick Man of Europe"; and, Tyrell [2] warns in the introduction, "as the United States has been on a similar diet, one might well ask if this nation is slated to go the way of the United Kingdom." Economist Robin Marris [3] makes light of the "self-interested fear of the dreaded Socialism that supposedly has ruined Britain" and uses the occasion of his review "to take up the challenge to explain what I think is really wrong with Britain." He argues that "the British economy has been in trouble since the turn of the century," and for this he offers a "sociological" explanation:

> Britain was first in the first industrial revolution, but dissipated her advantage through sociology. The entrepreneurs of the revolution bought country estates to keep their first sons out of trade, while second sons were exported to administer the Empire. Sons of all kinds were sent to public schools (i.e., private), basically upper-middle-class institutions whose values have consistently favored the career professions as against industry. . . . To sum up . . . the British industrial disease is a sociological syndrome in which an alienated but militant working class has combined with an inadequate managerial class to produce a heady recipe for economic failure. Great-grandchildren of the first industrial revolution, we have tried to abdicate from the mundane technostructure of the second. In short, the English disease is a malady to which America, of all countries, is unlikely to be susceptible for some time yet.[4]

American sociologist Daniel Bell [5] strongly supports this line of thought, even asserting that "in its social and political institutions, England has been a *traditional* society"! Bell [6] insists that "England never completed its bourgeois revolution or its industrial revolution"! One, of course, might be left wondering whether something as imprecise as an "industrial revolution" is ever "complete" or what the children of the great American robber barons are doing these days.

It is not my purpose to confront this "sociological" explanation, which, after all, may easily represent an additional dimension of the affluence-altruism syndrome that lies at the center of the present study.[7] The much more important point is that Marris's assertion that the British economy has been in trouble since the turn of the century is not inconsistent with Tyrell's thesis regarding the destructive role of welfareism. The British welfare state was essentially constructed between 1870 and 1914. Since about 1870, Britain's share of exports in world markets has been declining while its national production growth rate has been low compared with that of countries such as the United States and Germany. Today Britain's per capita income is also low relative to that prevailing elsewhere in Western Europe.

Britain's "take-off" into "self-sustained growth" began during the period 1740–90. By the end of the nineteenth century "the first industrial nation" had experienced an unprecedented increase in material wealth and with good reason was considered around 1870 to be the richest country in the world.[8] Mathias notes that Britain's industrialization could not be attributed to imported capital or to government policy directly promoting industrial growth. Indeed, "the state had its back turned to the economy," and Britain experienced its industrial revolution "spontaneously" and "by consent": "It owed nothing to planners and nothing to policemen."[9] D. C. Coleman[10] reports that the decay of the state's economic regulation was under way in the mid-seventeenth century and became evident by the end of that century. Neither did the industrial revolution owe very much to protection of "infant industries." The last vestiges of protection were dismantled in the 1850s, making Britain to all intents and purposes a free trade country until the twentieth century.

Economic historians have heatedly disputed the question of gains in living standards between 1790 and 1850. However, it is generally agreed that the "upper classes accumulated wealth as never before."[11] For the greatly enlarged mid-Victorian middle classes and skilled artisans who assumed a position of "relative comfort" there were, Pollard and Crossley[12] suggest, "no striking new fields of expenditure which were opened to them, though some particular developments stand out." They list among the consumption conquests of the latter half of the century a "remarkable" growth in the number of domestic servants; the purchase of landed estates or, at least, impressive suburban villas; and other items once the prerogative of the few, including jewels, gold, and

Eastern silks and spices.[13] Moreover, after 1850 a new social stratum of white-collar workers achieved incomes comparable with those of the professions. Bruce [14] describes the wealthy Edwardians as the "supreme hedonists of British history" and adds that "for many others the age was one of solid comfort." Perhaps it is true that the lower classes had up to midcentury experienced only a "marginal" alleviation of their condition.[15] But this cannot be true after 1850. "The national income was expanding so fast that, even with widening gaps between rich and poor probably developing, the poor were benefiting." [16] Mathias [17] states that in the period from 1860 to 1900 "the gain in real wages of the average urban worker was probably of the order of 60 percent or more—even allowing for unemployment." Beyond this an increasing proportion of wage earners were moving into better-paid occupations.[18]

Murphy [19] is unwilling to concede that the "pronounced upward trend in real wage rates" that was "more or less continuously maintained until the end of the century" delivered the working man to "prosperity," but he grants the status of "comfort." Mathias [20] describes the new consumption pattern:

> The age of Blackpool, as Lancashire's playground, had begun. Mass entertainment industries were growing, such as professional football and that greatest mass entertainment industry of all—betting on dogs and horses. One of the great British innovations of the nineteenth century was the Bank Holiday. All this was symptomatic of rising working class prosperity, as the petty luxuries long enjoyed by the rich became the necessities of the poor. . . . The habits, diet, clothes, entertainments, and holidays passed down the social scale.

During this period Britain approached the point "where wage earners are floated off to join the other classes as buyers over the whole range of consumer goods and services." [21] Pollard and Crossley [22] even see "distinct signs" including the sharp rise by 313 percent in the number of persons in "commercial occupations" from 1871 to 1911, "that the new age of high mass consumption began in Britain in the late Victorian era."

Surely in view of this background it will not come as a surprise to the reader that in the late Victorian era there was rapid growth of social conscience among the upper classes and an explosion in social amelioration.[23] Philanthropic bodies proliferated in the second half of the century to such an extent that a foundation was laid after 1869 for the growth of charity organizations.[24] In 1877 the guild of St. Matthew, a religious association with socialist leanings, came into being. In 1884 the Fabian Society (H. G. Wells's "open conspiracy") was organized and dedicated to the aim of convincing the public of the need for the "reorganization of the land and industrial capital from individual and class ownership, and the vesting of them in the community for the common benefit." Also born in 1884 was the Social Democratic Federation whose ultimate goal was a Marxian transformation of society. These societies, together with the Salvation Army (1878), were led by the comparatively comfortable classes and, for the most part, drew their membership from among the affluents.[25] The Social Democratic Federation, for example, was founded by Henry Hyndman, a wealthy intellectual.

The spirit of the times is captured well by Pollard and Crossley:[26] "The poor provisions for the social services came increasingly under attack. . . . The ideas of Free Trade were . . . coming to be questioned . . . and Imperialism found its accusers. . . . But at the time these weaknesses were seen not as signs of decline, but as a failure to use the growing wealth more fairly and more effectively." Most characteristically, at a time when the very poor "were almost certainly a smaller proportion of the population than at an earlier time, the existence of widespread poverty" was precisely documented and "forced upon the attention of a shocked public." [27] When income inequality was "almost certainly . . . just a little less extreme than it had been forty years earlier," critics in the early twentieth century rose to denounce it as "scandalous." [28] Even as late as 1908 Lloyd George felt the country should "shudder" at the "state of things" it "tolerated" when it was "rolling in wealth," and in the following year Winston Churchill felt that "wherever the reformer casts his eye he is confronted with a mass of largely preventable and even curable suffering." [29] Also in 1909, at the end of his budget speech, Chancellor of the Exchequer Lloyd George declared:

> This is a War Budget. It is for raising money to wage implacable warfare against poverty and squalidness. I cannot help hoping and believing that before this generation has passed away we should have advanced a great step towards that good time when poverty and wretchedness and human degradation which always follow in its camp will be as remote to the people of this country as the wolves which once infested the forests.[30]

Beginning in the last quarter of the nineteenth century, minimalism, or laissez-faire, could no longer be said to characterize the stance of the British government, which was becoming increasingly active in the economy.[31] Herbert Spencer's arguments notwithstanding, the scope of regulation and nationalization was greatly enlarged, as were expenditures on social services. "We are all socialists now," declared Liberal Chancellor Sir William Harcourt in 1894.[32] In large measure, the humanitarian reform movement was independent of political parties. Liberals, Laborites, Conservatives—all responded to the public demand. Ashworth [33] considers the change in policy to be "undeniable," "sharp," and "significant." The basis for this view is summarized below.[34]

In the 1880s the government began to set maximum rates that railway companies were permitted to charge for each class of goods traffic. Under the Railway and Canal Traffic Act of 1894 customers were given the right to challenge any charge higher than that prevailing at the end of 1892. Faced with an objection the railway company had to demonstrate the increase was "reasonable." Ashworth [35] notes that as factor prices rose the railway companies were put in a position of "some difficulty." In 1913 the companies were empowered to raise rates to meet rising labor costs. The Factory Acts of 1891 and 1901 constructed an elaborate code affecting most aspects of working conditions. Simultaneously the government was authorized to make even major changes in these regulations by administrative action alone. By the beginning of the twentieth century "such delegation of power to the executive was increasing enormously," and Ashworth [36] believes this "may well have been the greatest single source of the closer regulation of private activity." In 1908 came the first statutory regulation of the working hours of men apart from some railway workers—the Miners Eight Hours' Day. In 1912 the Shop Acts ordered all retail stores, restaurants, and the like to close one half day in each week in addition to Sunday. Also the working week in such establishments was limited to 60 hours.

In 1909 the government with little opposition enacted a minimum wage law and thereby established a "new principle so far as the economic history of the last one hundred years was concerned." [37] Central and local trade boards including employer, employee, and government representatives were established and given power to promulgate schedules of minimum wages for outwork as well as in the factory. At first only the so-called sweated industries, including ready-made clothing, paper box making, and artificial lacemaking, were covered. Within four years, however, the list was extended to include among others candy making, food preserving, and shirtmaking; the grand total of workers covered reached about 400,000. Meanwhile, in March 1912 a similar arrangement was made even for coal miners. Then during World War I, Agricultural District Wages Boards were created.

Economic regulation was accompanied by a growing government sector. In 1870, after twenty-five years of market development in the telegraph industry, the private firms were purchased by the government, which enforced a strict monopoly. When the telephone began to compete with the telegraph, the government dealt with the problem by purchasing all the main or trunk telephone lines and wires in 1892. Service inside the towns was left in the hands of the private sector, but in 1889 the government began to compete with private firms. Extensions of existing firms or establishment of new firms required a government license. Upon expiration of the license the government was authorized to purchase the plant. To add spice to the mixture the postal authorities were given the power to regulate telephone rates. The central government also intruded into the area of savings bank and money remittance services. Nor did the municipal authorities remain passive. The 1890s witnessed a proliferation in municipal operation of gasworks and waterworks, electric supply, electric tramways, steamboats, slaughterhouses, bathhouses, and so on. By the end of the century, government was well on its way to becoming a major employer.

The scope of government ownership was extended by the Development and Road Improvements Act of 1909. A Development Commission assumed responsibility for drainage, forest planting, "light railways" for local traffic, and much else. In 1919 the labor minister began to preside over a National Joint Industrial Council consisting of representatives of employers and unions. The council was recognized as the official consultative authority not only on specific industrial matters but in regard to all questions involving industry as a whole.

Turning finally to the social services, in 1870 a national system of elementary schooling, financed partly by local and central government, was inaugurated. Under an act of 1902 public support was extended to secondary schools. In 1906–9 school authorities were required to sell or give meals to children who came to school underfed. A series of laws from 1882 to 1894 involving Allotments and Small Holding Associations made it the duty of parish authorities to acquire, if need be by compulsory purchase, "allotments" (pieces of land usually from one-eighth acre to one acre). The latter in turn were to be rented out to poor or working-class families to cultivate in their spare time. After 1890, when the subsidy element in the rental was increased, the number of allotments grew rapidly. Under the terms of the Small Holdings Act of 1892 local government was empowered to buy small farms (up to 15 acres) and to rent them out to individuals deemed unable to pay the going market rental. In addition, the law called for the local authorities to meet the demand by purchasing small farms of from one to 50 acres, improving them, and then selling the farms on advantageous terms to cultivators. Nor was aid confined to farmers. The Small Dwellings Acquisition Act of 1899 permitted local governments to make loans to be repaid over thirty years amounting to four fifths of the cost of a small house. Earlier a growing number of localities had begun to build houses for workers under the provisions of the Housing of the Working Class Act of 1890. The Housing and Town Planning Act of 1909 prohibited the construction of back-to-back houses.

From 1884 onward all levels of government were called upon to pay fair wages to their industrial employees and to require their private contractors to do the same. In practice, fair wages meant union wages. In 1908 the central government unveiled a non-contributory scheme of old age pensions. All individuals at age seventy were eligible to receive from 1 to 5 shillings a week provided their means of support fell below a stated level (not more than £21 per year) and provided they were not receiving parish relief. Five years later the recipients (called "pensioners," not "paupers") numbered almost 1 million, with nearly all receiving the maximum amount permitted. In the first full year of the program the total cost was not the previously estimated £6 million but more than £8 million. This of course was taken as a "revelation of the amount of unsuspected poverty among the aged." [38] Winston Churchill provided the rationale for the scheme in 1909: "For a man in the prime of life, old age was far off and provision for it therefore seemed unnecessary." [39] A few years before, in 1906, Churchill as undersecretary for the colonies had called for a "line below which we will not allow a person to live and labour." [40]

In 1911 the National Insurance Act instituted compulsory insurance against sickness for all wage earners below a stated income level. The government assumed a portion of the cost for sickness and maternity benefits, but hospital treatment continued to be provided only by charity and Poor Law institutions. The same act also established compulsory insurance against unemployment, again with a government contribution (one third plus the administrative cost). At first the law applied only to the highly irregular building and engineering trades, constituting about one sixth of all industrial workers. According to Bruce,[41] that 111,000 workers applied for assistance in the first year "revealed the immense scale of underemployment." By 1913–14, over 2 million workers were covered. During the entire 1873–1914 period central and local government expenditure net of both national debt charges and the current expenditure of the "trading services" (nationalized industries) rose from 7 to 14 percent of gross national product.[42]

During the period from 1861 to 1899 productivity measured by real income generated per occupied person (national income per occupied person divided by the GNP deflator) rose at about the same rate in the United Kingdom, Sweden, and Germany (1.65 percent a year). But such similarity ended with the century when, in sharp contrast to the experience elsewhere, "the rise of productivity in British industry was halted abruptly in 1900, and the check persisted down to World War I." [43] But more remarkable is that in the United Kingdom productivity actually *declined:* in 1913 it was lower than twenty years before.[44]

On the other side of the coin of massive social amelioration, the period was one of deep social malaise. "Prosperity," notes economic historian R. A. Church,[45] "acted as a stimulant rather than as a bromide." Labor relations became increasingly bitter; government and opposition attacked each other with unexpected virulence; the militant women's suffrage movement adopted "novel methods of violence and defiance"; [46] revolutionary activity intensified; and more generally a paralysis of authority was noted. The Boer War (1899–1902) raised doubts about the military's capacity to war successfully against even a small nation. Hutchison [47] writes of an "Era of Ill-Feeling." As Roebuck [48] concludes: "The purity of the creed of freedom and *laissez-faire* had always been somewhat sullied by the inclinations of the liberals to succumb to their humanitarian, evangelical instincts, and it had been their quasi-liberal reforms of the nineteenth century which helped start England on the road to collectivism." Moreover, the very same "humanitarian, evangelical instincts" had become increasingly influential on the international scene. Michael Howard,[49] professor of war history at Oxford, notes that "by the end of the nineteenth century the passive liberalism of Cobden was as much on the wane in international relations as it was in domestic affairs." There arose a vigorous "new liberalism" embodied in the Gladstonian view that moral criteria should be applied to the activities of governments and that, in the last resort, a nation might justifiably go to war in defense of the "common interests of mankind."

In 1914 the British Liberals went to war with clear consciences: their government was fighting a just war to uphold "the public law of Europe." [50]

Interestingly, Daniel Bell [51] believes that the reasons for the dynamism of English society prior to the 1870s "are still not wholly clear." (The myopia concerning the role of markets is simply unbelievable in certain circles.) In the next two decades, Bell warns, Britain faces dilemmas threatening "an absolute decline in her standard of living" unless the *government* makes the correct decisions concerning the allocation of resources.

> Economically, any British government will have to choose between modernizing an antiquated industrial plant in order to compete with Germany, Sweden, and Italy . . . and making the leap to the newer post-industrial development by expanding banking, insurance, and trade services . . . or plunging blindly into the newer, and still uncertain fields of high technology, particularly telecommunications. [52]

Meanwhile, the *"new"* Cambridge Economics Policy Group proposes a "siege economy" (i.e., protectionism) to salvage a "senescent British industry"! [53]

CHAPTER 10

SWEDEN'S TIME OF TROUBLES

In both Britain and Sweden modern social policies were initiated amid broad-based and substantial improvement in real incomes. Despite all the qualifications that must be made, the welfare policies . . . are basically the accompaniments of affluence rather than poverty.

—Hugh Heclo

The efficiency or the growth of the Swedish economy along with the almost fanatical Swedish redistribution of income in the postwar period has been quite a remarkable phenomenon.

—Arthur M. Okun

We are at the end of a very long development. We live in a dangerous time. It is possible that everything will go to hell.

—Gunnar Myrdal

Contrary to popular belief, Sweden is not a socialist economy, at least in the traditional sense of having a dominant nationalized sector. The roughly 10 percent of Swedish industry in government hands includes telephonic and postal communications and most railway transportation. Government also plays a leading role in electric power, and firms in mining, iron and steel, shipbuilding, forestry, and banking.[1] Sweden's rapid industrial development,

112

which began relatively late (in the 1890s) occurred in the context
of an overwhelmingly market economy. Second, although held up
as the society most closely approximating the ideals of the welfare
state, Sweden's social welfare policy is quite similar to other "advanced" welfare states such as Norway and Denmark. "Nor has
Sweden," add Furniss and Tilton,[2] "always been a pioneer in the
development of social welfare policy; for example, its compulsory
health insurance program dates from 1955, or seven years after
the British National Health Service." Indeed up to the 1950s when
the Social Democratic government initiated truly significant programs in the areas of health insurance, pensions, children's allowances, and housing subsidies, Sweden's welfare policy had
been cautious, modest, inexpensive, and intermittent.[3]

Since 1950 the picture has changed dramatically. Sweden's per
capita income (apparently) passed and certainly approached that
of the United States, and, predictably, the Swedes discovered an
"underclass" an "other Sweden" that had not shared in the unprecedented general abundance.[4] Also characteristically, the government plunged heavily into environmental protection. For example, it was the first to enact legislation against most aerosol
sprays. The Swedish government sector has been the most rapidly
expanding in the Western World.[5] From 1950 to 1970 the ratio of
government expenditures to gross domestic product rose from
23.2 to 44.9 percent in current dollars, or 32.7 percent in real terms
(for 1971–73 the percentage was 33.9). The corresponding 1970
percentages for the United States are 30.0 and 23.8. Among the
major components, Swedish transfer payments increased in real
terms from 28.4 to 31.0 percent of total government expenditure
while, again in real terms, nondefense expenditure on goods and
services rose from 42.4 to 48.1 percent.

Surely incentives to produce, to seek opportunities, and to invest in improving job skills have been undermined by Sweden's
high tax rates and generous social security benefits. The latter are
illustrated in a study by Sweden's Central Statistical Office reported in the *New York Times*.[6]

It shows that a family with two or more children and with
one working parent can only marginally improve its standard
of living no matter how much family income is increased. For

instance, the head of such a family earning $7,000 a year would actually have a disposable income of $8,500 a year thanks to rent and other subsidies but this would rise only 17 percent if earnings were doubled. More striking is the case of a family with five children and one working parent, whose disposable income would remain almost unchanged whether earnings were $4,000 or $20,000 a year.

During the last ten years, "the tax bite has deepened . . . to an extent that, for executives, real income after taxes is now 25 to 30 percent lower than it was ten years ago." [7]

On the positive side Sweden has had, to the present, no equivalent of the Taft-Hartley Act, the minimum wage law, compulsory arbitration statutes, or national wage and price policies. Also absent is a compulsory national unemployment insurance program. To deal with unemployment the Swedes have relied on an "active labor policy" involving Keynesian techniques, industrial location policies, a state employment information service, retraining programs, mobility allowances, and the like. More ominously, however, Sweden in the past few years has begun to add significant direct controls over the workplace environment and private investment decisions to its impressive arsenal of public services and social insurance.[8] The full implications of a new law, known as the Codetermination Act, are unclear. However, it does require firms to give their employees information about "important company plans and negotiate such plans with the union before implementing them." [9] Another law requires employers to prove serious misconduct before firing a worker and to give up to six months' notice even when layoffs are due to declining market demand. Indeed the trend is to interpret full employment in terms of *property rights* in existing jobs. The government has also utilized national pension funds to influence private investment. Another step "unprecedented in recent Swedish history" has been for the government to take an active role in labor-management bargaining. It has "concluded deals describing the proper 'room' for wage increases in exchange for manipulating the tax system in beneficial ways," thus, according to Furniss and Tilton,[10] "raising the specter of a national incomes policy."

Whether social welfare measures and the more recent direct governmental interferences will "work" or, alternatively, worsen the already serious Swedish economic problems remains to be seen. But Swedish affluence does depend heavily on international trade (more than half of industrial output is sold abroad), and public intervention in collective bargaining has so far failed to restore Sweden's competitive status. Calculations by the business school of Stockholm University suggest that payroll costs grew by 160 percent in the last ten years.

> This meant that for an average hour of work Swedish employers paid out $8.91 in 1977—the highest figure in the industrialized world, according to the Organization of Economic Cooperation and Development. This compared with $7.39 in the United States. . . . The Swedish worker is absent from work and compensated for an average of 22 days a year. This rate, the employers federation maintains, is higher than in any other country.[11]

During 1975 and 1976 alone labor costs rose by a total of 43 percent as a result of increases in wages and social security charges, contributing to an inflation rate of 13 percent during 1977. Naturally export prices rose and, despite three devaluations during 1977, balance-of-payments difficulties continued. Import quotas on foreign textiles were imposed and the value-added (sales) tax was raised three points to 20.63 percent, making it the highest in Western Europe. The tax on petroleum was also raised precipitously.

Interestingly, despite its difficulties in financing oil imports, the government so far has refused to expand nuclear energy. Sweden is situated on the largest uranium deposits in Europe, but in 1978 the Swedish parliament preferred to consider a $9 billion, ten-year energy conservation bill that would encourage homeowners to pack mineral wool into wall cavities, convert double glazing into triple or quadruple glazing, and convert some dwellings to solar energy. In addition the 1977 and the 1978–79 budgets include hundreds of millions of dollars for experiments with wind and solar power. Environmental purity comes high! [12]

Reports for 1977 showed extensive losses in shipbuilding, steel, paper, and iron ore.

> In shipbuilding, for example, Svenska Varv, a state owned company . . . lost $491 million . . . the largest loss ever suffered by a Swedish company. . . . In the forestry business, every pulp mill in the country is now operating at a loss, according to Gunnar Hedlund, chairman of the North Sweden Forestry Owners Association. . . . LKAB, the state owned iron ore giant . . . lost $144.7 million, according to preliminary reports, and the steel industry is estimated to have lost at least double that amount.[13]

In 1977, under the (then) new "conservative" government, three of Sweden's largest shipbuilders were nationalized while the government took a 50 percent share in a new company formed by merging several of the nation's largest steelmakers. Similar actions are in store for the troubled electronics and textile industries.[14] In shipbuilding and steel the Swedes are losing out to Asians, in forestry to the United States and Canada, and in iron ore to Australia and Brazil. In 1977 total profits of companies listed on the Stockholm Stock Exchange fell by 90 percent, the gross national product dropped by 2.4 percent, and private consumption declined for the first time since 1931.[15] Further the same "conservative" politicians who said before election that market forces must be allowed to operate more freely spent more than $6 billion to support weak industries during the 1977–78 fiscal year.[16]

Within Sweden there is a pervasive feeling that the country has entered a long period of economic decline. Per Gyllenhammer, Volvo's managing director, concludes that Sweden has experienced a "deterioration of almost unparalleled swiftness in the competitive power of an industrial nation." [17] "This is no business cycle crisis," adds Sture Eskilsson, spokesman for the Swedish Employers Confederation, "the crisis is basic and structural." [18] Gosta Dahlstrom, a research economist for the trade union organization, admits that "many of our problems will never go away. . . . This could be for Sweden an historical decline. Yes. But it's too early to say." [19] Even the leading proponent of global amelioration, Gunnar Myrdal, is troubled! [20] And the Swedes appear to be yearning—and paying—for more trouble. This takes the form of a government-sponsored study carried out by a United States-based firm, the Boston Consulting Group. The study reaches the unremarkable conclusion that Sweden is a victim of "long term economic problems," but its policy recommendations are quite sensational: a national industrial policy involving consensus decision making, with "risk and returns to be shared across the economy as a whole, rather than assumed by an individual company's stockholders." [21]

CHAPTER 11

WILL THE UNITED STATES DECLINE?

Beneath the frenzied activism of the 1960s and the seeming quiescence of the 1970s, a Silent Revolution has been occurring that is gradually but fundamentally changing political life throughout the western world.

—Ronald Inglehart

The strange fact is that Americans are constitutionally free to do almost everything that our cultural tradition has previously held to be immoral or obscene, while the police powers of the state are being invoked against every aspect of the productive process.

—William E. Simon

In the end there is not so much difference . . . between saying that the decay of capitalism is due to its success and saying that it is due to its failure.

—Joseph A. Schumpeter

(1) THE NEW LITURGIES

Drained by Great Society-type programs, will the United States follow the altruistic path blazed by Greece and Rome and, in-

118

creasingly, create "liturgies" (literally folkworks) of its own? There are strong indications of such a trend, including the evolution of a "quota society." At this writing it is unclear to what extent the Supreme Court's ruling of June 28, 1978, that the University of California's Medical School at Davis must admit Allan Bakke [1] will reverse or retard the momentum of the oppositely directed forces that are discussed below.

Title VII of the Civil Rights Acts of 1964 as amended prohibits discrimination in employment (including hiring, training, referral, promotion, discharge, wages, and fringes) because of sex, race, color, religion, or national origin. However, the Supreme Court in a landmark Title VII case, *Griggs* v. *Duke Power Company* (March 1971), set forth an "adverse impact" doctrine: *in the event that an action has an adverse impact on a protected group, the employer must prove it is necessary for the safe and efficient operation of the firm.*[2] In 1978 Eleanor Holmes Norton, the chairperson of the Equal Opportunity Employment Commission, announced a change in strategy away from litigating individual complaints to a series of major class action lawsuits to end "patterns and practices" of discrimination in key firms and industries around the country. She added: "It is very difficult for a company that did not start hiring yesterday, literally yesterday, not to be in violation." [3] The lawsuits would be aimed at ending "discrimination" built into the institutional structure of business and the labor market in order to eliminate differences in indices of relative unemployment, occupational structure, and income distribution! [4]

President Carter's urban program announced in February 1978 included a provision that all federal agencies require goals and timetables for minority employment contracts. The part of the program under the supervision of the Department of Housing and Urban Development includes a 10 percent minority "set aside." [5] Earlier in 1977, the Department of Transportation made a 15 percent set-aside for minority-owned companies in the $1.8 billion program to rebuild the Northeast rail corridor.[6] A $4 billion public works program approved by Congress in the summer of 1977 requires the Department of Commerce to set aside at least 10 percent.[7] In June 1977 the Economic Development Administration approved $58 million for Los Angeles construction projects subject to a minority requirement.[8] The minority set-aside has been upheld by four federal judges, and eight more have refused to grant preliminary injunctions against it; a California and a Vermont judge have found the minority provision unconstitutional.[9] On May 21, 1979, the Supreme Court agreed to review a case *(Fullilove* v. *Kreps)* involving the 10 percent set-aside provision of the Public Works Employment Acts of 1977.

In October 1977 the Department of Health, Education, and Welfare's Office of Civil Rights charged that thousands of New York City classrooms were illegally segregated based upon the fact that they did not reflect the mix in overall enrollment. The Office of Civil Rights demanded a plan for reassignment of students so that "racially identifiable and/or isolated classes are desegregated." [10] The New York City School System was also asked to explain why black, Hispanic, and girl students are "greatly underrepresented" in the enrollment of its three most prestigious high schools—Bronx High School of Science, Stuyvesant, and Brooklyn Tech. Admission to these schools is based on a merit test, but for the last decade economically disadvantaged students who score just below the test cutoff but are "sufficiently motivated" to handle the difficult curriculum have been admitted. On June 16, 1978, the Office of Civil Rights withdrew its charges against the merit high schools and announced a major "agreement" under which ability grouping could continue.[11] Clearly, HEW had decided it did not wish to be cast in the role of the final destroyer of New York City's school system. But did this represent a major reversal in the trend of HEW's policy? An HEW official hastened to state that the agreement with New York City did not set a precedent for other school systems. Again, as in the case of the *Bakke* decision, we must await the unfolding of events.

In August 1978 and February 1979 the Internal Revenue Service proposed new rules under which private schools that failed to go beyond "paper policies" of nondiscrimination, and thus operated "contrary to public policy," might be deprived of tax exemption. The first step would be to classify a private school as "reviewable" if its percentage of minorities were less than 20 percent of the minority school-aged population in the community it serves. Alternatively, the school policy might be reviewable if the school were formed or substantially expanded within one year before or three years after the implementation of a public school desegregation plan. Then, to remove the IRS's "badge of doubt" and salvage its tax exemption:

> The "reviewable" school must prove to the satisfaction of the IRS that it is operating in a nondiscriminatory manner by showing the existence of *at least four of the following five factors:* (1) The availability of and, granting of scholarships or financial assistance *on a significant basis* to minority students; (2) a program of *active and vigorous* minority recruitment such as contacting prospective minority students; (3) *an increasing* percentage of minority student enrollment; (4) employment of minority teachers and professional staff; and (5) *other substantial activity and evidence of good faith* in combination with lesser activities such as significant efforts to recruit minority teachers, special minority oriented curriculum or orientation programs, minority participation in the founding of the school or current minority board members.[12]

HEW and the New York City School System entered into an agreement to assign teachers to schools on the basis of their race. In March 1978 the agreement was declared invalid by a federal district court judge on the ground that the required public hearings had not been held before signing the agreement. Later, on July 3, 1979, the judge, Jack B. Weinstein, upheld the agreement. At the same time it was revealed that since January 1979 the school board had assigned some 260 teachers on the basis of race.[13] The Los Angeles School Board has set up an "ethnic review committee" to consider cases in which a teacher's ethnic self-identification differs from the one in the files of the school system. In this event an "ethnic discrepancy report" is completed and the teacher appears before a committee consisting of two members from the ethnic group of record and three from the group the teacher wishes to be identified with. The ethnic review committee must be convinced of at least one-fourth ancestry in the desired ethnic group by means of documents or other evidence. This type of hearing may ultimately be adopted by the federal Civil Service Commission as part of its procedure for determining whether employee selection tests put minorities at a disadvantage.[14]

Several years ago a Charlotte, North Carolina, judge tied students to public schools on the basis of their race regardless of changes in residence.[15] More recently, the director of the Labor Department's Office of Contract Compliance Programs revealed that his office is drafting policy revisions to deal with firms that move their operations from central cities, where they are subject to minority hiring goals and timetables, to suburban communities that are mostly middle class and white. "We think they should not be absolved of their responsibilities to these central cities." [16]

The U.S. Civil Rights Commission in an August 17, 1977, letter reportedly asked several textbook publishers to submit those guidelines for their authors that instructed them on how to avoid racism or sexism. The information collected was to be printed in a "resource list." [17] It is feared by some that the "resource list" would provide a basis for denying federal funds to school districts not using federally sanctioned textbooks. At about the same time, in a report called "Window Dressing on the Set," the Civil Rights Commission accused the television networks of racial and sexual stereotyping, "perpetuated by the pursuit of higher ratings and higher profits." [18] In television drama white males had 65.3 percent of the roles and appeared more frequently in "serious roles"; white females had 23.8 percent of all roles and frequently portrayed characters who were "young, unemployed, underemployed, and tied to the family;" minorities had 2.9 percent of all roles and appeared primarily in "ethnic settings" or in otherwise "all-white" shows. Further, minority and female news correspondents rarely reported "crucial" national stories, and civil and women's rights received "minimal coverage" on network shows. Finally, the Federal Communications Commission was taken to task for only a "paper commitment" to end such practices and urged to consider a "variety of regulatory alternatives." [19] On January 31, 1978, the Carter administration announced a program to increase minority ownership of television stations and to divert more government advertising to minority-controlled stations and advertising concerns. The main elements in a petition submitted to the Federal Communications Commission by the Commerce Department and the White House Office of Telecommunications Policy were: deferral of capital gains taxes for broadcasters who sell their stations to minority entrepreneurs; permission of sales at reduced prices and on an expanded basis when the station owners face protracted license renewal hearings provided the purchasing syndicate is at least 50 percent black owned; preference to minorities in certain "competitive" applications for broadcast licenses.[20] The second and third elements were approved by the FCC on May 17, 1978.

The Justice Department on February 28, 1978, threatened to sue Brigham Young University and thirty-six private landlords for violating the Fair Housing Act of 1968 unless the Mormon school changed an off-campus housing policy forbidding single men and women to share apartments or to live next to each other within buildings or wings of housing complexes. A Justice Department official defended the threat but added: "Any suit that would try to put men and women in the same room would quite justly be classified as kooky. But that is not the case at all."[21] A Minneapolis volunteer for the Big Brothers charitable organization presented the name of a homosexual activist as a reference and would not deny being a homosexual. Big Brothers decided it would not bar homosexual volunteers but would inform the mothers and let them decide whether to accept the volunteer. The Minneapolis Department of Civil Rights ruled that this procedure violated a city ordinance forbidding any public accommodation to discriminate on the basis of "affectional preference." The department proposed that Big Brothers should: (1) no longer request or disseminate information about "affectional preferences"; (2) place special advertisements for volunteers in homosexual publications; (3) send its staff to an education seminar run by Gay House; (4) pay damages and attorney's fees.[22] Meanwhile, San Francisco mental health workers are objecting to being required to watch three films portraying homosexual acts as part of a training program. The complaining workers apparently doubt that the films are related to their jobs.[23]

There are, of course, 1,001 variations on the "liturgy" theme. Apparently one of the stronger reasons for President Carter's selection of G. William Miller to succeed Arthur Burns as chairman of the Federal Reserve Board is that Miller had advocated "selective economic controls" in an October 5, 1974, article in *Business Week*. Specifically, he proposed that bank loans be classified as low or high priority according to their social purpose: the lower-priority loans would be subjected to a higher reserve requirement and a mandatory interest surcharge. Along the same line, a study funded by the Savings Bank Association of New York State, conducted by the Harvard–MIT Joint Center for Urban Studies, reportedly suggests that racial lending quotas be established in order to combat discrimination in home financing.[24]

In a speech at Duke University in October 1977, Secretary of Commerce Juanita M. Kreps, a former Duke economics professor, stated that she intended to develop and publish a "social performance index" that would "give business a way of appraising the social effects of its business operations. Businesses might use the index, for example, to provide data on environmental controls, affirmative action, minority purchasing, consumer complaint resolution and product testing." Kreps went on to praise ten firms as having good track records and then, more ominously, suggested that for other firms "not to join" would, "I fear, continue to invite governmental regulation." (For the time being at least, the plan has been shelved in the face of intense business opposition.[25]) Only a few months later, in November and December 1977, the chairman of the Federal Trade Commission (FTC), former consumer activist Michael Pertschuk, made speeches in which he indicated the kind of regulation the Carter administration had in mind. Utilizing the broad language of the FTC Act's section 5 prohibiting "unfair and deceptive acts," his agency would implement a "bold" new "antitrust" policy that would be based, not on narrow economic concepts, but on a concern for "human values"—that is, for "social and environmental harms . . . including resource depletion, energy waste, environmental contamination, worker alienation, and the psychological and social consequences of market-stimulating demands." [26] In 1979 Chairman Pertschuk attacked the "insidious and intimidating effect" of professions ranging from architects to stockbrokers: "Our culture is dominated by professionals who call us 'clients' and tell us our needs," but who cannot be relied upon "to understand our unique preferences, our own particular willingness to trade quality against price, our unique aversion to risk." [27]

On May 1, 1978, former Harvard and Brookings Institution economist Barry F. Bosworth, the director of the Council on Wage and Price Stability, announced that in the interest of President Carter's plan for "voluntary" control of inflation the administration was ready to subpoena corporate records and publicly criticize companies that failed to hold prices down. Bosworth also said that the administration would pressure business executives to hold down increases in their own salaries to 5 percent. At the same time, increases for high-visibility unions in steel, automobiles, trucking, and railroads would have to be for less than 10 percent annually. Finally, Bosworth warned that doctors, dentists, lawyers, and other professional groups would be called upon "in the very near future" to hold down increases in their fees.[28] In January 1979, Bosworth threatened that "around the end of March" he would circulate a list of firms that had failed to comply with the "voluntary" price guidelines. Later he explained: "These firms are spending millions of dollars on public relations that could be wiped out if the finger is pointed at them. They don't want the image of being unpatriotic." [29] In April 1979 Sears, Roebuck publicly agreed to lower its prices, while two recalcitrants, Crown Zellerbach and Hammermill paper, were named in order to build credibility for the guidelines. Dr. Bosworth seemed genuinely relieved by the apparent confirmation of his economic model, which suggested that firms that sell directly to the public would be relatively easy to intimidate.[30] Can it be true? Is Bosworth really a specimen of Harvard McCarthyite?

A jury verdict in the *Berkey Photo-Kodak* case (January 1978) maintained that large firms, even in the absence of a demonstrated monopolistic position, must duly warm competitors of their intention to introduce new products or face antitrust action.[31] In November 1978 the Federal Trade Commission, having decided that Borden's ReaLemon mark gave it an unfair advantage over other competitors in the market for reconstituted lemon juice, enjoined Borden from charging "unreasonably" *low* prices.[32] We drift ever closer to a de facto implementation of a disastrous "no-fault" monopoly concept. Former U.S. Solicitor General Robert H. Bork and economist J. Fred Weston [33] have unhappily called attention to the tendency of the courts to twist antitrust law from restraining collusive price fixing in the interest of market efficiency toward protecting the status of individual producers and hence promoting market inefficiency in the interest of "equality." [34] Bork finds "no obvious stopping point in this process." But, even as things stand today, he warns, antitrust decisions are so suffused with an "egalitarian ideology" that their complete and consistent application would entail a "catastrophic destruction of wealth." [35]

For the not very distant future the public policy menu may reasonably be expected to include some of the delicacies outlined below.[36]

Difficulties in the introduction of new products and technologies will be intensified in order to exorcise anticompetitive, health, safety, and environmental devils.

Attempts may be made to restrict middle-class migration from deteriorating cities, or hamper it via double taxation, in the interests of permanently balancing communities with respect to race or limiting "suburban sprawl." Already there are signs that the growth of newer urban centers in the western states (e.g., Denver, Colorado) will be deliberately retarded by means of water development restrictions—in the name of the environment.[37] Nevertheless, many older urban centers continue to move inexorably in the direction of bankruptcy and federal dependency. As Rutgers University urban specialist George Sternlieb points out: "Even the *states* become very close to bankrupt: New York State simply isn't a big enough tug to move New York City. Inadvertently, aren't we going to have to end with Uncle Sam being the only taxing power capable of moving the ship? Are we not going to have a permanent dependency of a city like St. Louis or Cleveland on the Federal Government?" [38] Roger Starr [39] sees "somewhere down the road to the future" the possibility that the pursuit of racial integration will lead to "significant limitation of the freedom with which Americans choose housing. . . . Someone will be certain to advocate that whites be *assigned* to live where they will produce integration or, at least, forfeit any possible further federal assistance." Related policies might involve land-use controls such as government-mandated "moratoriums" on the construction of new suburban shopping centers,[40] parking lots, gas stations and so on. Graham [41] sees the "problem" as one of "How many and which eggs must be cracked to force the country to be built by new values and standards?" "New," of course, but one cannot help being reminded of the bitter fight waged by guild-ridden medieval towns and their royal allies to suppress the competing economic life of the countryside.[42]

Land-use controls in turn would dovetail nicely with what Briggs calls "The War Against the Automobile." This is indeed a war, and Briggs predicts it will continue to be pursued aggressively, even though "most air pollution is not caused by automobiles," "we do not know the effects of automobile emissions on public health," and "emission controls have reduced auto emissions to a fraction of their previous levels." [43] Automobile exhaust pollution levels have been reduced by about 80 percent since 1968 while raising the cost of the typical car some $400, but the Clean Air Act requires an additional 10 percent reduction by 1981 that will add an additional $350 to $400 to the average price.

Energy rationing is always on the horizon, and nationalization of the large oil companies has become a realistic political objective. On May 6, 1979, Representative Toby Moffett (D.—Conn.), a former Ralph Nader aide and current chairman of the House Government Operations Committee, told a national television audience that oil refineries were operating well below capacity, and he called upon President Carter "to force the production of more gasoline and heating oil." [44] One week later, on May 15, Governor Edmund G. Brown of California signed an order requiring large gas stations to stay open on Saturdays or Sundays. Richard Maullin, chairman of California's Energy Committee, warned gasoline dealers that "if the stick has to be used, then it will be." On June 19, Tina Hobson, the director of consumer affairs for DOE, warned oil companies they are "heading for nationalization." [45,46]

Now that industry is cleaning up, automobile pollution problems are fading, the long cherished "obsession" with economic growth has weakened, and officially defined income poverty is close to complete elimination (3 to 6 percent of the total population), some new "wars" must be invented to meet the continuing demand of the affluents. Robert L. Sansom recommends an attack on "lifestyle pollution." This, we are informed, has the proper credentials for a glorious revolutionary war "because it affects us all, requiring changes in how we live, travel, relax, and work, going right down to such details as the number of blankets we sleep under at night." Fellow affluents, the time has come to end "automobile dominance"; let us inscribe on our banners "Europeans have half as many cars per person as we do" or, perhaps, "New cars purchased annually in this country outnumber new babies by three to one"! [47]

For economist Robert Haveman the "natural sequel" to the War on Poverty would be a war on our "serious income inequality problem." After all, "in relation to other relatively developed countries . . . the inequality of final income is substantial." [48] Of course, any meaningful reduction in the inequality of income would require.tax reforms increasing the effective tax rate on high-income individuals. In addition, Haveman [49] foresees "pressures" for fundamental structural changes in the labor market ranging from "full worker participation in firms' investment decisions, plant location, wage scales, and work arrangements to more modest suggestions for increased on-the-job-training, constraints on firm layoff decisions." In the unfortunate event that such changes are precluded for "political reasons," efforts are likely to be made to supplement labor markets in order to achieve redistributive goals (i.e., wage rate subsidies and earnings supplements together with guaranteed "public service" employment). Haveman [50] appears rather optimistic regarding the commitment of Americans to the search for "cures of opulence."

Not nearly so optimistic and, indeed, more than a little frustrated, is John A. Brittain, a Senior Fellow of the Brookings Economic Studies Program. Brittain wishes to attack the "unfair" income inequality caused by the "inheritance of productivity" by means of higher tax rates. He does not propose "to attack the problem at its roots" by suggesting "that the influence of parents over the speech and dress of their children be reduced, or that parents be discouraged from developing the motivation and productivity of their children or that free choice be eliminated from marital selection." Brittain does admit, however, to feeling "ham-

pered" in his discussion of "policy implications" of inherited productivity "by the importance of nonobjective considerations and
by untouchable institutions"! [51] Indeed, Robin Hood altruists
more and more see political democracy in the United States as an
"untouchable institution" that is obstructing the attack on "unfair" income inequality. We find, for example, MIT economist
Jagdish Bhagwati [52] musing aloud:

> The dilemma . . . is that, while the developing countries by
> and large have centralized regimes and are able to formulate
> and coordinate resource transfers, the developed countries
> generally have democratic, decentralized regimes where re-
> source transfers must be justified to the electorates. These
> transfers cannot be defended when the neoconservative posi-
> tion assiduously tries to undercut the moral case for such
> actions and the liberal case is undermined by the insistence
> on performance criteria that are now rejected by the develop-
> ing countries seeking sovereignty. If only the developing
> countries had the democratic political regimes and the de-
> veloped countries had the centralized ones, the dilemma
> would disappear! This dilemma obtains chiefly in the United
> States.

Penetrating still more deeply into this policy fog, we encounter
zoology Professor Kenneth E. F. Watt, who in 1975 gathered with
a "team of physical and biological scientists" in beautiful Honolulu under the auspices of the East-West Center (a nonprofit educational corporation that receives its basic funding from the U.S.
Congress). Here they set out to "study the relationship between
culture and government." They concluded that the government
should set "upper limits on land holding, income, profits, and
consumption . . . beyond which no member of society would be
permitted to go." Of course the "team" expected to hear the inevitable protests in which the "familiar banners of freedom and
individualism will again be waved." [53] Deeper still, Furniss and
Tilton are encountered. Among the "must" items on their
"agenda for an American social welfare state" are "termination of
capitalist hegemony in the cultural sphere"; control of corporate

investment decisions "in the direction of greater economic efficiency and public utility"; "the elimination of commercial advertising on radio and television." Furniss and Tilton do assure their
readers that their list of "reform measures" is not meant to be
"comprehensive or final." [54]

At this point a brief digression is necessary lest the reader
falsely conclude from the preceding emphasis on "liturgies" and
regulation that the time-honored policy of throwing money at
problems has been abandoned. This is far from the case. Early in
1978 the congressional budget director, Alice M. Rivlin, cited estimates that it could cost $60 billion annually by 1983 to carry out
three programs being actively discussed in Congress ($18 billion
for revision of the welfare system,[55] $30 billion for a start toward a
comprehensive national health program, and $12 billion to help
the cities). Rivlin added that other proposals with substantial
backing (e.g., HEW wanted $60 million to combat the "national
epidemic of teenage pregnancies") together with more generous
funding of existing programs (e.g., farm subsidies) would add
many additional billions.[56] Also at this time one may only wonder
where the modified version of Humphrey-Hawkins bill with its
stated target of reducing the overall unemployment rate to 4 percent in 1983 will eventually lead us. Should the federal government become the "employer of last resort," we would be faced
with the problem of "too few producers," a problem that Bacon
and Eltis [57] blame for the recent severe deterioration in Britain's
economy.

Early in 1979 the Carter administration found itself faced with
the possibility that Proposition 13 portended a genuine tax revolt.
The political problem was how to insure against this risk while
maintaining its essential base of support among the affluents. Carter's advisors hit upon a bold strategy: the administration would
propose a $532 billion spending target for fiscal 1980 and pro-
claim this amount to be "lean" and "difficult"! [58] Only later did it
become evident that many of the spending cuts generated savings
for only one year.[59]

(2) A SCENARIO FOR ALTRUISTIC DESPOTISM

Extracting and underlining what appear to be the dominant present trends here is a scenario for the United States in "1984," in which already tottering interest groups such as the church, Armed Forces, and business will become impotent.

The Armed Forces have received multiple shocks in the forms of defeat in Vietnam; an end to the draft and consequent decline in recruitment standards; the emergence of a nine to five attitude among soldiers; appointment of "minority affairs assistants"; liberalization with respect to dress and hair styles; the 1976 West Point cheating scandal, engendering calls for substantive changes in military codes; and, as R. Emmet Tyrell, Jr., observes, the attempt to turn them into "international branches of HEW."

In 1977 President Carter ordered the first change in the Military Code of Conduct in more than twenty years. The way was opened for Americans taken prisoner to give the enemy more than name, rank, serial numer, and birth date if they are tortured. The change was made "to reduce guilt feelings in prisoners." [60] The West Point Study Group, a panel headed by army generals, criticized the institution for a "relatively humorless atmosphere" and suggested that "a certain grimness marks many of the cadets." The air force and the navy have introduced maternity uniforms, and the army is considering the matter. An air force spokesperson in Washington reported: "All our feedback is very good—the women seem to like it." [61] Life, however, appears to be most sparkling in the navy where Vice Admiral Robert Coogan, commander of the Naval Air Force in the Pacific, insists that today's sailors "are not spoiled brats and we are not mollycoddling them," but admits that "there is a lack of immediate obedience. It is thus more difficult to be a commanding officer." According to instructors at the Great Lakes Naval Training Center, "the reading level of our recruits is often below third grade. That means the sailor can't even read a warning sign in the ship's boiler room." [62] One cannot help being reminded that it was a continuing "labor shortage" that supposedly convinced Rome to make increasing use of "barbarians" in its armies. Moreover, as in the Roman case, serious questions regarding mobility have arisen because our troops at the front lines of defense are not only accompanied by large numbers of dependents (175,000 in West Germany alone) but also include thousands of pregnant soldiers.

The weakness and disintegration of the army has been described and analyzed in a thoughtful and disturbing book by Gabriel and Savage, both academicians and former military officers. Fundamentally, the problem seems to be a failure to comprehend the crucial role of "arational" traditions and rituals in the perpetuation of the kind of organization its members are willing to *die* for. General Motors can be "managed," but an army must be "led."

Perhaps the Armed Forces will regain their balance when the destabilizing shocks have run their course. However, whether the church can recover from radical breaks in traditional practices (e.g., the Episcopal church's ordination of women, one of whom is an avowed lesbian) or will be torn apart is again problematical.[63] More generally, Robert S. Ellwood, Jr., professor of oriental studies at the University of Southern California's School of Religion, sees an ongoing trend in which "today's large, monolithic religious structures" are being transformed "into smaller entities, both within society and within the believer's minds." As a result, he concludes, American religion is "becoming more and more separated from all other major components of American life— education, science, scholarship, letters, entertainment, economics, politics . . . and even from morals." [64]

In short, the influence of organized religion in American life is being brought to an end. There are many indications that the influence of business, too, has sharply declined. One indication remarked upon by Sansom [65] is the "extraordinary" failure of industry's attempts to defeat environmental reforms: "The automobile, steel, and energy industries demonstrated political impotence." Even more impressive is the complete cave-in of business in the face of Nixon's wage and price controls in 1971. It is true that business has shown several signs of recovering its nerve, including a successful 1978 battle against the creation of a Federal

Consumer Agency and the formation of tax-exempt public interest foundations to help business fight government regulation. But as the general counsel of one such group said: "Businessmen have to be radicals now, because they're the outsiders." [66] The extent of the ultimate recovery in business influence remains in doubt.[67]

Continuing weakness of Armed Forces, church, and business would undermine the present dualism of physical and intellectual force, thus clearing the way for the dominant mass media and prestigious universities, which together comprise what might be termed the "executive committee" of the affluents, to complete their encroachment upon, and capture of, the national government. The national media did, it must be remembered, challenge and defeat the national executive in the Pentagon Papers and Watergate conflicts. In the latter case Huntington [68] notes that "The press . . . played a leading role in bringing about what no other single institution, group, or combination of institutions and groups, had done previously in American history: forcing out of office a president who had been elected two years earlier by one of the largest popular majorities in American history. No future president can or will forget that." *The national media, by means of selective "investigative reporting," can destroy the career of virtually any professional politician who places him or herself on the wrong side of the "social issue."*

The essence of a new despotism is precisely the union of physical and intellectual power in the person of a president or, possibly, an Economic and Social Supreme Court,[69] perhaps with tenure in office for life, dedicated at all costs to better society by "going to the roots of social problems." Nisbet [70] warns that "in the name of education, welfare, taxation, safety, health, and environment . . . the new despotism confronts us at every turn." Its strengths lie not only in its "liaison with humanitarian rather than nakedly exploitative objectives" but in a "capacity to deal with the human will rather than mere human actions." In short, a government with a social justice mandate is capable of being as much or even more despotic than the historical despotisms of Pharaohs or kings, who even claimed a divine mandate or a mandate over hydraulic agriculture!

The Supreme Court has played a crucial role in speeding the evolution toward altruistic despotism by making use of the vague, "majestic generalities" of the Fourteenth Amendment, namely "due process" and "equal protection," to bring about what constitutional scholar Raoul Berger [71] calls a "truly extraordinary transformation" of the judicial system. The trend has been away from judicial supervision of procedure in the courts to *government by decree* in which the "demands of justice" and "humanitarian goals" override the "chains of the Constitution" and "arid legalism." [72] This "transformation of consciousness" during the postwar period was "far greater" than in any period since the Revolution, concludes Cambridge University historian J.R. Pole.[73] Berger [74] sees as the underlying premise that "the entire Constitution merely has such relevance as the Court chooses to give it, and the Court is truly a 'continuing constitutional convention' constantly engaged in revising the Constitution, a role clearly withheld from the Court." The possible deduction, he maintains, is that the justices have become a law unto themselves. In April 1978 the Supreme Court in a unanimous decision denouncing "judicial intervention run riot" instructed the Court of Appeals for the District of Columbia to stop blocking the will of Congress by erecting procedural barriers to programs it politically opposed, in this case nuclear power plants. This theme had previously been heard in several of Chief Justice Warren E. Burger's speeches. In 1976, for example, he said the problems leading to the Court's school desegregation ruling of 1954 and its one-person, one-vote decision in 1962 (both by the Warren Court) could have been resolved by Congress.[75] But he seemed to imply that since the problems were not in fact "resolved," the Court was justified in its activism. This implication has since received several striking confirmations.

In *Roe* v. *Wade* (1973) the Burger Court managed to discover in the Constitution an implicit right for women to have abortions. On June 15, 1978 Chief Justice Burger wrote the majority opinion halting completion of a $120 million Tennessee Valley Authority water project (Tellico Dam) because it would endanger 10,000 or so small perch called snail darters. But in his dissenting opinion

Justice Powell maintained: "There is not even a hint in the legislative history of the Endangered Species Act that Congress intended to compel the undoing or abandonment of any project or program later found to threaten a newly discovered species." [76] On June 23, 1978, the Supreme Court decided 8 to 1 that federal judges may limit the time state officials can keep prisoners in "punitive isolation." This decision represented a significant increase in the authority of the federal judiciary over conditions in state prisons. Justice Rehnquist, the sole dissenter, said the federal trial judge who had imposed a thirty-day limit in Arkansas prisons had exceeded his authority by moving "beyond the well-established bounds limiting the exercise of remedial authority by the federal district courts." [77] On March 27, 1979, the Court ruled 8 to 1 that it is unconstitutional for the police to randomly stop motorists in order to conduct license and registration checks. The decision represented a patently obvious attempt to stretch the Fourth Amendment in the interests of the total elimination of opportunities for systematic discrimination. This inference regarding the Court's motivation is based upon Justice Byron White's majority decision that asserts that states would remain free to set up roadblocks and check *all* motorists.[78] Finally, on June 27, 1979, the Supreme Court sanctioned reverse discrimination by private employers and thereby disregarded not only the legislative history but the letter of Title VII of the Civil Rights Acts of 1964. In *United Steelworkers* v. *Weber,* Chief Justice Burger found himself in the minority, and without noting the irony, he accused the majority of "totally rewriting a crucial part of Title VII to reach a desirable result."

The Court's seizure of power, together with the growth of regulatory activity, has already brought us close to a new day in which litigation becomes the primary method of solving all socially significant problems.[79] It is now widely recognized that the welfare state, with its proliferation of open-ended standards and general clauses, has encouraged the dissolution of the rule of law (defined by neutrality, uniformity, and predictability). Law is being replaced by ad hoc measures made to look like law in order to justify expenditures and to shield public servants from personal responsibility.[80] Simultaneously, Unger [81] notes, formalistic legal reasoning is being replaced by commonplace political or economic argument:

> The decline in the distinctiveness of legal reasoning is connected with the need administrators and judges have of reaching out to the substantive ideals of different groups, or drawing upon a conventional morality or a dominant tradition. These changes in the substance and method of law also help undercut the identity of legal institutions and of the legal profession. Courts begin to resemble openly first administrative, then other political institutions. Thus, the difference between lawyers and other bureaucrats or technicians starts to disappear.

Thus, the dissolution of law and the emerging cult of law represent different sides of the same phenomenon.

In order to move still closer to altruistic despotism the remaining powers of local government must be abrogated in order to prevent the "frustration of national majoritarian purpose." [82] Also the legislative, executive, and judicial powers must be rejoined in the interest of a "more unitary and resolute apparatus of public power" needed to pursue the "required social discipline." [83] Advocates of "mass democracy" such as Otis L. Graham, Jr., director of program for the Center for the Study of Democratic Institutions, assure us of course that the new leviathan will "preserve a tolerance of harmless individual thought and behavior." [84] And Lester Brown,[85] head of the Worldwatch Institute (which receives part of its funding from the federal government) adds that of course "political leaders will need to be in constant communication with their constituents, always explaining the reasons for change." An ominous note is struck by Graham's [86] "complex" view of freedom as the right to fulfill oneself "but not at the expense of the common good." He looks forward to a Marx-Engels kind of "freedom" to fulfill oneself "in part by contribution to the common good in a system of ordered freedom."

A vital link in the creation of an altruistic despotism or more generally in the chain of retro-development is the state's resort to compulsory "emergency" measures. Obviously these "quick solutions" are not solutions at all. At most, they are solutions to present problems in exactly the same perverse sense as the earlier less compulsive humanitarian reforms were solutions to the original ones. Minds regarding minimum wage laws, massive welfare systems, and the like as efficacious will, when circumstances become chaotic, easily be convinced of the need for generalized systems of wage and price controls, rationing, restrictions upon geographic and occupational mobility, and so on.

(3) THE PLANNING ALTERNATIVE

Consider an alternative, more optimistic interpretation of present trends. Planning (P) and the market (M) are, after all, alternative decision mechanisms (DMs). Each has its own costs. Real-world DMs are blends of M and P. Holding the amount of the produced "good" constant, substitution of one DM for the other will alter the total cost of production. Technological or other changes may have operated to lower the cost of P relative to M and, hence, to increase society's desired ratio P to M. Or possibly changes in the relative prices of goods or increases in income have increased the desired ratio P to M by altering the composition of desired national output in favor of public goods usually provided by the state.[87]

Current tendencies in the United States are (in the above framework) viewed as the birth pangs of a more intensively planned society (e.g., Myrdal's "The Trend Towards Planning"). The dynamic process of adjustment ("etatism") to a new social equilibrium is easily confused with the early warnings of retro-development. Problems arise primarily because reforms are still being introduced by well-meaning amateurs on a piecemeal basis. Confusion also reigns because previously blank areas in preference systems must now be filled and, as Mesthene[88] notes, because "where technological change alters the relative costs of implementing different values, it impinges on inherent contradictions in our value system . . . calling for deliberate attention to their resolution."

Based on the aforementioned, one perceptive observer, Otis Graham, described the "post–New Deal Broker State" as a "compromise system that contained the social programs demanded by contemporary liberalism but without the institutional capacity or political commitment required for coherent social management." [89] The pattern of Broker State incoherence follows from a modus operandi summarized by Graham: [90]

> A social problem reaches critical proportions . . . vague national goals are legislated in a preface to a new program, which is given to some nearly autonomous agency whose activities are never meshed with activities anywhere else in the government, and oversight is minimal and episodic. Citizens' advisory committees are formed from organized constituencies, a process of bargaining goes on between administrators and organized interest groups, and . . . a haven from competition is arranged for every group strong and persistent enough to arrange it.

But, according to Graham, the Broker State "non-Planning System" has been "run to the end" and will be replaced by "Planning." [91]

Graham's view of "Planning" is somewhat enlightened, permitting not only "public control of destabilizing change" but "some deregulation," allowing America to remain "capitalist." [92] For the reasons given in the next section, such a perspective is untenable.

(4) PLANNING OF THE AFFLUENTS: SOCIAL ENGINEERING

One strong, and well-known, argument against more comprehensive economic planning is its high cost (relative to markets), but this issue is put aside. The heart of the present problem is that in principle there is no difference between enlightened planning and enlightened use of the market. *The well-to-do Establishment that precipitates retro-development by altruistically rejecting the market will also reject planning.* Myrdal's [93] warning that "etatistic

liberals" in the United States "should be aware of the danger that
. . . reactionaries can exploit, at least partly and temporarily, the
popular dislike of tampering by the state and turn it into a resistance against the welfare state itself, and against planning" represents a misunderstanding of "liberals," and therefore, of the "next
phase of growth and perfection of the welfare state."

In order to determine social policy, scientific social knowledge
must first win the support of the affluents by confirming and
strengthening their vision of the way societies function. Accordingly, efficient planning would be viewed by the affluents as be-
trayal of the poor or unemployed, racism, fascism, despoiling the
environment, a scheme to enrich the oil companies or multina-
tional corporations ("corporization" is a favorite epithet of Ralph
Nader), and so forth. Policies that might contribute to urban revival would be hampered because they would give the superficial
appearance of favoring upper-income groups and industry at the
expense of the unemployed. A follower of philosopher John
Rawls, for example, might urge that the most productive individuals be allowed greater incentives in order to increase total
production and, consequently, to raise the absolute incomes of
poverty-stricken recipients of income transfers. But surely the proponent would risk being branded as a trickster seeking to fleece
the poor in the interests of the rich. The "marketplace" can be as
inhuman and destructive as it is "efficient," warns "new ethic"
advocate Lester Brown.[94] But this is equally true of planning.

A very clear test case is the minimum wage law whose harmful
effects (widespread teenage unemployment, especially among minorities—see chapter 3) are well understood by both economists
and legislators. Buchanan and Tullock [95] appropriately ask the
following question: "Would an 'Office of National Planning' . . .
be likely to produce significant change in minimum-wage restrictions?" They answer that such an office "would be no more likely
to produce effective action than those political institutions now in
existence, including the Department of Labor, the Council of Economic Advisers, or the United States Congress. And for precisely
the same reasons." These reasons are of course political, and the
"change in bureaucratic structure will not change one whit the
political interests."

As already argued, the reason for rejecting planning is based on solid grounds: the altruistic well-to-do lack the necessary insight into the way societies function and are insufficiently motivated to invest in acquiring it. Indeed, the extent of their grasp is limited to talk about an "era of limits," "age of crowding"; "exhausted resources"; and, in effect, to replacing the hoary Marxian labor theory of value by a mod, but equally inappropriate, energy theory of value. The "futurist" Victor Ferkiss [96] put it somewhat differently: "Consumerism joins environmentalism as a protest against the world liberalism has made." Similarly, in a work including every known pop-Marxist-Leninist cliché, Paul N. Goldstene [97] comments perceptively on the alacrity and even joy with which the shrinking resource perspective has won public acceptance. It must, he believes, reveal a "deep need" for the "ideological comfort" provided by a concept of scarcity. Even American "radicals," Goldstene adds, "saturate" their Marxism in scarcity, "perceiving revolution as the consequence of poverty not wealth." And why not, after all? To paraphrase English Chancellor Sir William Harcourt or Soviet Premier Nikita Khrushchev: "We are all affluents!" In a more sinister vein, John Shattuck, director of the Washington, D.C., Office of the American Civil Liberties Union, sees in the coming resource scarcity an opportunity for expanding what he calls "constitutional rights" to deal with the situation "in which the effective exercise of rights is impossible to those who cannot afford them." [98]

True, there has been much talk that favors planning or utilizing "tools that put a human on the moon" or "operations research" or "systems analysis," and about "technetronics." Nevertheless, contrary to the macroeconomic folklore, the federal government has by and large been unwilling to rely on or utilize the relatively simple tools of monetary and fiscal policy provided by neo-Keynesian economics through the Council of Economic Advisers. For each episode in which Congress apparently heeded the lessons of the "new economics" there is another in which they seem to have been ignored. Contrast the properly expansionary tax cut in 1964 with the refusal of Congress to cut spending or raise taxes in the overheated late 1960s or with the inflationary stimulus to the economy in 1972. Indeed it now appears that attempts by the political party in office to enhance its image just before elections by reducing unemployment are causing a "policy cycle." There is growing evidence, suggests MacRae,[99] of a politically motivated business cycle in which "macroeconomic policy *caused* fluctuations rather than eliminating them [italics mine]." Tufte [100] provides a variety of supporting evidence. Examining 1961–72 data, he found that in 19 of 27 democratic nations "short-run accelerations in real disposable income per capita were more likely to occur in election years than in years without elections." For the United States, the electoral-economic cycle from 1948 to 1976 (other than the Eisenhower years) consisted of "a two-year cycle of acceleration and deceleration in real disposable income" and a less sharply defined "four-year presidential cycle of high unemployment early in the term followed by economic stimulation, increasing prosperity, and reduced unemployment later in the term." [101] Whereas the unemployment cycle emerged from macroeconomic manipulation, the two-year real income cycle "is especially the product of election-year increases in transfer payments, administrative messing around with the timing of beneficiary programs, and decreases or postponements of taxes." [102]

Assar Lindbeck in his Richard T. Ely Lecture at the 1975 meeting of the American Economic Association "found it difficult to avoid the empirical generalization that inflationary policies followed by restrictive, unemployment-creating actions have been a dominant macroeconomic feature." [103] His understated conclusion, which as we shall see below is easily generalized, is that "the main problem is not that economists are unable to understand analytically what is happening, but rather that the institutional changes and the discretionary policies that are necessary for macroeconomic stability seem to be politically difficult to implement. The director of the Cost of Living Council, John T. Dunlop,[104] even suggests that "the traditional tools of macroeconomic analysis" are no longer relevant in an environment of pervasive and detailed government regulation: "Indeed, the whole complex of internal and external government interventions so complicates analysis that prediction of the consequences of general policies becomes hazardous."

Along similar lines, a 1978 Treasury study reveals that $15.8

billion in federal "countercyclical" revenue-sharing aid had been going not only to cities which, like Washington, D.C., are relatively immune to recession, but "in some instances may have become aid-to-the-government programs." [105] This "anti-recession" aid was terminated by Congress in 1978. Since then the Carter administration has been trying to gather support for a more narrowly focused program. Certain "high-strain" cities (including Boston, Buffalo, Chicago, Cleveland, Detroit, New Orleans, New York, Newark, Philadelphia, and St. Louis) will be hard hit by the program's termination. One way to measure the impact of withdrawal upon the severely "hooked" cities is the rise in the property tax needed to make up for the lost funds: an average $0.65 increase per $100 of full market value.

The "primitive nature" of *actual* government policies is illustrated at length in what follows. The U.S. Forest Service and the Bureau of Land Management have used the chaining technique to clear pinyon and juniper trees from thousands of acres of public lands in the southern Rocky Mountain states, presumably in order to foster the growth of more feed for livestock. According to Baden and Stroup,[106] however, while the "visual evidence of ecological disturbance is massive and compellingly obvious the cost of the chaining practice appears to exceed the value of the additional forage." Meanwhile, highway departments frequently conduct cost-benefit analyses, but "no effort is made to achieve optimality in the economist's sense of equating marginal cost and marginal benefit." [107] In a similar vein, it is interesting to note that "political considerations caused the interstate freeway system to contain large mileage of lightly utilized freeway, especially in the plains states, whereas the investment would have given society a greater return in the more populous areas." [108]

The Occupational Safety and Health Agency (OSHA), with its seven-foot-thick code, prefers costly mandated engineering controls (e.g., machine enclosures) to inexpensive but effective personal protection devices such as goggles or earplugs.[109] In order, for example, to reduce the level of exposure to cotton dust, OSHA mandated the installation of machinery to clear the air at an estimated annualized cost of over $600 million. The implied average cost of preventing a case of nonfatal byssinosis ("brown lung disease") is $380,000. Yet as *Regulation* [110] points out: "The economic impact statement reveals, and then ignores, an enormous difference between the costs of . . . individual respirators and the costs of engineering controls. About $222 million or $1,721 for each worker exposed could be saved by individual respirators." [111]

Again, OSHA's 90-decibel factory noise standard could cost industry as a whole $1.3 billion.[112] But this standard has not been justified in terms of estimates of the benefits to workers of a more pleasant environment and the prevention of hearing losses. Along the same line, recent studies by economists value a life at between $500,000 and $1.5 million, while the National Highway Traffic Safety Administration employs a figure of $270,000 per life saved in setting priorities. However, a coke oven emission standard promulgated by OSHA (which it is estimated will save twenty-seven lives a year) implicitly values a life at between $9 million and $48 million, depending on whether the costs of meeting the standard are closer to the OSHA estimate of $240 million or the industry estimate of $1.3 billion.[113]

Such illustrations (and I have supplied only a few) are not at all surprising, since in 1970 the Congress charged OSHA with assuring, "so far as possible, every man and women in the nation safe and healthful working conditions." In effect, this language treats safety and health as absolute values, which would seem to rule out considerations of economic costs and benefits.

Air quality standards, according to the Clean Air Act of 1970, must be based on public health, which at least in the judgment of the Environmental Protection Agency (EPA), prohibits any economic valuation of costs and benefits.[114] Current pollution control laws will require an expenditure of up to $500 billion over the next decade.[115] But no one has made a reliable estimate of the additional benefits of a cleaner environment. Further, the reliance on emission standards requiring treatment of air and water pollutants is not cost effective—that is, environmental objectives can be achieved at lower cost by means of effluent charges.[116]

According to a Brookings Institution study,[117] the Consumer Product Safety Commission has chosen an index of hazards that is "unbelievably arbitrary" and "without any rational foundation."

A death is scored as 2,516 points against a product, whereas a sprained ankle costs 10 points. This absurd hazard index was adopted under pressure from Congress "to begin regulating." Moreover, the CPSC, "reflecting in part the attitude of Congress, specifically rejected the use of economic analysis" of costs and benefits in creating a rationale for safety regulation.

Grabowski and Vernon [118] found some interesting things when they compared the benefit-cost ratios for twenty-one product classes (ratios that were available to the commission) with the CPSC's own action priority rankings. It would seem from the comparison that the CPSC believes "that the benefits of saving lives or preventing injuries for a product class like television receivers or extension cords (which are given high priority but have very low benefit-cost ratios) are worth several times more than the corresponding benefits obtainable from products like chain saws or drain cleaners (which have much higher benefit-cost ratios but are given considerably lower priority by the commission)." Certainly there is little evidence here of *cost effectiveness* in setting priorities. Similarly, Tollison does not find a very close relationship between the number of antitrust cases brought by the government against an industry and its ranking in terms of estimated monopolistic social welfare losses. He points out that over the 1945–70 period the Antitrust Division brought the largest number of cases against the food industry, which ranked only twelfth in terms of monopolistic social welfare loss.

In 1972 the Equal Employment Opportunity Commission (EEOC) promulgated guidelines making it unlawful for an employer to differentiate in fringe benefits (e.g., retirement, medical) even when the cost of a fringe was greater for one sex than for the other, for example, due to the biological capability to bear children.[119] As a final example, based upon the response in Congress and of the Food and Drug Administration to studies suggesting that drug regulation caused a significant lag in the introduction of new drugs,[120] even of the potential miracle variety, Seidman [121] concludes that "The potential impact of a comprehensive systematic analysis of the effects of policy is limited. If an analysis does not produce results consistent with the needs, preconceptions, and perspectives of policymakers, it is likely to be ignored—even attacked." Nevertheless, as Grabowski and Vernon [122] point out, the FDA's "safety imperative" makes it "almost inevitable that *marginal* costs will exceed benefits and that FDA policy will err on the side of being overly restrictive."

Of course it is quite true that since 1974 an executive order has called upon executive branch regulatory agencies (e.g., OSHA, EPA) to prepare an Economic Impact Statement (EIS) of estimated costs and benefits for each "major" new proposed regulation or legislative recommendation. However, the executive order does not apply to independent agencies (e.g., CAB, ICC), and, as seen above, there is no legal requirement for favorable cost-benefit ratios. Moreover, in November 1977, the Carter administration published a proposal entitled "Improving Governmental Regulation" in the *Federal Register* that *reduces* the modest discipline on the regulation development process. Instead of the existing requirement for a quantitative assessment of benefits and costs, agencies (including now the independent agencies) would be required only to analyze the "economic consequences" of the proposals and alterations.[123]

If macroeconomic policy and cost-benefit analysis have been treated in such cavalier fashion, there is even less reason for optimism regarding the utilization of systems analysis, which has been hailed by its promoters as a space age product. While systems-analytic techniques were diffused throughout the federal bureaucracy in response to President Johnson's 1965 directive, his own administration launched expensive new programs such as demonstration or model cities and rent subsidies without even analyzing costs and benefits.[124] Indeed, the use of systems analysis itself was not evaluated in terms of systems criteria! Hoos [125] notes that "Long before proof, or even adequate trial . . . the technique in its various forms became rigidified and entrenched as required procedure." While quite profitable for those of its practitioners able to win government contracts, systems analysis (outside the military) has become little more than a "demonstration of a particular administration's sophistication vis-à-vis modern management science." [126] "Moreover," Hoos [127] concludes, "because of the way in which systems analysis can be crafted to suit the occasion, the use of hired specialists may serve the politi-

cally useful purposes of masking bureaucratic ineptness and inadequacy, of providing support for a course of action already
decided upon, or of working as a red herring, diversionary tactic."

What remained of the Planning-, Programming-, Budgeting-
System after the fanfare subsided was "paper shuffling and wheel
spinning," and in the meantime the entire system too has been
largely dismantled.[128] The most notable exception [129] has quite
naturally been the Department of Defense, which as James
Schlesinger [130] once noted, "does not supply final goods and services highly valued by influential portions of the electorate."

Beyond misusing or ignoring scientific policy techniques, our
space age policymakers are not always above "cooking" data for
political ends. A little-noticed report entitled *Activities of the
Office of Energy Information and Analysis,* issued in 1977 by an
interagency task force of auditors, concluded that the Carter administration had manipulated the numbers that provided the
basis for its energy program. It is alleged that under the orders
or with the approval of White House energy advisor James
Schlesinger, twenty-one changes were made in the computer
model used to test policy options:

> The net impact of the 21 changes in the Project Indepen-
> dence Evaluation System model was to increase anticipated
> energy demand by the equivalent of 2.52 million barrels of
> oil a day by 1985 and to decrease anticipated supply by the
> equivalent of 1.44 million barrels of oil a day by 1985.[131]

Meanwhile, convincing evidence has surfaced that the U.S. Army
Corps of Engineers with the aid of Congress (section 7a of
the Transportation Act of 1966) has busily engineered cost-
benefit analyses justifying the expenditure of billions of dollars on
waterway projects. It would appear that benefits have been over-
estimated and costs underestimated in the interests of "horse-and-
buggy age" pork-barrel politics.[132]

Then, of course, there is the seat belt versus air bag controversy.
In October 1977 Carl Nash, special assistant to National Highway
Traffic Safety Administration chief Joan Claybrook, denied as
"poppycock" and "absolutely untrue" the claim of NHTSA en-
gineer Thomas H. Glenn that he was pressured to suppress a test

showing seat belts gave better protection than air bags, and then threatened with disciplinary action after he accused the agency of suppressing the test results. Agency officials conceded the belts showed better protection, but they claimed that the seat belts used in the test were cinched tighter than people normally wear them and that the air bags were an old model that has since been improved.[133] On October 12, 1977, the Senate voted to sustain a Transportation Department decision to require air bags or other "passive safety devices" to be installed in all new cars by the 1984 model year.

The government scientist who had the temerity to interfere with HEW Secretary Califano's pet crusade by revealing that there are "statistically tolerable levels" of cigarette smoking will, it appears, be permitted to retain his job.[134]

Another, more serious suppression of science charge against Secretary Califano surfaced in May 1979. Stephen K. Bailey of Harvard University, president of the National Academy of Education, revealed that Califano had buried a report entitled "Prejudice and Pride" because it expressed conclusions contrary to Carter administration desegregation policies. The report, which Bailey had coordinated, included the comments of Nathan Glazer and James S. Coleman, scholars who are not convinced of the benefits of compulsory school busing.

Taken together, the numerous studies of government programs and policies indeed present a "dismal picture of what government does and how government does it." University of Wisconsin economist Robert H. Haveman [135] reports that he is "left with a dominant impression that serious problems of inefficiency and inequity afflict program after program." Indeed, given the pervasiveness of the errors, Haveman is inclined to reject "the hypothesis that the documented performance shortfalls are extreme observations in a distribution with a quite satisfactory average." Two Harvard University public policy researchers, Nichols and Zeckhauser,[136] have concluded that "on virtually all counts, OSHA has not done its job well." Costs have been driven up a great deal, and "little has been accomplished for occupational safety and health."

The chain of causality in the creation of OSHA ran from perceived crisis, through political pressure, to regulatory response. At no juncture did basic conceptual questions relating to market performance or failure, and the appropriate role for government to assume in response, play an important role in the debate.

Summarizing the attempts by the OEO and HEW to subject the programs included in the War on Poverty to scientific evaluation, Brookings Institution economist Henry J. Aaron [137] writes that "evaluation was a political instrument to be trotted out when it supported one's objectives or undercut one's opponent's and to be suppressed, if possible, when it opposed one's objective or strengthened one's opponents." The "painful lesson" for economists, according to Nichols and Zeckhauser,[138] "is that *however relevant or powerful economic concepts may be, they are likely to be ignored when political passions are strong* [italics mine]." [139] Miller [140] adds that the "reluctance of some agencies to go beyond analyzing costs appears to be caused more by pressures from constituents than by an inability to cope with technical problems of economic analysis." Similarly, *Business Week* [141] points out that "seemingly logical proposals for cost-benefit analysis are controversial." The Consumer Subcommittee of the Senate Commerce Committee, chaired by former Senator Frank Moss (D–Utah), attacked such studies as "oversimplified, biased, incomplete, and inaccurate," and in effect recommended that they should not be used at all. "No law maker running for reelection," *Business Week* points out, "wants to be accused of putting too low a value on human life or health—or any value at all, for that matter."

Nichols and Zeckhauser's lesson regarding the irrelevance of powerful economic concepts for actual policymaking finds additional confirmation in the rather obvious bias displayed by government in the method chosen to carry out its numerous "social interventions." According to economic theory, the desired end may be achieved either by a centralized regulatory apparatus (e.g., directly setting product or production process characteristics) or by appropriate alterations in private incentives (e.g., effluent charges to reduce pollution, injury rate charges to improve occupational safety). In practice, as Schultze [142] concludes, "our political system almost always chooses the command-and-control response and seldom tries other alternatives regardless of whether that mode of response is appropriate." The reason is that the humanitarian well-to-do to whom the political system is responding completely misunderstand the working of markets. To the affluents, injury rate charges are "licenses to maim." Thus OSHA head Eula Bingham: "The idea of using workers' bodies to drive the wheel is a philosophy untenable to me. I am in the business of preventing sickness and injury not using bodies to drive up the cost so that business will find it more profitable to comply." [143]

Indeed S. Prakash Sethi, the director of the Center for Research in Business and Social Policy of the University of Texas, sees a "significant change in legal interpretations" in recent cases involving the newer areas of enforcement, such as environment: "Increasingly, the courts, Congress, and the regulatory agencies are placing the blame for corporate law-breaking on the top boss, holding him personally responsible and even jailing him." [144]

For the above reasons, what looms on the present political horizon is not planning at all, but social engineering. This spurious form of planning can be defined in various ways, but is viewed here as an attempt to ameliorate social problems in accordance with quantified but superficial "plans." In these plans econometric analyses of society are largely replaced by scenarios based on mathematical extrapolations of past trends. Such trend extrapolations are notorious for their frequent inadequacy,[145] but this fact seems to be forgotten amid the aura of computer printouts. Roberts [146] adds rather neatly: "Modern oracles employing computer models instead of dead birds have looked into the future and seen inevitable constraints on economic growth," but in "such exercises, with appropriate postulates, you can make the answer come out as you wish."

If the pro-planning talk misses the mark with respect to the actual direction of current political forces, so equally, I believe, does the smokescreen of pseudo-laissez-faire rhetoric that emanates from conservative officeholders and seekers during elections and other ceremonial occasions. Once in power the same conservatives increase intervention in the economy but, of course, only to deal with an "emergency," and only in the interests of a welfare state that would be "consistent" with "conservative principles." In the United States, former President Nixon comes immediately to mind as a politician who spoke "right" but acted "left"; but the fact is that nowhere in the West has there been a general retreat from welfareism.[147] Britain has experienced a rapid growth in public sector employment since 1961. But Bacon and Eltis emphasize that the

> shift has been as rapid under Conservatives as under Labor governments and employment in education increased more rapidly when [Conservative] Mrs. Thatcher was Secretary of State for Education and Science [1970–74] than in 1969–1970; and during the same period, when [Conservative] Sir Keith Joseph was Secretary of State for Social Services, employment in the provision of health and welfare services grew 8.2 percent faster than employment in general.[148]

Then there are Sweden's strange "new conservatives" who embraced the "full employment" philosophy of the Social Democrats even more fervently than their ousted predecessors.[149] "They have stolen our clothes," complained longtime Social Democrat Gunnar Myrdal.[150] In the American intellectual sphere, in order to be accepted as a "neoconservative" one must firmly draw a line and proclaim the need for a welfare state in today's complex society while judiciously opposing welfare excesses.[151] With, I think, a great deal of justice, Lipset and Raab [152] contend that the neoconservative orientation "might just as accurately be called neoliberalism."

The reason for this pattern is forcefully stated by J. R. T. Hughes: [153] "The control bureaucracy is part of our modern social fabric, carefully woven in over many decades. It will not go away, and the people would not tolerate its abolition since they at least believe that it serves them." Norman Birnbaum,[154] an Amherst College sociologist, put it nicely: these days when the "right" in the Western world takes power all that happens is that "the revolution is moved indoors."

The January 1978 *New York Times*/CBS News national telephone survey did reveal growing disquiet with at least one aspect of the welfare state. In 1964, 42 percent of the public agreed with the statement, "The Government has gone too far in regulating business and interfering with the free enterprise system," and 39 percent disagreed. But in the January 1978 survey 58 percent agreed, and 31 percent did not.[155] Nevertheless, despite the panic (or scare tactics) of the vanguard of the affluents, which of course includes the *New York Times,* there is as yet no hard evidence of a grass-roots rebellion against the welfare state. For example, from 1962 to 1977 (approximately the period in which public opinion turned against excessive regulation of business) the percentage favoring government-imposed limits on profits in competitive industries rose from 25 to 55 percent.[156] Moreover, as Nisbet notes, "There are a great many Americans who, although willing to identify themselves . . . right of center . . . are nevertheless unwavering in support of this or that piece of Federal welfare." [157] In 1973, when respondents were asked whether they would agree to higher taxes to finance the many programs they favored, the majority expressed willingness.[158]

Does the June 1978 decision of California's voters to slash property taxes by 60 percent (Proposition 13) portend a genuine tax revolt against the welfare state? Despite all the fanfare and political rhetoric, the national impact has so far been marginal.

Also at this time, the political distillation of the "Rage Over Rising Regulation" is clearly selective. Deregulatory pressure is strongest when the regulations are viewed as benefiting the regulated firms (as in the New York Stock Exchange, airlines, savings and loan associations, eyeglass industry, trucking, railroads, licensing requirements, restrictive advertising practices by doctors and dentists, and so on). Thus, Michael Pertschuk, the chairman of the FTC, says his agency will fight vigorously to eliminate "both private and state regulation which is essentially *dictated by the interests of the professions themselves* [italics mine]." [159] Where the regulations are seen as harming the regulated firms, as in oil and natural gas, the resistance to deregulation has been fierce. For example, Stuart E. Eizenstat, assistant to President Carter for Domestic Affairs and Policy, explained that the idea for a "windfall" profits tax was the result of a search for action that would make decontrol of domestic crude oil prices "less risky in the court of public opinion." [160] But the rapidly growing "public interest"-ori-

ented regulation in the areas of health, safety, and the environment is quite another story. Here the deregulation movement
remains virtually invisible, and it is likely to remain so. A survey
conducted by the *New York Times* [161] in 1979 showed that of
eighteen states considered, environmental outlays were scheduled
to rise in eleven (including California, the home of Proposition
13), to remain roughly constant in six states, and to decline only in
New York.

Of course, some deregulation is better than none, and it is un-
wise to examine gift horses too carefully. The point is that deregulation is unlikely to be carried very far by a movement
deriving a major part of its political clout from an altruistic crusade against business. This will bear watching. Meanwhile, I
would agree with Kristol that "there is far less to 'deregulation'
than meets the eye." [162]

(5) UTOPIANISM OF THE TECHNOCRATS

An interesting and ironic side effect of the rise of mathematical
superficiality is the "decline of the intellectual." [163] In fact, this
decline can be interpreted as the emerging technological unemployment of the "masters of the written and spoken word," as
purveyors of social progress. The intellectuals are reduced to carp-
ing against the "dehumanizing effects of science" while the "active shaping of the future passes into the hands of a socially
somewhat conservative but disinterested, technologically innovative elite." [164] Something along the same line is presented as the
"Humanistic Left–Responsible Center Confronation" by Kahn
and Briggs.[165] It is worth noting that this "technologically innovative elite" is basically utopian.

Given political realities, true planning is unlikely despite often
repeated calls of prospective policy experts and scientific decision
makers for a "restructuring of our political institutions" in order
to "increase the governability of democracies"—that is, *for planning by administrative law.*[166] In this connection Brzezinski's [167]
"prediction" in 1968 is interesting for its unstated assumptions:

Our existing post crisis management institutions will probably be increasingly supplanted by *pre* crisis management institutions, the task of which will be to identify in advance likely social crises and to develop programs to cope with them. This could encourage tendencies during the next several decades toward a technocratic dictatorship, leaving less and less room for political procedures as we now know them.

Similarly, but much more cautiously, Brzezinski's [168] introduction to the 1975 *Report on Governability of Democracies to the Trilateral Commission* remarks on the emergence of

a situation in which the needs for longer-term and more broadly formulated purposes and priorities, for a greater overall coherence of policy, appear at the same time that the increasing complexity of the social order, increasing political pressures on government, and decreasing legitimacy of government make it more and more difficult for government to achieve these goals.

In the same volume's appendix, Brzezinski [169] also refers to a "need to restore a more equitable relationship between governmental authority and popular control." (What does "equitable" mean in this context?) But the problem lies much more in the preferences of the affluents than in the presumed flaws of democracy as a political system.

What our scientific technocrats fail to explain is how they will be able to win and retain power without the support of the well-to-do. Isn't this sheer utopianism on their part? As Feikiss [170] aptly put it: "The cultural and political struggle for the reordering of American society is in large part a war for the soul of the middle class and a struggle over the continuance of its dominant role in American culture." Social values constrain policy choices, and systems dynamics can no more transcend this problem than any other method of decision making. The technocrats cannot determine the ruling values, and consequently they are in no position to revolt against the affluents. Today, as in 1919 when

Veblen [171] saw little in the situation to flutter the hearts of the affluents, no technocratic Lenin or "Soviet of Technocrats" is visible on the horizon. To win the "soul" of the affluents (i.e., to get their attention) and with it power, fame, and wealth, technocrats must renounce science in favor of social justice, worldwide egalitarianism, and so on. They must promise a golden age in which the kinds of activities and values desired mainly by the affluents would (presumably) flourish.[172] Also they are forced to immerse themselves in almost cannibalistic warlike behavior, a style of politics Weaver has called "adversary government" and the "politics of complaint." In this condition goals must be " 'pure'—uncontaminated by such mundane and unedifying concerns as cost, feasibility, and the whole swarming host of competing values that, at one point or another, collide with any one goal when it is taken in extreme"—in a word, uncontaminated by the concerns of the true planner, who as Weaver [173] well notes seeks "not the maximum, but the optimum." The problem of the technocrat is well illustrated by the behavior of government regulators, who according to two experienced participants, Lilley and Miller,[174] exhibit a "tendency to propose or promulgate 'extremist' and/or 'nonsense' regulations, for fear that failing to leave any stone unturned would raise questions about the regulators' 'commitment' to the social objective."

In short, to remain in power the technocrats must use science to dissipate the remaining political opposition to the "solution" of "major" social problems. Hoos [175] adds the ominous conclusion that "there will always be willing mercenaries, some of them academic and all with an entrepreneurial bent interested in using closed-book, mission-directed analysis as a vehicle for personal fame and fortune."

Lewis Lapham [176] beautifully sharpens our focus by calling the technocrat hired by the government "to conduct studies and issue reports" a "courtier" and by adding the warning that "only the provincial scholar forgets that these commissions constitute patronage and that he might as well be making gilded furniture or porcelain shepherds." [177]

(6) THE MALAISE OF THE U.S. ECONOMY

Examination of estimates for the periods 1948–66, 1966–73, and 1973–77 (the last is preliminary) reveals that the growth rate of real output per manhour in the U.S. domestic business economy had declined continuously. The annual rate of increase in productivity stood at 3.5 percent in 1948–66, at 2.1 percent in 1966–73, and at only 1.4 percent in the final period. A more comprehensive but less familiar measure of productivity, total factor productivity, which takes account not only of the contribution of labor but of capital and natural resources, displays a broadly similar pattern: from 2.7 to 1.6 to 0.7 percent in the 1973–77 period. Other data show that the United States has performed poorly relative to other major industrialized countries. During 1960–75 output per manhour in manufacturing increased more slowly in the United States (2.9 percent per year) than in any of eleven other countries. Moreover, although in a number of these countries average annual productivity growth increased after 1966, in the United States it declined by 45 percent—far more than in any of the other countries.[178]

In order to aid in the appraisal of recent growth experience, Edward Denison, Senior Fellow of the Brookings Institution, has attempted to measure the productivity impacts of three changes in the business environment. He concluded that output per unit of input in the nonresidential business sector was 1.8 percent smaller in 1975 that it would have been in the 1967 environment: one percentage point of the drop is ascribable to new requirements for environmental protection and four tenths of one percentage point each for new employee health and safety programs and to increases in the crime rate. From 1973 to 1975 these three changes subtracted 0.47 percentage points—half due to pollution abatement—from the growth rate of output per unit of input. Note that we are dealing here with a substantial impact on the growth rate: nearly one fourth of the annual growth rate of output per unit of input from 1948 to 1969 (2.1 percent). But Denison cautions that other new governmental controls (e.g., consumer protection) have led to an as yet unmeasured portion of the observed decline in U.S. growth rates.

There is also evidence that in addition to this considerable slowing of growth in factor productivity the position of the United States as a world leader in new technology has been slipping. According to a National Science Foundation compilation ("Science Indicators—1976"):

• Patents of international significance are being issued to foreigners relatively more often than in the past. In 1963 patents were issued to Americans by foreign governments 4.5 times more often than the United States issued patents to foreigners. In 1975 the United States patent advantage dropped to a ratio of two times more.

• A survey of the 500 most important innovations (e.g., double-knit fabrics, electron beam welding, urethane foams) to enter the market in six industrial noncommunist countries found the U.S. contribution down from 80 percent in the 1950s to below 60 percent in the early 1970s.

• United States research and development (R&D) spending dropped from 3.0 percent of the gross national product in 1963 to 2.5 percent in 1976.

Even granting a possible element of special pleading by the NSF for an increase in government-supported R&D, there is a disquieting note in the suggestion of science historian Derek de Sola Price of Yale that the United States faces the impending "loss of our scientific and technological empire." Price added that his calculations showed that the U.S. contribution to "world science" in 1967 was 33 percent of the total but at present only 25 percent.[179]

Meanwhile, J. R. T. Hughes [180] in his recent book, *The Governmental Habit*, regards "stagflation" to be the logical consequence of government controls.

The original conception of the controls was always government action which was complementary to private economic decisions. What our bureaucracy *cannot* do is substitute itself and its decisions for the private economy. But it now forms a barrier of enormous proportions between individual decision-makers and the objects of their decisions, all the way from the individual taxpayer to the giant conglomerate. The result is a relatively stagnant, under-employed economy, kept inflated by yearly government expenditures in excess of tax receipts.

Klein [181] even speaks of a "New Victorian" United States! Near the end of Britain's Victorian era productivity slowed down, technological leadership eroded, and the economy became "vulnerable simultaneously to both inflation and recession."

Will retro-development come to pass?

CONCLUSION

Does this mean that freedom is valued only when it is lost, that the world must everywhere go through a dark phase of socialist totalitarianism before the forces of freedom can gather strength anew? It may be so.

—F. A. Hayek

Those who wish to maintain the capitalist system must endeavor to teach the world a little history, and remind it, and especially the young, that though man's achievements are great they are never as solid as they look. If man makes the wrong choice, there is always another Dark Age waiting for him round the corner of time.

—Paul Johnson

I have sought to demonstrate that decline is more than just another scary futuristic scenario. The analysis does not depend upon arbitrary assumptions that transfer natural resource limits on growth from the far distant to the near future. Neither does it involve ignoring history by assuming that technological progress is incapable in the foreseeable future of pushing out limits. Indeed, the increasingly common calls for a deliberate retardation of the economic growth rate and for a worldwide egalitarian leveling of incomes are best viewed as integral components of the decline process. The argument, put forward and supported by historical evidence, relies on an income-elastic desire for altruism, a growing role for political altruism, the rational ignorance of the

158

affluent-altruists, and the counterintuitive nature of complex societies.

Altruism, or the "taste" for helping others, is one of the higher needs described by the psychologist Abraham H. Maslow. An examination of the implications of modern consumer-choice theory, together with the review of a substantial body of behavioral evidence, suggests that affluence markedly increases the altruistic desire. Several considerations, including that of inefficiencies associated with the private provision of a public good, cause affluent societies to substitute amelioration by the state for private wealth transfers. Adolph Wagner's law predicting a rising share of government expenditures seems to hold for altruism. Unfortunately, there is good reason to believe that the persistent and massive nature of the effort to eliminate social problems and improve people's lives ultimately jeopardizes the health of the society.

A great deal of evidence has been presented linking humanitarian motives with social disruptions. In order to grasp the reasons for this linkage it is necessary to take account of both rational ignorance and the counterintuitive nature of complex societies. Given the difficulty of comprehending how societies operate and, of equal importance, the negligible influence that *one* individual can exert on social policy, it is predictable that even the most altruistic person would likely conclude that the cost to him or her of becoming more informed exceeded the expected return in social improvement. But to improve complex societies one must first understand them! Complex societies are like battlefields mined with hidden causes whose impacts run counter to the desires of the rationally ignorant reformer. All too often the plausible-sounding reforms supplied to the well-meaning but naive affluents by profit-seeking politicians and intellectuals have effects opposite to those intended or, by suppressing one symptom, of causing new and more serious problems to surface elsewhere.

The history of Rome and of other societies suggests that perverse reforms can trigger retro-development—a dynamic feedback process leading from affluence to altruism to atrophy! Roughly the chain of events is as follows: affluence increases the demand for altruistic but perverse reforms; lower-class impatience with the rate of progress leads to social strife; simultaneously, the precedents set by the reforms unleash demands for new reforms to benefit left out groups; continued deterioration of economic and political performance due to the reforms themselves and the over-crowding of government lead to further disaggregation of interests and rent-seeking behavior, with a possible accompanying invitation to aggressive, predatory behavior by internal adventurers and by foreign states; emergency measures subjecting individuals to compulsions of various kinds lead to new declines in output and economic efficiency; temporary compulsive measures are extended until they become permanent; repetition of feedbacks until equilibrium with a low-level economy and society that is tradition, localistic, and other-world oriented.

How can we avoid this fate? By this time it should be evident that conventional political approaches at best substitute reluctant interventionists for eager interventionists. The broad ethical questions arising in the choice between collectivism and individual liberty no longer seem to concern most people, and in any event, high-flown moral crusades are singularly incapable of coming to grips with concrete social problems. The growing movement seeking constitutionally mandated spending and taxing limits on governmental bodies is much more promising. Such limits would reduce undesired spending and thus narrow the gap between the existing level of government activity and the level of public services genuinely desired by the public. Government bureaucrats would find it more difficult to implement their pet projects, and possibly, destructive rent-seeking behavior by special-interest groups might be contained.

However, while constitutional limits can mitigate some of the epiphenomena arising in the retro-development process, I do not believe that they can reverse it. There is only one way in which the underlying problem can be solved: increased and more widely diffused understanding of the way markets and societies operate. There are indications that the desire for wisdom and knowledge, like that for altruism, is one of man's higher desires. Perhaps we have now reached a point at which the desire to fulfill this desire can break the apparently immemorial affluence-altruism-atrophy cycle. Certainly new winds are blowing, agonizing reappraisals are taking place, and the monopoly of the liberal reformers in the marketplace of ideas is finally being challenged. Hopefully this study will take its place in an ongoing national dialogue that leads to conscious decisions to alter the trajectory of our society. In any event, even if the light at the end of the tunnel is still very dim, there is something to be said for knowing a little more about its size and shape.

APPENDIX 1

THE CONTROVERSY REGARDING AID IN KIND VS. AID IN CASH

Smolensky has noted that the disutility of poverty is not confined to the poor and that with respect to the demand for federal antipoverty programs "the primary objective may very well be efficiency in the Pareto sense." He suggests that the rise in the so-called poverty line (or standard by which the society judges the welfare of the poor) would "be such that were the incomes of the poor to rise at the same rate, the poor would, by voluntary market actions, satisfy the evolving desires of the community due to changes in its income level for those things in which there are externalities in consumption; e.g. housing." [1] An interesting idea, but note the assumption concerning the nature of utility function interdependence. Quite plausibly the utility index of the rich is taken to depend on specific commodity bundles consumed by the poor rather than (or in addition to) the poor person's utility index or money income.[2] But, to proceed with this line of thought, why then rely on *voluntary* market actions by the poor? As Rivlin [3] correctly points out, the marginal propensity to consume goods in which there are externalities in consumption (housing, medical care, nutritious food, etc.) is less than unity. Might not, she concludes, *aid in kind* cost the affluents less than aid in cash?—certainly a viable explanation for this policy choice. Indeed, it is a sufficient explanation unless one is prepared to argue that the

162

leakage of money into nonexternality goods is *always* offset by higher administrative cost (including that of preventing the subterranean resale of externality goods [4]) or externality measurement costs of giving goods rather than money. To say the least, the evidence pointing in this direction is inconclusive. Browning,[5] however, does argue that "administrative costs tend to be lower with cash transfers generally around 3 percent, as compared to 10 percent for in-kind transfers. Thus, we can actually get 7 percent larger subsidies to the poor at no additional cost to taxpayers by using cash rather than in-kind transfers." And Smeeding [6] estimates that in 1972 the cash-equivalent values to the recipients of in-kind transfers of food, housing, and medical care are respectively 88,56, and 68 percent of their market value. Moreover, some of this aid finds its way to households above the official income poverty lines: only about 31 cents out of each dollar of benefits (cash-equivalent value to the recipient household) accrues to the pre-transfer poor.

Unfortunately, even if all this were accurate and complete we do not know to what extent the return to donors from a dollar's worth of externality goods exceeds that from a dollar in cash.[7] In an empirical study of public housing, Muth [8] does ask whether it "may produce beneficial effects for the community at large." However he ignores direct consumption benefits to donors and considers only effects of slums on other property values and on municipal expenditures. Contrary to Muth [9] and Aaron [10] when both costs and benefits are taken into account, in-kind aid may prove to be efficient, while a "simplified" system of cash assistance might "waste resources."

Friedman [11] seems to reply that undesirable externalities might be discouraged by a tax (e.g., on slum housing) rather than by subsidies (e.g., for decent housing). The rejection of such extra taxes on the ground that they would bear on the poor is taken to mean that "public housing is proposed not on the ground of neighborhood effects but as a means of helping low-income people. If this be the case why subsidize housing in particular?" This is a peculiar argument. Surely "housing externalities" would not evaporate if higher taxes forced the poor to freeze on the streets instead of on the inside! External benefits analysis casts grave doubts on the validity of "libertarian" advocacy of a "negative income tax." [12] Also undermined are explanations of aid-in-kind in terms of "paternalism," [13] preservation of "middle-class values" disguised as "maintaining incentives to work and save," [14] desires of politicians to look as if they are "doing something about social problems," [15] and creation of jobs for civil servants. Explanations of redistribution in terms of the *self-interest of the poor* are weakened as well. For, as Rodgers explains, "recipients always would prefer the cash equivalent of any in-kind subsidy." [16,17] Browning [18] simply misses the point with his argument that if the poor "aren't capable of intelligently making relatively simple choices concerning their own consumption needs, how can they be deemed capable of making the more difficult and important decisions called for in the voting booth?" Aside from the other errors made here, the real issue, of course, is neither "capability" nor "intelligence" but whether different consumption goods provide different external benefits to those that are transferring their income. Browning [19] himself provides 1960 data showing that families with incomes below $3,000 spent 3.1 percent of their budgets on alcohol and tobacco. Interestingly, this is about the same as the percentages spent by the $5,000 to $7,499 class (3.5) and the over $15,000 class (3.0). Are we to believe that an altruistic donor will receive the same benefit from a transfer of $100 in housing, medical care, and so on, as he will receive from a transfer of $100 in cash, $3 or $4 of which will be spent on alcohol and tobacco?

In completing this digression on aid in kind vs. aid in cash, it is in order to ask why a libertarian would tell people they should not spend their money to spread middle-class values. Collard's [20] reply is the "ethical proposition": "Their preferences are their business, not mine." But if one *should not* be his brother's keeper, why not the "ethical proposition": "Their welfare is their business, not mine"?

APPENDIX 2

PROBLEMS IN EVALUATING PUBLIC SECTOR GROWTH

Beck [1] has argued that even the constant-price estimates of the growth since World War II of the national income share of government expenditures on "civilian" programs may, to some extent, exaggerate the *real* growth of the welfare state. This possibility arises because according to his data the price of government-provided services rose substantially more than the price index of total output. Beck asserts that the real size of the *entire* public sector rose from 20 percent of gross national product in 1950 to 24 percent in 1970. The latter "real" figure for 1970 must be compared with a current dollar share of 31 percent. But Dubin points out that Beck understated the growth in real government expenditure, since he deflated transfer payments as well as final government "consumption" expenditure by the implicit price deflator for government consumption. When transfer payments are deflated by the implicit price deflator for *private consumption,* the ratio of government expenditures rises from 22.8 in 1950–52 to 26.8 in 1968–70. (The ratio is 26.7 in 1971–73.)

Of course the continuing growth of the welfare state in the face of the presumed "substantial" rise in the relative price of political altruism would testify to the great strength of the underlying demand. Further, although Beck does not separate welfare state expenditures from all other government expenditures (including national defense, interest on public debt, etc.), his data do indicate that transfer payments grew more rapidly than government "consumption" (i.e., purchases of goods and services).

Questions may also be raised as to whether Beck is correct in assuming that comparatively high prices for government inputs are merely inflationary. Beck [2] states that the two major and equally important sources of the comparatively large rise of the government price index were the "productivity lag in the government sector" and rising salaries of civil servants. To this Buchanan and Tullock add the finding that during the period the wage levels of public employees, especially on the federal level, rose relative to service wages generally. Thus, as they remark: "We confront a puzzle. Why did the salaries of civil servants rise so rapidly over this period?" [3] Their explanation is that increases over time in the number of civil servants has enhanced their political power, which in turn has been employed to win income transfers from the public. But an alternative hypothesis can be defended: the disproportionate rise in wage levels of government employees (i.e., rising expenditure) is not, as Beck believes, merely inflationary; it instead represents a rising demand for quality and/or quantity of governmental output. Federal government civil service ranks run from 1 through 18. A national survey taken by the Bureau of Labor Statistics suggests that in March 1977 private attorneys at the GS-13 level of competence and experience averaged $30,973; chemists, $30,526; personnel directors, $29,188; and engineers, $29,376. The average GS-13 salary is comparable, ranging from $26,022 to $33,825. But the number of government lawyers, for example, has been increasing sharply, reaching 14,312 in 1977.[4] *Time* [5] remarks that Washington, D.C., "is overrun with lawyers—13,000 now, up from 7,000 in 1972." More generally, *U.S. News & World Report* [6] says that "Experts explain higher federal salaries in part by noting the growing trend of government agencies' contracting with private industry for support functions such as janitorial and guard services while increasing professional staffs as a result of automation. This pushes earnings higher, on the average." It is also reported that "the larger agencies with proportionately more high-paying jobs are those employing mostly professionals, such as scientists."

The truth undoubtedly lies somewhere between Beck's position and the alternative hypothesis.

APPENDIX 3

ALTRUISM AND INCOME: ANTECEDENTS

Herbert Spencer linked the "growth of feelings which find satisfaction in the well-being of all" to the emergence of complex industrial societies in which the "well-being of each is more bound up with the well-being of all." [1] He believed that the nineteenth-century extension of political rights in England was facilitated by an increase among the ruling classes of the "highest altruistic sentiment," namely "justice." "The ultimate explanation of the rise of humanitarianism," according to William Graham Sumner,[2] "is the increased power of man over nature by the acquisition of new land, and by the advance in the arts." When this happens men "are willing to adopt ideas and institutions which make the competition of life easy and kindly." For Veblen [3] the economically sheltered position of the "leisure class" favors the exercise of the "motives of charity and of social good-fellowship . . . or, in more general terms, the various expressions of the sense of human solidarity and sympathy." Schumpeter, in his great work *Capitalism, Socialism, and Democracy,* suggests that in response to capitalist development "our inherited sense of duty . . . becomes focused in utilitarian schemes about the betterment of the masses." [4] Like Schumpeter, Nisbet [5] believes affluence "is a fertile ground for the spread of equalitarian philosophy" because it arouses in "a great many of us . . . strong guilt feelings which are in no way anchored in piety . . . but, rather, in contemplation of

168

the plight of the poor." As a final example, Kristol [6] has stated that "those who benefit most from capitalism and their children, especially experience a withering away of the acquisitive impulse" in favor of "acquiring power so as to improve the quality of life."

Schultz,[7] relying on modern microeconomics, has explained the rise over time in the so-called poverty line as representing "an increase in the demand for welfare services for the poor, . . . this increase in demand as it is revealed by the social-political process is a function of the rise in per capita income which can be treated as an income elasticity." Along the same line, Fabricant [8] suggests that philanthropic giving may be "the kind of 'good' which people tend . . . to devote a larger share of their income when they become richer." Banfield in his *Unheavenly City Revisited* has cited the positive impact of income on the desire to "do good" politically. Still another microeconomics-type explanation is advanced by Allvine and Tarpley,[9] who reminds us that "it was in the euphoria of the booming 1950s that the recent wave of societal laws was initiated." They go on to link strong economic conditions with the focusing of attention on "higher order societal issues": "During such halcyon times public attention can be diverted from production and consumption activities toward correction of imperfections." Allvine and Tarpley conclude that "concern over the environment, human resources, and marketing practices is a luxury that tends to increase as affluence rises."

Buchanan [10] has emphasized the "samaritan's dilemma" in twentieth-century Western society. Altruism here takes the form of a loss of strategic courage, "the unwillingness to force members of a group to abide by the rules" or to make the choices "required to prevent . . . exploitation by predators of one's own species." At least in part the origin of the dilemma is to be found in the "increasing affluence of choice-makers" that has allowed them to select the "soft options" (superior economic good) instead of the hard option, "strategic courage" (inferior economic good).

APPENDIX 4

SOCIAL INTERACTIONS AND THE DEMAND FOR ALTRUISM

Becker's model of social interactions does not rely on any conception of needs arranged in order of "relative prepotency," but the implications for the income elasticity of demand for altruism are similar to those of growth actualization theory. Individuals are viewed as spending, according to the usual marginal conditions, own income (earnings, etc.) on own goods *(X)* and on altering the relevant characteristics of other persons *(R)*. R can be interpreted as the living standard of other persons. Becker then shows that social interaction implies that the own income elasticity of demand for X would be low relative to the elasticity of demand for expenditures to alter R.

The latter finding depends on the assumption that an individual receives "free" psychic income benefits (or losses) from his "social environment" *(D)*, that is, from characteristics of others *not* resulting from his own direct efforts. Note that in this case the percentage increase in R would be less than the percentage increase in the individual's contribution to R, since R is the sum of the individual's contribution and a fixed D. Thus, Becker [1] concludes the elasticity of demand for expenditures to alter R would be "certainly larger than the elasticity resulting from equal percentage changes in own income and the social environment."

Two difficulties present themselves in applying this analysis to altruism. First, unlike growth actualization theory, social interaction theory does not determine the *sign* of income elasticities: altruistic behavior may be a superior or inferior good. Of course it does not seem very likely that most consumers would view the services provided to them by altruistic behavior as lower-quality members of some broader family of services. I am not convinced that the passive enjoyment of other people's living standard (free "social income") is fully equivalent to what is understood by altruism (see chapter 1). To some extent, the individual may have to feel a sense of participation in doing good to satisfy the desire (the "Kantian" motive). Conceivably, passive enjoyment (the "public goods" motive) might play only a secondary role.[2] It is difficult to explain voluntary income transfers to organized charities and the like, without believing that the donors receive satisfaction from participation, since, as noted in chapter 1, the living standard of each recipient is a *public* good and consequently subject to "free-rider" behavior. The smaller the fraction accounted for by free "social income" in fulfilling the desire for altruism, the weaker the implications of social interactions theory regarding the relative magnitudes of the income elasticities of own consumption and contributions to the consumption of others (i.e., altruism).

After expressing the doubts and qualifications, the fact remains that the growth actualization and social interactions theories have reinforcing implications for the income elasticity of demand for altruism: positive and greater than that for amenity.

NOTES

INTRODUCTION

1. Page 52.
2. Page 4.
3. Page 203.
4. Pages 746–51.
5. Pages 371–72.
6. Page 549.
7. 1978, page 244.
8. Pages 746–51.
9. 1970, page 2.
10. Chapter 6.

CHAPTER 1

1. Breton; Johnson, 1965 (b); Silver, 1967.
2. Silver, 1975.
3. Monsen and Downs.
4. Page 45.
5. See Coase, 1976, pages 529–30.
6. Pages 225–26.
7. 1969, page 249.
8. Wilson, 1975, pages 110–20.
9. Aronfreed, pages 139–40; Barash, page 78; Wilson, 1975, pages 121–29.
10. Barash, page 313.
11. Page 228.
12. The difficulty of genetic discrimination is also illustrated by the extension of the universal "taboo" on sexual intercourse between brothers and sisters to genetically unrelated individuals. In view of the heavy physiological

172

penalties imposed should there be inbreeding among offspring, evolutionary theory predicts the spread of any genetic predisposition to avoid incest.
Studies of Israeli kibbutzim suggest, however, that sexual aversion de-
velops even between unrelated individuals who have lived together at the
early ages (see Wilson, 1978, pages 36–38). This process appears to depend
upon a maturational device. "Thus in chimpanzees, where sexual play is
common among juveniles, when females reach sexual maturity they begin
to repel their brother's approaches, but display keen interest in males of
other groups" (Young, page 221).

13. Page 109. Midgley, a professional philosopher, makes the same kind of
point in her critique of "Drosophilosphy" or the "atomizing approach to
impulses": "If you believe that the tendency to each specific sort of action
is inherited separately, then all tendencies carrying personal danger are
surprising, because it should have been possible to eliminate them while
keeping all the rest. But in fact there seems no reason to suppose that these
(complex) tendencies are inherited in such small units, however convenient
that arrangement might be to games theorists" (page 132). "How could
there be different *kinds* of motivation for rescuing first cousins, and strangers? Cousins, after all, can *be* strangers; so, indeed, can uncles and brothers" (page 141).

14. Aronfreed, page 140.

15. Macauley and Berkowitz have published a number of studies dealing with
the question of altruistic "need" versus altruistic "norm."

16. Alchian and Allen, 1967, pages 135–42; Boulding, 1973.

17. Manne, 1975, pages 131, 138.

18. Becker, 1974; Pollak; Schwartz; and others.

19. Ireland, pages 28–30.

20. In Salter, page 8.

21. Gray, pages 24–25.

22. van Houtte, page 128.

23. Ashley, chapter 5; Garraty, pages 24–26.

24. Hands, page 15.

25. Gray, page 25; Jordan, page 85.

26. Gray, pages 31–33; Bruce, pages 28–31.

27. Ashley, page 360.

28. Lipson, pages 418–19.

29. Bruce, page 163.

30. In Hands, pages 44–45. See also Arrow, pages 16–19.

31. Ireland (page 20) calls the desire to perform a good act as distinguished
from its result, the "Kantian" motive after the German philospher, Im-
manuel Kant. It is this motive rather than the "public goods" motive that
he considers to be "the truly philanthropic motive."

32. But Ireland (page 23) points to the theoretical possibility "that individuals
might voluntarily contribute for the provision of a public good in excess of

the amount of the public good which would be justified by non-Kantian efficiency conditions."

33. Page 995. See also Tullock, 1970, pages 253–55.

34. Orr performed a multiple regression analysis adjusted for both state per capita income and total number of AFDC recipients. The (statistically significant) estimated elasticity of transfers with respect to the recipient/transfer ratio was about −0.12.

35. Pages 995–96. The infeasibility of forming an "altruist contract" during an emergency situation may explain why bystanders so frequently fail to intervene despite their concern with the plight of the victim and the obvious efficacy (i.e., low cost) of group action. See also Landes and Posner on the law of rescue.

36. In the last few years several "alternative" philanthropic foundations have been founded by affluents, including an heir to the Pillsbury flour fortune. One of these, the Vanguard Public Foundation in San Francisco, even published a book titled *Robin Hood Was Right* in 1977 *(New York Times,* June 10, 1979). See also Tullock, 1970, pages 248–49.

37. To the extent that the motive for charity is "Kantian" (as opposed to "public goods"), those economists who calculate an "optimal" income tax are, consciously or not, adopting the "Robin Hood" altruist's perspective. The assumption that taxpayers will reduce their labor supply amounts to an admission that taxpayers are *unwilling* to contribute.

38. Page 82.

39. Pages 51–52, 202–4.

40. Page 50.

41. Furniss and Tilton, pages 158–60.

42. 1969, page 312.

43. Pages 26, 31.

44. *Historical Statistics,* H-398; *Statistical Abstract,* 1976, no. 510.

45. Weisbrod and Long, pages 17–18.

46. *Historical Statistics,* H-1–2.

47. Borcherding (a), page 32.

48. Beck, 1977. See appendix 2 for a discussion of some of the problems that arise in measuring the growth of the public sector.

49. See Batchelder, pages 160–69.

50. Friedman and Hausman, pages 28–29.

51. Friedman and Hausman, page 28.

52. 1977, page 14. See also Lynn, page 95.

53. Pages 22–24.

54. 1977, page 13.

55. Pages 94–95. See also Paglin, page 22.

56. 1978, page 40.

57. Pages 17–18.

58. 1975.

59. Page xii.

60. Borcherding (a), pages 28, 32. See also appendix 2.
61. *New York Times,* January 22, 1978.
62. See Weaver, 1977.
63. Pages 52–53.
64. Lilley and Miller. page 50. Note that regulations are published several times in the *Federal Register,* but this kind of duplication is absent from the *Code.*
65. *Washington Post,* December 26. 1977.
66. Lilley and Miller, pages 49–51.
67. *Time,* January 2, 1978.
68. *Business Week,* April 4, 1977; *New York Times,* March 20, 1978.
69. *Los Angeles Times,* November 22, 1978.
70. *New York Times,* March 20, 1978.
71. January 22, 1978.
72. January 29, 1978. From 1967 to 1976 civil suits in federal courts have grown 84 percent with much of the increase stemming from key acts by Congress in the areas of environment, civil rights, health, consumer safety, and so on.
73. DeFina (page 12) stresses the need for additional research, since his estimates "cover only a fraction of the regulations in force and in some cases only a part of the regulatory activities" and because in many areas (e.g., Antitrust Division, Consumer Product Safety Commission) "no cost estimate was available for any part of the regulatory activity." The quote in the text is taken from a summary of the paper in *Newsday* (March 2, 1978). Some of the data have been published by Weidenbaum, who has cited estimates of total regulatory cost in 1979 of more than $103 billion!
74. *Newsday,* June 8, 1978.

CHAPTER 2

1. 1970, pages 53–54, 57.
2. 1970, pages 38–46.
3. 1970, page 46.
4. 1965, pages 103–7.
5. Page 251.
6. Page 44. See, however, Pryor's apparently conflicting evidence. He presents correlations for a sample of 60 widely scattered "primitive and peasant" societies indicating that "noncentric transfers of goods appear more frequently in societies at the lower end of the [economic] development scale" (page 276). On the other hand, the index of economic development is positively related to the frequency of centric transfers of goods, but "in the more developed societies they usually act in a regressive fashion, in marked contrast to ... noncentric transfers" (page 304).

7. Cohen himself doubts that the ubiquity of altruism reflects "innate psycho-logical aspects of human beings" and prefers an explanation in terms of a "learning response to socio-cultural norms" (page 55). He attributes the difference in "affective intensity" to "family and household composition, and their effects on socialization" (page 47).
8. Pages 88, 91.
9. Page 39.
10. Page 73.
11. Page 36.
12. This discrepancy would be narrowed if "amenity" were more time inten-sive as a consumer good than "other's necessaries." Mishan (page 161) notes that "consumption of the plethora of consumer goods, churned out by affluent economies, is itself a time-absorbing activity."
13. 1976, page 38.
14. Page 215.
15. See Murray, pages 148–49.
16. See Coase, 1976, page 540.
17. Collard (pages 90–93) has attempted to reach conclusions about the size of income transfers by increasing the specificity of assumptions regarding the form of utility interdependence. He selects a multiplicative utility function of the Cobb-Douglas type in which the proportion of income given away by individual i to individual j is:

$$t = v - (1 - v)^{1/r}$$

where r is the proportion if i's income to j's and v is the weight attaching to j's utility in i's utility function. Given certain special assumptions it follows that t increases with income at a decreasing rate which, in the limit, ap-proaches v. This is an ingenious and fascinating exercise, but I would agree with Collard that it is "probably unrewarding business" and that the actual patterns of donation must be considered.
18. Goode, page 164.
19. Page 126.
20. See Abrams and Schitz; Taussig; and Schwartz.
21. These results are derived from tax return data. Several recent studies cir-cumvent some of the associated problems by analyzing survey data for charitable giving. In 1976 Feldstein and Clotfelter utilized a 1963–64 na-tional survey of households conducted by the Board of Governors of the Federal Reserve System. In one regression in which permanent income is represented with an instrumental variable estimator (current income) the income elasticity is 0.95 (t = 5.1). Most recently, Reece employed data for a large sample of households from the 1972–73 BLS Consumer Expendi-ture Survey. The results of his multiple regressions, which include price and other variables, are quite impressive: the income elasticity of "Char-ity" (i.e., contributions to nonreligious charities) is 1.67 (t = 10.5)!

22. Some evidence is provided by a Conference Board survey of 417 major U.S. corporations published in 1976. In this survey, corporate chairmen and presidents were apparently asked to check the *"most important reasons from a company viewpoint"* for undertaking contribution activities in three fields: United Funds, higher education, and the arts. The percentages of corporate leaders checking "practice altruism with little or no direct or indirect company self-interest" were 10, 8, and 15, respectively (see Harris and Klepper, page 16). But the troublesome question is how a corporate executive would distinguish between "company" as opposed to "individual" interest.

23. 1971, page 386. See also Stigler, 1970.

24. 1975, page 121.

25. Dickinson, page 95.

26. See Bar-Tal, page 78; Mussen and Eisenberg-Berg, pages 134–36.

27. See Rodgers, pages 190–91.

28. Barash, pages 78–89.

29. Page 20.

30. See Collard, pages 110–14.

31. The corresponding estimated income elasticities (at the point of means) are 0.65 and 1.17. The regressions, it should be noted, are adjusted for both the recipient/taxpayer ratio and the total number of recipients. But see the comments of Southwick, Schiller, and Spall and Orr's reply in the *American Economic Review* of December 1978.

32. See Greene.

33. See Crain and Ekelund, page 824.

34. Borcherding (b) (page 56) estimates that the rise in the relative price of public services (assuming a price elasticity of -0.5), increased affluence (assuming an income elasticity of 0.75), and population changes probably explain 50 to 60 percent of the increase in the public sector's real spending over the last 70 years. (He adds that "these factors explain why about one-fifth of our GNP is spent through the public sector, but not a third.") Borcherding attributes the remaining 40 to 50 percent growth in government to "political variables" that admittedly are theoretically and empirically rather intractable (pages 57–69). Thus, it is worth noting that the importance of such variables, together with the "gap" that must be explained, decreases when higher, probably more realistic, values are assigned to the income elasticity.

35. Page 996.

36. Page 64.

37. The effect of heterogeneity of tastes is illustrated by Chester's finding that in countries where Catholics are a minority, the government tends to spend a smaller fraction of the national income for nonmilitary purposes. Obviously, minority Catholic populations experience difficulty in prevailing upon governments to participate in the support of Catholic-oriented social organizations, including schools and hospitals.

38. Page 186.
39. In addition, it appears that in West Europe's welfare states, ideological hostility contributes to this trend. A story in the *New York Times* (July 2, 1978) revealed that "increasingly in Western Europe, philanthropy is acquiring a bad name. Leftists assert it delays the expansion of government-controlled social benefits. . . . Even moderates are voicing disapproval of what they call the elitism of 'philanthropists and their foundations' dispensing large amounts of money and patronage without the controls of electoral mandates or the accountability of government bureaucrats." Most West European governments (but not England) refuse to allow income tax deductions for large individual contributions.
40. Owen, chapter 19.
41. Real taxes and government employment have both risen faster than U.S. real GNP since at least 1900 (Meltzer and Richard; see also Peacock and Wiseman; Chester).
42. Page 66.
43. Page 207.
44. The myth of an "era of limits" has had at least one very realistic outcome. Affluent groups pursuing "New Age" life-styles have sharply increased the market demand for consumer goods that are "durable, repairable, recyclable, energy cheap, authentic, made with simple technology," and, of course, "esthetically pleasing." All this is recounted in the most serious manner by Carter Henderson, who is codirector of the Princeton Center for Alternative Futures, Inc. *(Newsday,* August 17, 1978).
45. 1970, page 4.
46. Page 205.
47. Pages 198–202.
48. 1970, page 101.
49. Page 217.

CHAPTER 3

1. Pages 277–78.
2. Collard, chapter 4; McKean.
3. Page 3.
4. *New York Times,* January 16, 1978.
5. A *New York Times* editorial (January 31, 1977) entitled "The Welfare State Enhanced" is worth quoting. "New York States's ban on pay toilets is a preeminently civilized measure, and we applaud the Court of Appeals for upholding it. Though our society has done much to meet diverse human needs, when it comes to public conveniences there is nothing to brag about. Travelers can testify that on this count, we do not stand high among the advanced nations. The visitor, or indeed the native, who has difficulty

finding a public toilet in any of our cities may attribute the lack to oversight; to find one and then be barred for want of a coin must stir suspicions of sadism. So away with locks. Even in a market economy, welfare measures have their place." However, the paper's news columns told a different story only a few weeks later, on March 6, 1977. Businesses began to replace the outlawed coin locks with token locks. The token is given away free upon request by the proprietor because "stores, filling stations, bars, and bus stations,—just absolutely must have some sort of security over their toilets." To get a token, toilet users must now "look the proprietor straight in the eye."

6. Boulding, 1964, page 57.

7. A recent ruling by the New York State Supreme Court (upheld in the appellate division) has established that the duty of the state's welfare inspector general to uncover fraud does not supersede a welfare recipient's right to a confidential relationship with a social work agency. It seems that the inspector general investigating a case of fraud tried to compel the Community Service Society to reveal whether one of its "clients" was married and employed. Justice Arnold L. Fein ruled the privilege of confidentiality for communications between a client and a certified social worker granted by state law belongs not only to the social workers but to the agency and to the client "who here asserts it." Georgia McMurray of the Community Service Society hailed the ruling as "a landmark decision" *(New York Times,* August 28, 1977, December 7, 1978). Federal Judge Charles E. Stewart, Jr., ruled invalid a procedure whereby welfare payments for dependent children would be stopped if the parents refused to appear for an interview with authorities about possible welfare fraud *(New York Times,* September 15, 1977). Harrison J. Goldin, the comptroller of virtually bankrupt New York City, has reported that welfare checks are being sent to prisoners in city jails. He called this "an intolerable condition whereby taxpayers are needlessly paying for the subsistence of individuals twice." Unfortunately, the City's Human Resources Administration, which had forwarded the checks, hesitated to match its own lists with those of the City and State Corrections Departments because "there is a problem of confidentiality with regard to obtaining any information on youthful offenders, since these records, by law, are not available for review" *(New York Times,* January 29, 1978). In a related development, the Carter administration, concerned about violating the Federal Privary Act, delayed its plan to turn over to private bill collectors $430 million in student loan defaults *(New York Times,* February 12, 1978). Later HEW said it would launch a pilot program for San Francisco and Atlanta, but the private agencies would have to find the addresses of the defaulters by themselves. "We will not release to them addresses obtained through the Internal Revenue Service," said Undersecretary Hale Champion *(New York Times,* April 30, 1978).

8. Page 8.

9. Manne and Wallich, page 9.
10. Sternlieb and Burchell, page xxiv.
11. Page 144.
12. 1976, page 94. Interestingly, Hayek's line of explanation was anticipated by none other than Friedrich Engels, who wrote in the preface to the first German edition (1884) of Marx's *The Poverty of Philosophy:* "The social demand ... remains an unknown magnitude to [the capitalist], both in regard to quality, the kind of objects required, and in regard to quantity.... Nevertheless, demand is finally satisfied in one way or another, well or badly, and taken as a whole, production is finally directed toward the objects required. How is this reconciliation of the contradiction effected? By competition [i.e., markets]. And how does competition bring about the solution? Simply by depreciating below their labor value those commodities which in kind or amount are useless for immediate social requirements, and by making the producers feel, through this round-about means, that they have produced either absolutely useless or useful articles in unusuable, superfluous quantity" (pages 19–20).
13. Pages 76–77.
14. Page 262.
15. 1977, page 41.
16. See Molnar, page 134. Stripped of the hostile, anti-middle-class rhetoric, this may be the kind of phenomenon various social critics refer to as "imposing middle-class values on the poor" (for an example of this, see Johnson, 1965) (b).
17. 1969, page 9. In *The Man versus the State* (1884), Herbert Spencer made essentially this point, but in a less systematic way. Spencer pointed to the many ways in which commonsense inferences about social affairs are flatly contradicted by events, which he linked to the property of a "spontaneously-formed social organization" that "is so bound together that you cannot act on one part without acting more or less on all parts." He cites numerous examples of perverse reforms in chapter 3 on "The Sins of Legislators."
18. Forrester, 1969, page 9.
19. Page 234.
20. Welch provides a concise summary of the recent empirical literature on the employment effects of minimum wage laws. In addition, he takes account of the rising proportion of workers covered, from 43 percent in 1938 to 84 percent in 1978, in devising an index of the impact of minimum wages which forms the basis of the disturbing suspicion that "if general wage growth continues at its average rate of the last decade ... then by 1981 the impact of the hourly minimum will exceed anything we have seen before" (page 30).
21. This aspect remains to be quantified.
22. Page 147.
23. 1978, page 92.

24. Pages 10–12.
25. Page 58.
26. Page 58. See MacDonald and Sawhill for a survey of the mixed evidence bearing on the relationship between AFDC benefits and aspects of family structure. Anderson (page 149) reports that "one striking result of the guaranteed income experiments was a sharp increase in the number of broken marriages" for the participating low-income families. *None of this means that such families would tell an interviewer or themselves recognize that AFDC was responsible.*
27. Blaydon and Stack, page 151.
28. Freeman, page 12.
29. Doolittle, Levy, and Wiseman, page 69. In 1978 Dr. Blanche Bernstein, the former New York City Human Resources administrator, cited a figure of "the equivalent of at least $8600 a year" *(New York Times,* May 15, 1978). Of course recipients place a higher value on a dollar in cash than on a dollar of in-kind benefits.
30. Anderson (pages 44–45) points out that as a result of income testing, "people on welfare now face higher effective marginal tax rates on earned income than even those making $100,000 or more."
31. See Cain and Watts, page 74. Almost all studies predict that transfer payments sizably reduce the labor supply of female family heads and of older men.
32. See Anderson, page 121. Masters and Garfinkel have utilized two nonexperimental sample surveys of individual cross-section data—*Survey of Economic Opportunity* (SEO) and University of Michigan Institute for Social Research Panel Study of Income Dynamics, Office of Economic Opportunity (ISR–OEO)—and two simulation techniques, to estimate the reduction in labor supply resulting from a negative income tax with a guarantee at the poverty level and a tax rate of 50 percent. For the specified demographic groups the effect was found to be a reduction of from 2.4 to 4.1 billion hours of work. In percentage terms, the decline in hours ranges from 12.0 to 20.8.
33. Page 123.
34. Page 121. Bishop suggests that Anderson has "mishandled" the bias adjustments. He adds that under alternative assumptions all bias guesstimates would have to be reduced by half.
35. Page 119.
36. *New York Times,* February 12, 1978.
37. See the excellent analysis by Spencer Rich *(Washington Post,* December 27, 1977). *Time* (June 12, 1978) adds: "Under mounting pressure from claimants and their congressional allies, the definition of disability has been stretched to a point where it can cover a case of nerves, lingering depression. . . . Disability claims are now swamping HEW, which has had to hire 650 administrative judges to hear all the appeals—more judges than the entire federal court system uses." In April 1979 the prestigious Social

Security Advisory Council, headed by economist Henry Aaron of the Brookings Institution, and including economists Joseph Pechman of Brookings and Gardner Ackley of Michigan University, recommended further relaxations of eligibility requirements that could add several billion a year to the cost of the disability program *(Washington Post,* April 21, 1979).
38. 1977, pages 106–7.
39. Pages 113–14.
40. Schultze, page 64.
41. Friedman and Hausman, page 32.
42. The food stamps story is quite similar (see Friedman and Hausman, pages 32–33). On July 18, 1978, the House Commerce Committee amended the administration bill to remove mandatory controls on hospital costs. In 1979 the Carter administration launched an intense lobbying campaign to secure the passage of similar legislation.
43. *Business Week,* April 4, 1977.
44. See *Regulation,* July/August, 1977, pages 9–10.
45. *Washington Post,* April 13, 1978.
45. Gilder, page 38.
47. Page 717.
48. Page 147.
49. September 5, 1977.
50. *New York Times,* September 17, 1977.
51. 1969, page 123.
52. Proposals to end "rent gouging" via rent control were defeated by the Los Angeles City Council in March 1978 in a rather turbulent session. The disappointed backers, however, chanted, "We will be back" *(Los Angeles Times,* March 22, 1978). They were. One year later, in March 1979, Los Angeles Mayor Bradley signed a rent control ordinance. One of its sponsors predicted that other Western cities would now "have the courage to come to grips with real estate speculation which has had such a devastating effect on so many people" *(Los Angeles Times,* March 16, 1979). By April of the same year Jane Fonda, Tom Hayden, and Ralph Nader were leading their "young veterans" in cheering Santa Monica's passage of the "strictest rent control law in the nation" *(New York Times,* April 15, 1979).
53. *U.S. News & World Report,* May 8, 1978.
54. Page 21.
55. *New York Times,* October 6, 1977.
56. It is sometimes alleged that rent controls protect tenants from monopolistic exploitation by landlords, but no such monopoly exists. In New York City, for example, Roger Starr (1978) points out that the city's own Housing Authority owns about 10 percent of the total stock, while among thousands of private owners no one landlord owns more than 5 percent.
57. Starr (1977, page 100) adds that in the era of former New York City Mayor John Lindsay a special Housing Court was established to handle all cases

involving landlords and tenants, and he cites reports that "the Mayor suggested to those whom he appointed to that bench that it was not in the public interest to put families out on the sidewalk even for nonpayment of rent."

58. 1977, page 100.
59. Starr, 1977, pages 100–101.
60. 1977, page 101. New York City's current Mayor Edward Koch reportedly found it outrageous that 60 percent of the tenants in city housing did not pay rent. The problem will soon assume even more massive proportions, since the city expects that by June 1980 it will have taken over 75,000 housing units from landlords who failed to pay their real estate taxes. The mayor threatened evictions (into "temporary facilities") and called upon Congress to repeal a law prohibiting the city from issuing two-party checks to more than 20 percent of its welfare recipients. The city told of its plans to ask HEW to conduct an experiment requiring all welfare recipients in a given area of the South Bronx to receive two-party welfare checks *(New York Times,* May 4, 1978, January 7, 1979). But on February 27, 1979, this "no-nonsense" reforming mayor urged the City Council to extend rent control for another three years. It did so. Then in April of the same year, the Carter administration placed its seal of approval on this incompetent housing policy by ruling that Mayor Koch could set aside $100 million in federal community development funds to help maintain the housing it owned as a result of foreclosure proceedings *(New York Times,* April 10, 1979).
61. Pages 32–33. See Ravitch and "A Response to the 'White Flight' Controversy" *(Public Interest,* Fall of 1978, pages 109–15) for a methodological and empirical treatment of the issue.
62. Coleman, page 33.
63. *New York Times,* April 16, 1978.
64. Page 33.
65. But are the following objections to busing racist? A Cleveland mother wants to know: "Why should I put my kids on a bus and send them across town? What happens if they get hurt? I'm at work all day and my mother-in-law isn't going to drive down Hough Avenue to get them" *(New York Times,* April 16, 1978). In Wilmington, Delaware, a citizen claims that the judge's decision that not only orders busing but that remedial programs not be segregated would reduce all instruction "to the lowest possible denominator" *(New York Times,* February 2, 1978).
66. *New York Times,* November 13, 1977.
67. Page 34.
68. *New York Times,* November 20, 1978.
69. *Washington Post,* June 24, 1978.
70. *Washington Post,* October 9, 1978.
71. Coleman, pages 31–32.
72. *New York Times,* February 5, 1978. A *New York Times* article on "Ten-

sions in Textiles: A Challenge from Asia" ("International Economic Survey," February 5, 1978) stated that "the developing world's gain is the developed world's loss and in the current period of economic stagnation, the developed world is not willing to suffer that loss for a half-hearted altruism called free trade." Thus, 200 years after Adam Smith, the *Times* still does not understand that an uncoerced exchange benefits both participants.

73. *Time,* January 2, 1978. On May 22, 1979, the U.S. Steel Corporation not only agreed to spend $400 million on air and water pollution control equipment for nine western Pennsylvania plants but accepted liability for a civil penalty of $18.6 million for violating federal anti-pollution standards in the Pittsburgh area. The company will now be permitted to construct new facilities in the region. According to the company, the agreement will add $25 per ton to the cost of producing steel by the end of 1982 *(New York Times,* May 24, 1979).

74. *Business Week,* April 4, 1977.

75. *New York Times,* February 5, 1978.

76. January/February 1978, page 56. Meanwhile, in an attempt to lower raw materials prices the steel industry has begun to lobby for export controls on cobalt-bearing scrap and molybdenum *(Business Week,* July 2, 1979.

77. August 21, 1978.

78. Page 178.

79. Page 109.

80. Baden and Stroup (page 24) point out an unintended and unmeasured by-product of controlled natural gas prices in the form of "environmental damages due to the extra electricity production, multi-billion dollar Alaskan gas pipeline, or conversion of coal to gas, all of which are promoted by the shortage."

80. It has been estimated that the redistributive gains to one group of consumers are of the same order of magnitude as the losses to the other group (see Owen and Braeutigam, pages 82–83).

82. Another sort of leakage encouraged by the price controls is the importation of liquefied natural gas (LNG) from OPEC countries at prices above that of regulated domestic natural gas.

83. Page 187.

84. Page 88.

85. Forrester, 1970, page 222.

86. Page 18.

87. 1970, pages 210–11.

88. Pages 388–89. See also Tumlir, pages 30–33.

89. Yet Charles Lindblom concludes his otherwise excellent study of *Politics and Markets* with the extraordinary assertion that the "pivotal" problem of the current American political-economic system is the "ease with which opponents of any positive policy to cope with a problem can obstruct it" (page 346). "A veto of a solution to a collective problem—say, of an energy

policy," he warns, "may put society on the road to catastrophe" (page 347). If we are on this road, however, it is certainly not because we have "vetoed" so-called positive policies. Just the reverse is the case!

CHAPTER 4

1. Schumpeter, page 147.
2. Molnar, page 8.
3. Berger, pages 6–9.
4. Kahn and Briggs, page 28.
5. Burnam, page 302; Carson, pages 16–19; Molnar, page 132; Voegelin, pages 169–70.
6. Dolan, pages 220–21.
7. Page 30.
8. Page 1. For Gouldner (pages 32–33) the "negativity" of the intellectuals is only an "opening move" in their replacement of the "old class."
9. Pages 30–31. Tullock adds, in private correspondence, that Shakespeare was so much a royalist that he was sometimes called in to doctor plays which were having trouble with the censors while Milton spent a good part of his life as an official for the most totalitarian government England ever had.
10. Page 216.
11. Fawtier, pages 219–20.
12. Page 34.
13. Carson, pages 489–92; Freeman, page 9; Tullock, 1971, pages 389–90. "In the face of divergence of scientific findings . . . one of the divergent views (which like its rivals enjoys some degree of scientific confirmation) confirms or is confirmed by some people's ordinary knowledge. They then take that view as authoritative, thus act on it. It appears that a great deal of Professional Social Inquiry offered to problem solvers is of just this kind" (Cohen and Lindblom, page 554).
14. 1979, page 34.
15. In a *New York Times* interview (January 29, 1978), Yale University's Charles E. Lindblom asserted that social scientists have failed to analyze the threat to democracy arising from the undue power of business. Asked if this could be, as Marx suggested, because intellectuals tend to be the servants of the privileged classes, he replied, "Marx was right about a number of things." He surely was! But which are the privileged classes? A few months later Robert Lekachman, Distinguished Professor of Economics at Lehman College of CUNY, resorted to the spurious corporate monopoly power "explanation" of inflation, which succeeds only in confusing "high" with *rising* prices, in order to teach the readers of the *New Republic* that "there isn't much left except some sort of incomes policy" (page 21). This

untenable thesis, which Weintraub (page 216) traces back to Jean Bodin and even Aristotle, serves only to demonstrate that conspiratorial theories are not monopolized by the John Birch Society.
16. 1978, page xii.
17. Page 7.
18. *New York Times,* February 19, 1978.
19. 1977 (b).
20. Page 163.
21. *Washington Post,* June 12, 1978.
22. Jordan Kurland, associate general secretary of the American Association of University Professors, benignly reports that since the mid-1960s "the number of professors with Marxist or strongly anti-establishment ideologies has multiplied tremendously," and he adds contentedly that "increasingly they are being judged on academic merits" *(U.S. News & World Report,* November 6, 1978).
23. Page 94.
24. Keyfitz's research was financed by the Ford Foundation.
25. 1977, page 36.
26. Lipset and Dobson, page 147.
27. The "supply" may be of a nondeliberate or as-if kind when formal empirical data diverge. The *lucky* scientist will "do well" because his or her honest pursuit of truth leads to "doing good"--i.e., to stressing those findings that confirm the preconceptions of the affluents.
28. Page 171.
29. Page 263.
30. Page 153.
31. *Washington Post,* January 9, 1978.
32. 1970, page 89.
33. Page 47.
34. Page 73.
35. Page 74.
36. *New York Times,* August 6, 1978. *U.S. News & World Report* (September 25, 1978) goes so far as to award HEW Secretary Joseph Califano the title "Most Successful Self-Promoter" in President Carter's cabinet." "Among the orders to his public relations staff: Put out a story featuring Califano nearly every day." It has been revealed that HEW spent $100,000 (not the announced $15,000) in celebrating its 25th birthday in 1978. According to the *Washington Post* (April 10, 1979): "The birthday party featured an outdoor celebration starring Big-Bird of the HEW-financed 'Sesame Street' television show and HEW Secretary Joseph Califano."
37. Page 483.
38. Page 29.
39. *Harper's,* June 1978, page 58.

CHAPTER 5

1. Sources on prosperity of the Roman Empire: Carcopino, 1952, page 37; Clark, pages 652-84; Dolan and Adams-Smith, page 51; Frank, 1940, pages 21-22; Hardy, pages 80, 95; Hodgett, pages 41-47; Louis, page 214; Percival, pages 45-46; Starr, 1954, page 278; Stobart, pages 254-58; Trever, pages 433-36, 541-42, 681-83; Walbank, 1969, page 21.
2. Ferrero, 1909, page 216; Frank, 1940, page 21.
3. 1952, page 49.
4. Sources on technical progress: Gimpel, pages 7-9; Kiechle, pages 341-45; Viljoen, page 70.
5. Page 343.
6. Page 258.
7. Pages 659, 662, 678.
8. Based on Clark, table VII, page 678.
9. III, pages 215-16.
10. Sources on the "Good Emperors" and Severi: Abbott, pages 192-93; Bernardi, page 79; Cochrane, pages 140-41; DeBurgh, page 250; Dill, 1956, pages 2-3; Frank, 1923, page 499; Grant, pages 258-59; Hands, page 140; Louis, page 213; Mazzarino, pages 129-31; Mazzolani, pages 182-86; Pirenne, pages 386-87, 399-402; Rostovtzeff, 1957, pages 170, 370, 405; Starr, 1954, page 110, 1971, page 126; Stobart, page 280; Trever, pages 505-10, 597-98, 634-35; Walbank, 1952, page 53. It must, however, be noted that scholars such as Hands express doubts concerning the altruism of emperors and affluents, stressing instead such motives as "the lure of honor" (page 48) and "military requirements" (page 114).
11. Page 39.
12. Attempts to aid the poor during the second century B.C.E. (e.g., by the Gracchi) were associated with *declining* rather than rising real wages of citizen laborers. The decline was brought about by the competition of slaves whose numbers had been greatly increased by the Roman conquests of the times. See Hicks (page 133) on this point.
13. Page 28.
14. See also Hands, pages 47-48.
15. In Pareto, footnote 33, page 114.
16. Sources on the low-interest child support (or alimentary) program: Barrow, page 104; Frank, 1932, pages 99-100, 1940, page 66; Garzetti, pages 349-50; Pirenne, page 387; Trever, pages 512-13.
17. Pages 109-17.
18. Page 133.
19. Page 185.
20. Frank, 1932, page 104.
21. Rostovtzeff, 1957, page 270.

22. DeBurgh, page 250.
23. Sources on the guilds: Abbott, page 233; Frank, 1923, page 540; Hadley, pages 293–96; Hodgett, pages 38–40; Levy, page 97; Mazzolani, pages 209–10.
24. Louis, page 214.
25. Levy, pages 76, 79; Toutain, pages 262–63.
26. 1967, pages 72–73.
27. Sources on dole and *congiaria:* Bernardi, page 33; Carcopino, 1952, pages 30, 40–43; Frank, 1940, pages 68, 72, 76–77; Hardy, pages 100, 107; Latouche, page 9; Levy, page 96. In an especially lavish *congiaria* Trajan distributed more than a third of his Dacian booty to Rome's urban poor. According to Frank (1940, footnote 13, pages 66–67), this war booty might have amounted to more than three times the annual budget of the state. The state also spent a great deal on Athens, and Hadrian even instituted a state dole there.
28. 1940, page 206.
29. Finley, 1969, page 171. This seems to parallel the present situation in the United States in which husbands "desert" their families to obtain welfare payments.
30. Sources on the urban crisis: Bernardi, pages 33–34; Boak and Sinnigen, pages 324, 374; Ferrero, 1914, pages 89–90; Hodgett, pages 36–40; Johnson, pages 186–87, 208; Pirenne, page 395; Robinson (a), page 382; Rostovtzeff, 1957, pages 146–47, 391, 464–65; Trever, pages 517–19, 532; Viljoen, page 83.
31. Pages 34–35.
32. Sources on Diocletian's edict on prices and wages: Abbott, pages 150–78; Frank, 1923, pages 557–58; Hadley, pages 295–96.
33. Abbott, page 155.
34. 1968, pages 148–49.
35. Is President Carter a contemporary counterpart of Diocletian? On September 24, 1977, while Senate liberals were leading a filibuster to prevent action favorable to deregulation, President Carter was telling a crowd in Norfolk, Virginia, that he would "protect their interests" against the "power of the gas company lobbyists" by vetoing a gas deregulation bill *(Time,* September 25, 1977). Characterizing his political philosophy, Carter said: "I vote on each issue as it arises. I make my judgment on the basis of merit" *(Miami Herald,* September 25, 1977). Later, on October 13, in a press conference widely noted for its "problem solving" and "pulpit tone," Carter savaged the petroleum industry using words like "profiteering" and "ripoff" and "grabbing for gross profits" and pointing to the "oil lobby" in terms of "potential war profiteering" in the face of "an impending energy crisis" *(New York Times,* October 14, 1977). Similar rhetoric accompanied the 1979 gasoline crisis.
36. 1940, page 57.
37. Heichelheim, III, pages 294–95.
38. If prices are expected to rise at a rate of x percent a year, the lender must

receive an interest rate of x percent simply to do as well as by holding goods. But the restriction on the nominal rate of interest to 12 percent during a period of hyperinflation prevented the appropriate adjustment. The evidence suggests that earlier, during the second century, the interest rate had risen from a normal 6 percent to the legal limit (Homer, pages 54–55).

39. Heichelheim, II, page 310.
40. Louis, page 213; Rostovtzeff, 1957, page 512. Julian, who was proclaimed emperor in 360, sought to reduce tax rates and expenditures by mass discharges of court personnel, reductions in state employees, and curtailing the postal service. However, less than twenty years after Julian's death, the number of state employees again rose precipitously (Bernardi, pages 66–69).
41. Johnson, pages 198; Roztovtzeff, 1957, pages 380, 405, 407, 448–50.
42. Louis, page 297.
43. Walbank, 1952, page 53.
44. Bakers were forbidden to marry any but the daughters of bakers.
45. Ardant, page 197.
46. Mazzolani, pages 211–14.
47. Frank, 1923, pages 540–41; Hadley, page 295.
48. Johnson, pages 206–7.
49. The rates are not known for Constantine's *chrysargyron*, a poll tax combined with a tax on capital equipment, but it is accepted that it bore most oppressively on merchants and craftsmen (Jones, 1974, pages 170–76; Louis, page 290).
50. Johnson, page 198.
51. Page 202.
52. Dill, 1958, page 247.
53. Hodgett, pages 40–41; Latouche, page 28.
54. Mazzolani, page 210.
55. Dill, 1958, book III.
56. Bark, pages 56–57.
57. Scattered evidence indicates that toward the end of the empire the tax on agriculture had risen to between a quarter and a third of the gross yield of the land (Jones, 1974, page 83).
58. Bernardi, pages 56–57.
59. Page 532.
60. Bernardi, page 73.
61. Bark, page 53.
62. Page 76.
63. Historian Paul Johnson (1977, page 78) has suggested that one reason why the Eastern Empire remained viable was that "the degree of compulsion was much more marked in the West than the East."
64. See Goffart (pages 425–26) for a brief discussion of the decline of openhandedness by the rich Romans.

CHAPTER 6

1. Sources on economic growth: Elvin, Part Two; Fairbank, Reischauer, and Craig, pages 127, 132; Hartwell; Ho, pages 30–31; Hucker, pages 272–78; Kracke, 1969, page 10; Liu, 1959, pages 1–10; Liu and Golas, page ix; Shiba, pages 1, 45, 212; Williamson.
2. Elvin, page 113.
3. Page 39.
4. Page 179.
5. Needham, page 202. Some controversy exists on this point.
6. Pages 272, 277–78.
7. Page 1.
8. Page 167. Tullock informs me that about this time periodic redistribution of agricultural land among families according to their size, etc., was replaced by more secure private ownership.
9. Chan, page 21.
10. Pages 149–57.
11. Page 279.
12. Page 32.
13. Liu and Golas, page xiii. The military prowess of the Mongols must not, however, be completely discounted.
14. Pages 179, 204.
15. Page 355. The Mongols appear to have restored the earlier inefficient system of periodic redistribution of agricultural land (see footnote 8 above).
16. Page 203.
17. Sources on reforms: Balazs, page 43; Cotterell and Morgan, page 147; DeBary; Eberhard, pages 216–19; Fairbank, Reischauer, and Craig, page 129; Franke, page 229; Hsu; Hucker, pages 274–75; Kracke, 1969, page 13, 1970, page 70; K'o, page 51; Lee, pages 73–92; Li, pages 208–9; Lin Yutang; Liu, 1957, 1959; Meskill, pages xi–xii; Miyazaki; Nivison; Williamson, II, page 182.
18. DeBary, page 91.
19. Kracke, 1975, page 70.
20. Page 100.
21. Pages 216–17.
22. Pages 80–81.
23. Meskill, page xi.
24. Page 43.
25. Lin Yutang, page 74.
26. Liu, 1959, page 10.
27. Page 210.
28. Page 219.
29. Page 86.

30. Lee, page 87.
31. See Elvin, pages 62–63.
32. Page 356. But according to Goodrich (page 162) the salvaging of Wang's reforms did not come "soon enough to save China from losing the northern part of her empire."

CHAPTER 7

1. Sources on fifth-century prosperity: Bolkestein, pages 145, 153–54; French, pages 156–61, 172–73; Glotz, 1926, pages 146, 168–69, 286, 1929, pages 311–12; Heichelheim, II, page 33; Levy, page 22; Meiggs, chapter 14; Starr, 1977, chapters 2–4; Viljoen.
2. 1977, page 4.
3. Page 70.
4. 1977, pages 83–84.
5. Meiggs, page 258.
6. Ferguson, page 14.
7. 1926, page 169.
8. Page 156.
9. 1926, page 286.
10. II, page 33.
11. Pages 161, 172.
12. Pages 160–61.
13. Sources on the polis and the market: Bolkestein, pages 135–38; Heichelheim, II, pages 149–53; Homer, pages 34, 40; Laistner, page 383; Starr, 1977, pages 174–77.
14. Starr, 1977, page 191.
15. It appears that Solon's reform (c. 594 B.C.E.) removed all restrictions from rates of interest and loan transactions with the exception that personal slavery for debt was forbidden. During the fifth century interest rates on low-risk loans ranged from 10 to 12 percent per annum.
16. II, pages 152–53.
17. Sources on social welfare expenditures: Andreades, pages 225, 265–66; Bonner, 1927, page 39; French, pages 148–53; Glotz, 1926, pages 147–50, 1929, pages 17, 239–42; Heichelheim, II, pages 135–37, 143; Jones, 1964, pages 17, 50; Michell, page 367; Rostovtzeff, 1963, page 208.
18. Page 151.
19. 1933, page 37.
20. Robinson (b), pages 271–72, observes during the Periclean Age "a considerable increase in the scope and volume of litigation" to the point that by the fourth century "the litigious habits of the Athenian became in fact, one of his most pronounced characteristics." The parallel with the present United States is sharpened by the evolution of "an unpleasant type of

man," the sycophant, who, playing the "part of the modern detective and crown-prosecutor rolled into one" devoted his time to "bringing suits against persons with whom he was in no way directly concerned." While the sycophant presented himself as a watchdog and public benefactor, it is nevertheless true that a successful suit (or a credible threat) might open wide the doors to political power and wealth via hush money or a share of the proceeds from the conviction of those violating the laws regarding commerce or public property (Bonner, 1927, chapter iv). Bonner notes that many of the victims belonged to the "better class" and that it became commonplace for the jurors to be "warned that democratic institutions are in danger, that the defendant is trying to put himself above the laws and is insulting the constitution and courts" (1927, pages 66, 78).

21. Page 153.
22. II, page 143.
23. Sources on the depression of the fourth century: Clark, pages 682–83; Ehrenberg, page 87; French, page 169; Glotz, 1929, page 213; Heichelheim, II, page 34; Levy, page 31; Meiggs, page 260; Rostovtzeff, 1963, pages 209, 275; Smith, page 91.
24. But Calhoun (page 44) believes that having taken shelter in the city and tasted its amenities and stipends for state service, the peasant farmers "were in many cases disinclined to return to the countryside to reclaim their ruined lands."
25. Sources on social welfare in the fourth century: Andreades, pages 258–61, 358–63; Ehrenberg, page 87; Glotz, 1929, pages 309–27, 339–41; Heichelheim, II, page 144; Jones, 1964, page 50; Levy, pages 31–32; Rostovtzeff, 1963, pages 276–77.
26. Starr, 1977, pages 47–48.
27. Page 87.

CHAPTER 8

1. 1952, page 63.
2. Page 182.
3. 1960, page 67.
4. Pages 400, 403.
5. Page 27.
6. Pages 363–64.
7. Page 364.
8. One line of reconciliation is that exploitation declined not through lack of opportunities (rising costs) but as a result of lack of desire to exploit—i.e., humanitarianism. With respect to the decline of slavery, Finley (1973, page 86) rejects the "curious assumption" that Germans, unlike the earlier "barbarians," were unsuited to slavery.
9. 1954, page 362.

10. Pages 79–83.
11. Page 58.
12. It appears that civil strife occurs because the reforms, or rather the expectations they raise and the publicity given to the evil and unnecessary nature of the specific problem, make the prospective beneficiaries impatient with the rate of progress. The result is the well-known "rising expectations" or, perhaps, "the world owes me a living" syndrome (see Kahn and Weiner, pages 202–3).
13. Potential revolutionaries quite rationally regard these goings on as signals of weakness or submission on the part of the ruling Establishment. The beneficiaries of the reforms and the revolutionaries come to feel not only that they have the right to the donors' wealth but also that the latter will not resist attempts to expropriate them. (This line of argument, together with supporting historical evidence, is presented in Silver, 1974; see also Buchanan, 1975, on "loss of strategic courage.").
14. See Cipolla, 1970, pages 13–14.
15. Writing about the *Roman Government's Response to Crisis,* MacMullen (page 122) notes that the "government's grasp of the economy was loosened by shocks of its own making, and a vast range of problems developed in the third century beyond its comprehension."
    16. This sort of world has found its elitist glorifiers in economists as disparate as Karl Marx and E. J. Mishan. How ironic that the other-world, anti-growth ideology increasingly serves as the "new opiate of the masses"! Interestingly, medieval historian Norman Cantor observes that the recent "neo-humanist, anti-industrialist attitude" is "one that in a peculiar way is actually very close to the interpretation of modernism that prevailed in nineteenth- and early-twentieth-century Catholicism. This Catholic interpretation condemned the modern world as materialistic, as putting business above divine values, as placing pragmatic social dictates above man's conscience" (pages 303–4).
17. 1976, pages 142–43.
18. Page 145.
19. Having noted this trend Reynolds and Smolensky (pages 35–36) describe a "stylized life cycle" of a transfer program that first targets "on a relatively small, 'deserving' group, who may or may not be poor—for example, the aged. If the poor are not explicitly included initially, they are often brought in by stretching eligibility or benefits a little bit. Taxes seem to proceed from the opposite pole, with coverage gradually extended down the income distribution."
20. Krueger, page 302; Buchanan, 1977.
21. Pages 43–44. See also Balassa.
22. Pages 372–73.
23. Complaining that the meaning of the term "minority" has been destroyed, the National Association of Black Social Workers vowed to stop using it to describe black Americans *(New York Times,* April 22, 1979).

24. Page 1.
25. Pages 11–12.
26. Page 13.
27. Page 15.
28. 1977, page 222.
29. Page 345.
30. Rostow, pages 13–14.
31. Later on, Rostow (page 105) observes "much similarity between the economic policies of the rulers of ancient states, on the upswing of their cycles, and those of the rulers in Early Modern Europe."
32. Page 113.
33. "Economic solipsism" is, however, what Karl Polanyi (pages 14–15) called the view that "Men would barter unless they were prohibited from doing so, and markets would thus come into being unless something was done to prevent it." Perspective is gained by remembering that Polanyi was revolted by the market system of the modern West, which he saw as having turned both man and nature into fodder for the "satanic mill" of the "self-regulating market system." Polanyi's editor, Harry W. Pearson (page xxxvi), explains that "The driving force behind all his historical work was the conviction ... that it had been possible to produce and distribute the livelihood of man while maintaining the integrity of society, and that pre-market history offered many clues to the possibility of returning the mandate for man's fate to the variegated social, political, and cultural institutions of society." By "premarket" Polanyi had in mind the pre-nineteenth-century West or Hesiodic Greece or Amos's Israel; in fact, he was more than a little fuzzy on this question (see pages 58–59, 73). Indeed, Polanyi complained that economic solipsism barred the recognition that the early role of the state in the economic field was "the maintenance of a centralized economy without bureaucratic oppression" (page 16) that opened up "a sphere of personal freedom formerly unknown in the economic life of man" (page 74).

CHAPTER 9

1. See Bacon and Eltis; Brittan.
2. Page 1.
3. Page 23.
4. Pages 24, 28.
5. 1978, page 60.
6. Page 62.
7. A. L. Levine presents a detailed analysis of industrial retardation and entrepreneurial conservatism in Britain during this period. McCloskey in his work on *Economic Maturity and Entrepreneurial Decline* rejects any "sociological" hypothesis of entrepreneurial failure for explaining the

performance of Britain's iron and steel industry during 1870–1913. Indeed, considering the late Victorian economy as a whole, he sees "nothing ominous for Britain in the faster growth of two large industrializing countries," namely the United States and Germany (page 127).

8. See, for example, Best, chapter 1.
9. Page 4.
10. Chapter 10.
11. Murphy, pages 654–55.
12. Page 212.
13. Pages 211–14.
14. Page 135.
15. Murphy, page 655.
16. Mathias, page 222; see also Best, pages 91–99.
17. Page 378.
18. Ashworth, page 247.
19. Pages 711–12.
20. Page 381.
21. Murphy, page 719.
22. Page 230.
23. Fraser, pages 115–23; Hutchison, chapter 5.
24. Sayers, page 122.
25. Cheyney, page 327.
26. Page 225.
27. Ashworth, pages 249, 253; Fraser, pages 123–28.
28. Ashworth, page 248.
29. Bruce, page 16.
30. In Fraser, pages 145–46.
31. Murphy, page 708. David Roberts (page 315) traces the origins of the British welfare state back to the early Victorian period in 1833; by 1854 "none of the governments of Europe intervened so decisively to regulate the hours of labor in factories, to systematize poor relief, and to promote the public health."
32. In Fraser, page 132.
33. Page 219.
34. The sources utilized include: Ashworth, pages 124, 219, 223, 225–26, 228, 258; Bruce, pages 153, 155, 164, 170, 186–87; Cheyney, pages 304–6; 311–19; 337–39; 346–49; Fraser, pages 144–63, Murphy, pages 707–9; Roebuck, pages 53, 74–75.
35. Page 223.
36. Page 223.
37. Cheyney, page 347.
38. Bruce, page 155.
39. In Bruce, page 153.
40. In Bruce, page 14.
41. Page 164.

42. Murphy, page 707. During the same 1873-1914 period in the percentage share of the military in total central and local government expenditure (other than national debt charges) fell from 34 to 25 while that of social services (i.e. education and health) rose from 8 to 23. In 1913 the share of the "trading services" (postal, water, gas, electricity, transport and harbors) was 26 percent of total expenditures (Murphy, page 708).
43. Brown, pages 174–75.
44. Brown, pages 115–18.
45. Page 75.
46. Ashworth, page 258.
47. Chapter 10.
48. Page 75.
49. Page 57.
50. Howard, page 72. Howard (page 132) dismisses myths regarding the origins of the world wars: "As for the clash of capitalist interests, few historians would today see this as a major factor in the origins of either world war. In particular, the part played by imperial rivalries in both was minimal. In both, indeed, the British found more hostility to their imperial interests among their allies than they did among their enemies."
51. 1978, page 51.
52. 1978, page 63.
53. See, for example, *New York Times,* April 5, 1979.

CHAPTER 10

1. Schnitzer, page 218.
2. Page 124.
3. Heclo, 1974, chapter 4; Schnitzer, pages 135–49.
4. Heclo, 1974, pages 323–24; Furniss and Tilton, pages 148–50.
5. Beck, page 18; Dubin. Over the 1960–74 period Sweden's estimated average percentage point increase in government expenditure as a percentage of national income was 1.84. The corresponding rates for Denmark (1950–74), Norway (1951–74), and the United States (1950–74) were, respectively, 1.42, 1.38, and 0.51 (Nutter, page 12).
6. August 5, 1977.
7. According to a survey reported in the *New York Times,* March 24, 1978.
8. Furniss and Tilton, pages 125–27, 137.
9. See Furlong, pages 92–97.
10. Page 138.
11. Reported in the *New York Times,* March 24, 1978.
12. *Los Angeles Times,* April 22, 1978.
13. *New York Times,* March 24, 1978.
14. *Time,* May 1, 1978.
15. *New York Times,* March 24, 1978.
16. *New York Times,* March 25, 1978.
17. *New York Times,* March 24, 1978.

18. *New York Times,* March 24, 1978.
19. *New York Times,* March 24, 1978.
20. See the chapter headnote.
21. *Wall Street Journal,* December 11, 1978.

CHAPTER 11

1. The Carter administration in September 1977 filed a brief as friend of the court, in which the use of race as a criterion in university admissions was defended. The Supreme Court ruled that the school had illegally discriminated against Bakke, but Justice Powell's opinion suggested that the benevolent, nondecisive use of race as one factor in an admissions program is permissible.
2. Such demonstration is not yet impossible. (1) The Second U.S. Circuit Court of Appeals held that men who do heavy commercial cleaning can be paid more than women who do light cleaning jobs. The ruling was made on a motion by the New York State Labor Department to bar Columbia University from continuing its 30-year-old policy of pay differentials for heavy and light cleaners *(Washington Post,* October 7, 1977). (2) In a 5 to 1 decision the California Supreme Court ruled in April 1978 that requiring police officer candidates to scale a six-foot wall does not discriminate against women *(Los Angeles Times,* April 14, 1978). (3) The Supreme Court in January 1978 upheld, by 5 to 2, South Carolina's right to use a teacher-testing system that disqualified 83 percent of the black applicants but only 17.5 percent of the whites *(New York Times,* January 17, 1978). (4) On June 11, 1979, the Supreme Court ruled unanimously that Southeastern Community College's associate degree nursing program could constitutionally reject a deaf applicant on the ground that the ability to understand speech without reliance on lipreading is necessary for the safety of patients *(New York Times,* June 12, 1979).

   However, Kenneth Keniston and the Carnegie Council on Children (page 97) urged that Title VII be amended so as to require employers to prove not only that their employment criteria predict future job performance but that "there are no other selection mechanisms available that will serve as well or better to predict job performance but with less discriminatory effects." Somehow, Keniston never quite makes clear how an employer would go about proving the required negative (see page 98).
3. *New York Times,* January 5, 1978. Apparently Sears, Roebuck & Co., reached the same conclusion, for in January 1979 the firm filed a suit against Ms. Norton and the heads of nine other government agencies that charged that government equal employment policies were so confusing, contradictory, and arbitrary that they could not be complied with *(New York Times,* January 25, 1979). The suit was dismissed in May of the same year. Ms. Norton commented: "There was never any doubt in the legal community that this suit would be dismissed. The equal opportunity laws

are too serious to be entangled with frivolous litigation" *(New York Times,* May 16, 1979). The threat to equal opportunity policies also played a crucial role in a federal appeals court decision upholding the right of the Carter administration to deny contracts to companies that disregard voluntary wage-price guidelines *(Newsday,* May 31, 1979).

4. *New York Times,* January 9, 1978.
5. *New York Times,* April 2, 1978.
6. *New York Times,* November 13, 1977.
7. *New York Times,* February 2, 1978.
8. *New York Times,* April 2, 1978.
9. *New York Times,* April 2, 1978; *Washington Post,* October 4, 1978.
10. *New York Times,* October 8, 1977.
11. *New York Times,* June 16, 1978.
12. Senese, page 76.
13. *New York Times,* April 8, 1978, July 4, 1979.
14. *New Republic,* October 15, 1977.
15. Glazer, 1975, page 115.
16. *New York Times,* May 26, 1978.
17. *Chicago Tribune,* October 14, 1977.
18. Speaking of stereotypes, University of Minnesota psychologist Dr. Ellen Bersheid refers to a "strong physical attractiveness stereotype: Attractive people are assumed to be kinder, more genuine, sincere, warm, sexually responsive, poised, modest, sociable, and sensitive" than less attractive ones. She concluded that "as with any form of discrimination, you have to determine that it's occurring before you can take steps to combat it" *(New York Times,* March 18, 1978). One wonders how long it will take HEW to swing into action to solve this social problem. Mr. Leslie Bialler suggests bumper stickers: "Don't Forget—Hire the Ugly." Of course a more radical method was chosen by Praxagora, in Aristophanes' *Assembly of Women.* She issued a regulation requiring that a person sleep with an unattractive person before being permitted to sleep with an attractive one.
19. *New York Times,* August 16, 1977.
20. *New York Times,* February 1, 1978.
21. *Los Angeles Times,* March 22, 1978. "Kooky," certainly, but quite consistent with the logic of the threatened suit. Let us linger with the "kooky" theme. A regional HEW office objected to a father-and-son dinner in Arizona, and another office in Connecticut objected to a boys' choir as violating Title IX of the sex discrimination law *(New York Times,* November 8, 1977). On December 3, 1978, HEW Secretary Califano announced the deletion from the regulations against sex discrimination of a section forbidding discrimination "in the application of any rules of appearance." Accordingly, it would appear that schools will be legally permitted to require boys to wear neckties without requiring girls to wear them as well! But during the same month Califano proposed regulations calling for equal per capita expenditures for male and female intercollegi-

ate atheletics including the major revenue-producing sports such as football and basketball. Then in May 1979 a federal judge, Raymond J. Pettine, ruled that a male high school senior had been unconstitutionally barred from the girls' (?) volleyball team. He ordained that the young man be permitted a share of the net. But the Justice Department, in a friend-of-the-court brief, suggested that Judge Pettine had erred by failing to consider whether the "overall athletic opportunities" for boys at the school were previously limited. In June 1979 U.S. District Court Judge William Hoeveler denied the motion of the Miami Dolphins Football Club (National Football League) to dismiss a suit brought by a man who wishes to become an NFL cheerperson. Mr. Glen Welt alleged that he is a victim of sex discrimination, since he is a dancer with sex appeal. Finally, on the ground that the school system of Bellevue, Washington, had implemented its corporal punishment policy more frequently against boys than against girls, HEW has charged discrimination and threatened to end $1 million in federal education aid unless a satisfactory "plan" is forthcoming.

22. *Wall Street Journal,* March 16, 1977. Also in Minnesota, the Department of Human Rights ruled that a Roman Catholic landlady had violated a state law prohibiting discrimination on the basis of "marital status" when she refused to rent a Minneapolis apartment to an unwed couple *(Washington Post,* June 22, 1979).
23. *Los Angeles Times,* February 1, 1979.
24. *Washington Post,* December 8, 1978.
25. *New York Times,* December 29, 1977; *Newsday,* February 1, 1978.
26. Gellhorn, pages 38–39.
27. *New York Times,* March 8, 1979; *Regulation,* March/April 1979.
28. *New York Times,* May 2, 1978.
29. *Los Angeles Times,* January 4, 1979; *Time,* March 5, 1979
30. *New York Times,* April 28, 1979. On June 28, 1979, the Uniroyal, Goodrich, and Firestone rubber companies were cited for "probable noncompliance."
31. Berkey had charged that Kodak's introduction of its 110 Pocket Instamatic cameras, with a new color film and processing equipment was anticompetitive and that Kodak had the obligation to give competitors information sufficiently early and in sufficient detail so that they would be in a position to market comparable products and services. "The decision raises far reaching questions about the nature of antitrust law and about the whole notion of a free enterprise economy," concluded Keith I. Clearwaters (a former deputy assistant attorney general of the Justice Department's Antitrust Division) in an article appropriately entitled "Better Mousetrap Builders Beware" *(New York Times,* February 26, 1978). However, in June 1979 the United States Court of Appeals for the Second Circuit ruled unanimously that the Berkey-Kodak presiding judge, Marvin E. Frankel (since resigned), had committed "several significant errors" that required reversal. In his decision Judge Irving Kaufman rejected Berkey's conten-

tion that Kodak was required to give advance notice of innovations to competitors. Berkey may carry the case to the Supreme Court *(New York Times,* June 26, 1979).

32. According to *Regulation* (March/April 1979, page 10): "No one mentioned the possibility . . . that people might know and trust the ReaLemon brand and be willing to pay a few cents more . . . for this familiarity and reliability."

33. *Wall Street Journal* April 14, 1978.

34. But George Gilder (page 41) insists there is still a way to strike it rich, namely the civil suit: "malpractice, product liability, whatever, . . . *Caveat producer* is the new rule"! Consider, for example, how close Berkey came to striking it rich ($7 billion!).

35. Pages 420–24.

36. See Briggs, 1976, pages 291–92; Haveman (b), pages 13–14.

37. *New York Times,* May 26, 1978.

38. *New York Times,* June 18, 1978.

39. 1977, page 95.

40. At the White House Conference on Economic Growth in 1978, then Governor Michael Dukakis proudly "told of how he personally had intervened from Boston to see that 'they put that damned shopping center in downtown Pittsfield!' " (Graham, 1978, page 55). In the same year a permit to construct a suburban shopping center outside Burlington was denied on "environmental" grounds by a Vermont district environmental commission despite having met all the requirements with respect to landscaping, water pollution control, and energy conservation. The commission supported this denial with the novel argument that the proposed shopping center would have an "adverse environmental impact" on business within the city of Burlington! *(Time,* November 13, 1978). It is also reported that the federal government has blocked suburban malls that would have competed with Charleston, West Virginia, and Duluth, Minnesota, by refusing to provide access roads and other improvements.

41. 1978, page 59.

42. In August 1978 California Governor Edmund G. Brown declared that "the lifeblood of corporate America is in the hands of the executive branch and when those hands start squeezing, the corporate lifeblood will flow in the right direction. It's that simple" *(Los Angeles Times,* August 9, 1978).

43. Page 101.

44. *Washington Post,* May 7, 1979.

45. *New York Times,* May 15, 1979; *Washington Post,* June 21, 1979. At about the same time Senator Edward M. Kennedy launched a vigorous attack on oil decontrol: "Is it fair to ask poor elderly citizens in Northeast Washington to shift to cat food so they can afford to pay their heating bills? . . . [Decontrol] is the worst form of rationing because it is rationing by price" *(Washington Post,* May 13, 1979). On June 19 Governor Hugh

Carey of New York issued an order for gas stations in a nine-county area to stay open at least one weekend day.

46. The main media portray the decontrol conflict as one between the valiant proconsumer opponents and the lobbyist-ridden probusiness or free enterprise forces. For example, the *New York Times* (May 23, 1979) described opponents of oil price deregulation such as Thomas P. O'Neill (D.–Mass.), John Brademas (D.–Ind.), and John D. Dingell (D.–Mich.) as "taking the consumer side." On the other hand, James C. Wright (D.–Tex.), who maintained that removing price controls would increase domestic production and induce conservation (exactly what is predicted by economics) was described as "a strong defender of oil industry interests." The public in general cannot see beyond the announced *motives* of the antideregulation forces and does not even suspect the possibility that the proconsumer policies are in their *effect* anticonsumer.

Speaking of lobbies, the fight against natural gas deregulation was spearheaded by Energy Action, which according to the *New York Times* (October 2, 1977) is the "brainchild of a loosely-formed group of California businessmen who made fortunes in such fields as computers and real estate." This group (which also includes actor Paul Newman) moved from the antiwar movement, to the McGovern presidential campaign, to environmental issues. "The long-range goal of Energy Action is to break the large oil companies," a goal its lobbyist, James Flug, a former aide to Senator Edward Kennedy, is confident will be achieved. Continuing on the subject of lobbyists, Ralph Nader comes to mind. According to a story in the *Washington Post* (February 10, 1978), when Representative Patricia Schroeder, a liberal Democrat from Denver, wrote to Nader's organization questioning some provisions of the proposed Consumer Protection bill in 1977, she "suddenly" found that "major contributors" were calling her and demanding to know why she had "sold out" to big business.

47. Pages 2, 147–48. Sansom (page 181) believes the "only 'balanced' community one can see in America is Colonial Williamsburg, tastefully restored with Rockefeller money near Virginia's coast." All must deeply ponder this thought. Of suburbia, Sansom (page 195) writes: "We cannot enjoy it; hours are spent getting to or from work or driving the children to their distant school, sports, or social activities. Before suburbia, adult social relationships and camaraderie were enjoyed in the cafes, night spots, movie houses, and churches of our cities. Now it is vainly sought from the television set or in the shopping center parking lot." Where does he live?

48. Haveman, 1977a, page 14.

49. 1977a, page 21.

50. 1977a, page 12.

51. Pages 28–29. Sometimes truth is science fiction! Another Brookings economist, Joseph Pechman, seems impatient with complaints of a growing tax burden on the middle class. He considers the main difficulty to be that

the real income of the middle class "has not nearly kept pace with their rising expectations" *(Time,* January 8, 1978). So the problem is in their minds, but does this not apply to the poor as well? On May 23, 1979, Brookings president B. K. Maclaury wrote to the *Washington Post* that it is "misleading" to suggest there is a " 'liberal claque' at Brookings."

52. Page 12.

53. Page 257. Other team recommendations to meet the "public need" include "a 100 percent tax on revenue gained through the use of computers" [including their own?], which would raise billions for "social services" while decreasing the "growthmania obsession with automation" [page 258]; a "social management tax" to eliminate "excessive construction of luxury hotels" [even in Honolulu?] (page 258); and "People's Action Programs" that would make sure that government policies "are consistent with the current needs of society" [What about the needs of the team?] (page 263).

54. Pages 192–95.

55. President Carter's 1977 proposal for a Program for Better Jobs and Incomes (PBJI) died in Congress. In May 1979 he submitted a "scaled-down" welfare reform proposal with an announced projected cost of $5.7 billion.

56. *New York Times,* January 19, 1978, June 18, 1978.

57. Page 24. President Carter's May 1979 welfare revision plan called for the creation of 400,000 newly funded public service jobs and training slots at an average salary of $7,200 per year in 1979 constant dollars.

58. See the *New York Times,* January 23, 1979.

59. A Brookings Institution analysis revealed that the so-called austerity budget "looks like a one-time effort" *(Washington Post,* May 21, 1979). Nevertheless, Representative Donald R. Obey (D.–Wis.), who led a fight against Carter's budget, stated that the resistance "indicates that a majority of the Democratic Party in the House does not feel it's necessary to abandon the elderly and the poor and the kids and give the Pentagon everything on its wish list" *(New York Times,* May 24, 1979). In a "compromise" the Senate agreed to add $350 million to spending for educational and social programs.

60. *New York Times,* November 4, 1977.

61. *New York Times,* May 6, 1979.

62. *Time,* May 8, 1978.

63. In 1978 a special study recommended to the 2.6 million member United Presbyterian Church that practicing homosexuals who otherwise meet the requirements for the clergy be ordained. This study was chaired, not surprisingly, by the wife of a retired Kodak executive. *Time* (January 30, 1978) placed the issue in perspective: "For conservatives, including the growing Evangelical forces and many adherents of the waning neo-orthodox theology, the policy on homosexuality is crucial. . . . Since the Bible is so explicit, they wonder if the church will have any biblical basis

for imposing restrictions on human behavior if it votes moral acceptance of active homosexuality." For liberals, however, the Bible verses condemning homosexuality "merely express the opinions of the Jewish priestly writers and Paul who were conditioned by time and place."

In June 1979 a study commission of the Episcopal church recommended that homosexuals be ordained if they lead a "wholesome life." Meanwhile, Episcopal defections continue to increase. Political scientist Paul Seabury has traced the background of the rupture in this church and provided a pithy description of the part played by Bishop Paul Moore of New York, a millionaire prototype of the "radical-chic" Establishment.

64. *Los Angeles Times,* May 2, 1978.
65. Page 9.
66. *New York Times,* February 12, 1978.
67. No doubt business influence will be strengthened by the May 1978 Supreme Court decision striking down a Massachusetts law forbidding corporations from using their funds to influence a referendum not directly related to their business or property.
68. Pages 99–100.
69. Buchanan and Tullock, page 266.
70. 1975, page 197.
71. Page 249.
72. Berger, page 288.
73. Pages 325–26.
74. Page 408.
75. *New York Times,* April 9, 1978.
76. *New York Times,* June 16, 1978.
77. *Washington Post,* June 24, 1978.
78. *New York Times,* March 28, 1979.
79. See "The Chilling Impact of Litigation," in *Business Week* (June 6, 1977). But not only socially significant problems are now being litigated. In May 1978 a San Francisco woman was sued for $38 by a man she broke a social date with *(New York Times,* May 23, 1978). A Milwaukee couple legally divorced their teenage daughter *(Newsday,* November 10, 1978). But all is not yet lost, for in December 1978 the Arkansas Supreme Court overturned a $13,000 verdict awarded a woman who slipped, fell, and sprained her back when she fell while standing on a loose toilet seat at the Russellville hospital *(Los Angeles Times,* December 12, 1978).
80. Poggi, page 143.
81. Page 200.
82. Graham, 1976, page 316.
83. Graham, 1976, page 317; but see also Silver, 1977.
84. 1976, page 317.
85. Page 326.
86. 1977, page 9.
87. See Auster and Silver, pages 7–9.

88. Page 53.
89. 1976, page 297.
90. 1976, page 229.
91. 1976, page 301.
92. 1976, page 302.
93. 1960, pages 92, 101–2.
94. Page 310.
95. Page 258.
96. Page 50.
97. Page 108.
98. Pages 18–19. Harvard Law School professor Charles Fried (page 15) notes that those who see no difference between lack of means or opportunity and coercion "will not long hesitate to propose solutions for social problems that involve directing people how and where to live their lives."
99. Page 239. Tufte's evidence is currently being evaluated in the profession.
100. Page 11.
101. Tufte, page 57.
102. Tufte, page 57.
103. Page 17.
104. Page 14.
105. *Washington Post,* February 8, 1978.
106. Pages 31–32.
107. Hilton, page 171,
108. Hilton, page 147.
109. Lilley and Miller, page 57.
110. July/August 1977, page 7.
111. Over the objections of his Council of Economic Advisers, President Carter decided in favor of engineering controls. Carters's so-called compromise followed in the wake of Ralph Nader's denunciation of the economic advisors as "pink cheeked academics who don't go beyond their callous calculators" and who wish to "stick it to the sick and the weak" in order to fight inflation *(New York Times,* June 9, 1978). When OSHA's head, Dr. Eula Bingham, was asked whether the "compromise" meant that future rules might be less stringent, she replied: "Oh no, it means that we will have to be more persuasive about the value of what we are doing" *(New York Times,* November 26, 1978).
112. *Business Week,* April 4, 1977.
113. *Business Week*, April 4, 1977.
114. Lilley and Miller, page 57. After their much-publicized agreement with U.S. Steel in May 1979, EPA officials were asked to comment on the company's estimate that the agreement would add about $25 per ton to the cost of producing steel. They replied that "it sounded 'a little high,'" but added they "had no way of determining just what the price impact might be" *(New York Times,* May 24, 1979). A few days later, on May 25, the

EPA introduced rules requiring all newly built coal-burning plants, *including those burning low-sulfur western coal,* to install "scrubbers" to remove sulfur dioxide. The EPA estimated that the new rules would add $3.3 to $3.6 billion to the annual total cost of electricity production. When officials at President Carter's Council on Wage and Price Stability were contacted, they could not comment on the new rules because they had not yet had time to study them *(New York Times,* May 26, 1979).

115. *Business Week,* April 4, 1977.

116. One study of the Delaware estuary found that an effluent charge of 10 cents a pound of BOD (a standard measure of water pollutant) would reduce the real costs of water cleanup by 50 percent *(Business Week,* April 4, 1977).

117. Cornell, Noll, and Weingast, pages 483–85.

118. Page 287.

119. See Wallace, pages 131–32.

120. Since the passage of the 1962 Kefauver-Harris Amendments to the Food, Drug, and Cosmetic Act (1938) the "annual rate of new drug introduction in the United States has fallen to less than one-third the rate which existed in the early 1960s" (Grabowski and Vernon, page 287). Grabowski and Vernon (and Thomas) have completed a study concluding that "increased regulation has been a major factor underlying declining innovational performance in the drug industry" (page 287). In addition, of 27 new drugs introduced over the 1965–75 period that were classified by the FDA in 1974 as *important therapeutic advances:* "Fifteen had prior introduction in a foreign country, eight became available here and abroad in the same year, and only four were initially available here first" (page 288).

121. Page 35.

122. Page 288.

123. See *Regulation,* January/February 1978, "After Economic Impact Statements—What?," pages 12–13. Miller's (page 4) "personal and unsystematic appraisal" is that policy-makers now appear to be taking the economic implications more seriously than they used to," but he admits that while cost estimates are reasonably good those for benefits are needlessly weak. But Miller's reply to a letter *(Regulation* January/February 1978) seems to indicate that the EIP are primarily window dressing. The alleged "substantial effects" of EIP "did not flow from the agency's relying on the analysis at the proposal stage, but rather from the agency's knowing it eventually would have to expose its proposal to the sunshine of such analysis." See also note 115 above.

124. Schlesinger, pages 286–87.

125. Pages 46–47.

126. Hoos, page 11.

127. Page 243. See also Cohen and Lindblom (page 556): "The closer Professional Social Inquiry moves to direct engagement in social problem-

solving—as, for example, when the practitioner takes a policy-making organization as client—the more difficult it is to find examples . . . that are in their impact unquestionably pre- rather than post-decision."

128. Weidenbaum and Rockwood, pages 66–69.

129. But see Hoos, pages 60–63.

130. Page 289. In other words, scientific knowledge can win the day only when the preconceptions of the affluents do not raise "positive obstructions" to its "authoritativeness" (see Cohen and Lindblom, page 549).

131. Reported in *Miami Herald,* December 21, 1977.

132. *Business Week,* February 19, 1979.

133. *Newsday,* October 11, 1977.

134. *Newsday,* August 29, 1978.

135. 1973, page 4.

136. Pages 62, 67–68.

137. 1978, page 32.

138. Page 68.

139. Shortly after the accident at Pennsylvania's Three Mile Island nuclear power plant a panel of nuclear scientists learned a similar "painful lesson" when they sought to present their views on the safety of nuclear power to the House Science and Technology Committee. With the agreement of the other panelists, Dr. Edward Teller stated that "Nuclear reactors are not safe but they are incomparably safer than anything else we might have to produce electric energy." Dr. Eugene Wigner added: "Coal plants put out more radioactivity than Three Mile Island did. . . . Why not forbid mining and burning coal?" But all this only succeeded in eliciting a know-nothing retort from Representative Richard Ottinger (D.–N.Y.): "Some of you" took part in the Manhattan Project which developed atomic bombs "that caused thousands of deaths" *(Washington Post,* May 7, 1979). Jane Fonda has become the true image of an atomic scientist.

140. Page 16.

141.. April 4, 1977, page 95.

142. Page 13.

143. *New York Times,* February 19, 1978.

144. *New York Times,* February 12, 1978. See also "Developments in the Law—Corporate Crime: Regulating Corporate Behavior Through Criminal Sanctions." *Harvard Law Review* (April 1979), pages 1229–1375. J. V. Stalin, who was completely liberated from the traditional (bourgeois) principle of *mens rea* (evil mind), must, of course, be given the credit for perfecting the use of physical punishment against "wreckers" who failed to fulfill his grandiose economic plans. Can we not learn from this great teacher how to deal with "white-collar criminals" who sabotage "economic justice"?

145. Mishan (page 81), however, considers the "prudent" conclusion with "reference to Malthus on the population question and to Jevons on the coal reserves question" is that "they were premature rather than really

wrong"! For those enamored of trend extrapolations, here is a rather chilling one from *Business Week* (January 1977). Professor John Barton of Stanford Law School estimates that if the growth rate of appeals to federal courts remains constant, by the year 2000 there will be 1 million appeals decided each year. Given the current case load, this would require 5,000 federal appeals judges as opposed to the 97 we have today. Assuming appeals continue to run at 10 percent of the total cases initiated, this would mean 10 million cases annually, which would collapse the system.

146. Page 32.
147. See Heclo, 1974 page 23.
148. Page 14. An important figure in Prime Minister Thatcher's brain trust is economist Douglas Hague, who describes himself as a "reluctant interventionist" *(New York Times,* April 29, 1979).
149. *U.S. News & World Report,* February 20, 1978.
150. *Washington Post,* May 23, 1978. To the complaint that the Swedish Conservatives nationalized more industries in their brief tenure than the Labor government had in 44 years, the response of government officials was that they had no choice if they hoped to be reelected *(New York Times,* August 2, 1978). In the cases of the "rightist" French government elected in March 1978 and Mrs. Thatcher's Tory government elected in May 1979, we will have to await events.
151. Kristol, page 136. This is parallelled in the East by the assertion that Stalinism represents an aberration from true socialism.
152. Page 45. Sociologist Christopher Jencks regards the "neoconservatives" to be conservatives: "Their distinctiveness . . . really does derive from the recency of their conversion. Having spent much of their adult life among liberals and radicals, they still tend to think and write for this audience. . . . Because of their past experience, they know how to sway such an audience far better than say, William F. Buckley does" *(New York Times,* Book Review, July 1, 1979). Henry Fairlie, perhaps a bit jealous of the celebrity of the neoconservatives, writes that they "turn out to be nothing but a bunch of liberals who have 'made it' . . . to the 'style' section of the *Washington Post" (New York Times,* January 1, 1978).
153. Page 229.
154. *New York Times,* April 4, 1978.
155. *New York Times,* January 22, 1978.
156. *Public Opinion,* September/October 1978, page 34.
157. 1978, page 96.
158. Katona and Strumpel, page 144. A great deal of supporting evidence has been assembled by Lipset and Raab (pages 44–45): "In 1960, about 64 percent of the people endorsed the proposal that 'the government ought to help people to get doctors and hospital care at low cost.' In 1978, 81 percent of those interviewed by the *New York Times*/CBS poll agreed. In a 1970 Harris poll, Americans approved (46–34) the proposition that welfare should be abolished, and that welfare recipients should be made to go to

work. But the same respondents overwhelmingly supported (56–28) the idea that government programs should be increased to help the poor. Again, in a 1976 survey, Harris found that 62 percent favored (and only 23 percent opposed) 'a major cutback in federal spending.' However . . . substantial majorities of the same respondents *rejected* cutbacks in spending for education, health, environmental protection, and product safety. It was only on welfare that a majority (56–35) favored a cutback. . . . In 1977, the white population was evenly split (39–39) on whether welfare programs should be greatly decreased, but three-quarters of them said the government should spend money for job incentives for the poor (Roper). In 1977, the American public approved by 80–13 percent the idea that all able-bodied people should be removed from the welfare rolls, but also stated by a similar majority that the government should provide public service jobs, with tax money, for those who could not find jobs in private industry. . . . *There was no significant difference in the answers to these questions by self-styled conservatives and self-styled liberals* [italics mine]."

159. *Business Week,* July 10, 1978. Pertschuk told a convention of investigative reporters to check the appointment calenders of lawmakers in order to see if they are spending disproportionate amounts of time with "moneyed interests," and to correlate this with whether their voting records reflect corporate positions *(Newsday,* July 3, 1979).
160. *New York Times,* April 30, 1979.
161. June 3, 1979.
162. Page 107. Some straws in the wind: In a sharp departure from rulings of other appellate courts, a federal appeals court in New Orleans set aside the OSHA's benzene exposure guideline on grounds that OSHA failed to demonstrate a "reasonable relationship" between expected benefits and costs *(Washington Post,* October 17, 1979). In September 1978 Congress enacted legislation that would permit manufacturers to sell pesticides without meeting EPA safety standards for up to 15 years and, in addition, calls for a series of negotiations before a pesticide is banned *(Newsday,* November 2, 1978). A federal judge, in November 1978, disqualified Chairman Pertschuk from participating in FTC hearings on children's advertising because his hostile "prejudgment taints the entire proceeding" *(Newsday,* November 4, 1978). In January 1979 the Interior Department postponed for six months the implementation of expensive restrictions on strip-mining *(New York Times,* January 7, 1979). Also in January 1979 the EPA relaxed the smog standard cities must meet under the Clean Air Act. However, a Petroleum Institute spokesman maintained that even the new standard would not "provide any substantial relaxation of impossible controls in many areas of the country" *(Los Angeles Times,* January 22, 1979).
163. Brzezinski, 1971, page 139; Molnar, pages 321–22.
164. Brzezinski, 1970, page 248.
165. Pages 82–85.

166. See Buchanan and Tullock, pages 266–71.
167. 1971, page 137.
168. Page 7.
169. Page 174.
170. Pages 266–67.
171. 1921, page 169.
172. See Simmons, page 207.
173. Weaver, 1976, pages 31–33.
174. Page 59.
175. Page 243.
176. Page 13.
177. A rather pathetic illustration is provided by a letter to the *New York Times* (February 20, 1979) from a government research contractor, Leonard M. Greene. Greene, the president of the Institute of Socioeconomic Studies, was evidently in mortal fear of bankruptcy for inappropriate findings. He heatedly denied that his firm's analysis of the Seattle and Denver income maintenance experiments showed that work effort is reduced significantly. Greene even attacked his own product: "The figures and conclusions are quite tentative"; "another government contractor on the project . . . has issued a broad criticism of the studies' methodology"; the data are "highly ambiguous"; and so on. Finally, he prostrated himself and pleaded that his findings not be "used to block the modest welfare proposal forthcoming from the Carter administration."
178. The percentage changes in average annual productivity growth in manufacturing for 1966–76 versus 1960–66 are as follows: United Kingdom (−16), Canada (−19), Switzerland (+76), France (+5), Sweden (−20), Italy (−21), Germany (−3), Netherlands (+32), Belgium (+62), Denmark (+48), and Japan (+1). The source of the productivity data is the New York Stock Exchange, Office of Economic Research, *Reaching a Higher Standard of Living* (1979), plus the detailed paper specially prepared for the study by John W. Kendrick, entitled "Sources of Productivity Growth and of the Recent Slow-Down."
179. *Los Angeles Times*, April 16, 1978.
180. Page 239.
181. Page viii.

APPENDIX 1

1. Pages 371–72.
2. See Rodgers (pages 180–89) for a useful summary of the literature.
3. Page 397. See also Rowley and Peacock, pages 54–55. Brennan and Walsh have shown that redistribution in kind is *consistent* with the Pareto optimality criterion that both donor and recipient get better off. But any Parcto-desirable redistribution must be effected in generalized purchasing

power. That is, only cash will do in situations in which efficiency considerations *require* redistribution (i.e., for the donor to get better off it is *necessary* to make the recipient better off as well).

4. See Collard, pages 131–33.
5. 1977, page 16.
6. Page 365.
7. An innovative attempt to measure this differential by using simulation techniques to estimate recipient benefit-weights has been published by Smolensky, Stiefel, Schmundt, and Plotnik. The authors tentatively suggest that in-kind transfers do not greatly alter recipient consumption patterns and, therefore, that they cannot be rationalized on donor benefit grounds.
8. 1973, pages 31–37.
9. 1976, page 179.
10. *New York Times,* December 12, 1977.
11. 1962, page 178; but see also page 191.
12. M. Friedman, 1962, pages 191–95.
13. M. Friedman, 1962, page 178.
14. Johnson, 1965(a), page 544.
15. Chickering, pages 333–34.
16. Page 185.
17. Intrahousehold conflicts regarding consumption patterns would, perhaps, permit exceptions to this rule.
18. 1977, page 16.
19. 1977, page 16.
20. Page 122.

APPENDIX 2

1. 1976.
2. 1976, page 16.
3. 1977, page 148.
4. *New York Times,* February 12, 1978.
5. March 6, 1978.
6. February 20, 1978.

APPENDIX 3

1. 1897, pages 609, 616–18.
2. Page 39.
3. 1934, page 33.
4. Page 127.
5. 1975, pages 90, 202.
6. Page 136.

7. Page 511.
8. Page 22.
9. Page 176.
10. 1975, page 74.

APPENDIX 4

1. 1974.
2. 1974, page 1090. Reece attempted to test Becker's social interactions theory by including in his charity regressions a measure of the household's social environment: the consumption level of potential charity recipients as measured by the lower quintile income of the SMSA within which the sample household resides. This rough variable exhibits the expected inverse relationship with "Charity," but the regression coefficient is extremely insignificant.

BIBLIOGRAPHY

Aaron, Henry J. *Politics and the Professor: The Great Society in Perspective.* Washington, D.C.: The Brookings Institution, 1978.

Abbott, Frank Frost. *The Common People of Ancient Rome.* New York: Biblo and Tanner, 1965.

——— and Allan Chester Johnson. *Municipal Administration in the Roman Empire.* New York: Russell and Russell, 1968.

Abrams, Barton A., and Mark D. Schitz. "The Crowding-out Effect of Governmental Transfers on Private Charitable Contributions." *Public Choice.* Vol. 33, Issue 1 (1978), pp. 29–39.

Adkins, A. W. H. *Moral Values and Political Behavior in Ancient Greece From Homer to the End of the Fifth Century.* London: Chatto and Windus, 1972.

Alchian, Armen A. "Economic Laws and Political Legislation." In Siegan, ed., *The Interaction . . .* , pp. 139–48.

——— and William R. Allen. *University Economics.* Belmont, California: Wadsworth, 1974.

Allvine, Fred C., and Fred A. Tarpley, Jr. *The New State of the Economy.* Cambridge, Mass.: Winthrop Publishers, 1977.

Anderson, Martin. *Welfare: The Political Economy of Welfare Reform.* Stanford: Hoover Institution, 1978.

Andreades, A. M. *A History of Greek Public Finance.* Vol. I. Cambridge, Mass.: Harvard Univ. Press, 1933.

Ardant, Gabriel. "Financial Policy and Economic Infrastructure in Modern States and Nations." In Charles Tilly, ed., *The Formation of National States in Western Europe.* Princeton: Princeton Univ. Press, 1975, pp. 164–242.

Aronfreed, Justin. *Conduct and Conscience.* New York: Academic Press, 1968.

Arrow, Kenneth J. "Gifts and Exchanges." In Phelps, ed., *Altruism . . .* , pp. 13–28.

Ashley, Sir William. *An Introduction to English Economic History and Theory.* Vol. II. London: Longmans, Green, and Co., 1920.

212

Ashworth, William. *An Economic History of England: 1870–1939.* London: Methuen, 1970.

Auster, Richard, and Morris Silver. "Collective Goods and Collective Decision Mechanisms." *Public Choice* (Spring 1973), pp. 1–17.

Bacon, Robert, and Walter Eltis. *Britain's Economic Problem: Too Few Producers.* New York: St. Martin's, 1976.

Baden, John A., and Richard L. Stroup. "The Environmental Costs of Government Action." *Policy Review* (Spring 1978), pp. 23–36.

Baechler, Jean. *The Origins of Capitalism.* New York: St. Martin's, 1976.

Balassa, Bela. "World Trade and the International Economy: Trends, Prospects, and Policies." World Bank Staff Working Papers. No. 282. Washington, D.C.: May 1978.

Balazs, Etienne. *Chinese Civilization and Bureaucracy.* New Haven: Yale Univ. Press, 1964.

Banfield, Edward C. "Welfare: A Crisis without 'Solutions.'" *Public Interest* (Summer 1969), pp. 89–101.

———. *The Unheavenly City Revisited.* Boston: Little, Brown, and Co., 1974.

Barash, David P. *Sociobiology and Behavior.* New York: Elsevier, 1977.

Bark, William Carroll. *Origins of the Medieval World.* Stanford: Stanford Univ. Press, 1958.

Barkun, Michael. *Disaster and the Millennium.* New Haven: Yale Univ. Press, 1974.

Barrow, R. H. *The Romans.* Chicago: Aldine, 1964.

Bar-Tal, Daniel. *Prosocial Behavior.* New York: Wiley, 1976.

Barton, Allen H. "The Emerging Social System." In George W. Baker and Dwight W. Chapman, eds., *Man and Society in Disaster.* New York: Basic Books, 1962, pp. 222–67.

Batchelder, Alan B. *The Economics of Poverty.* 2d ed. New York: Wiley, 1971.

Bauer, Raymond. *Second-Order Consequences.* Cambridge, Mass.: M.I.T. Press, 1969.

Beck, Morris. "The Expanding Public Sector: Some Contrary Evidence." *National Tax Journal* (March 1976), pp. 15–21.

———. "Letter." *New York Times.* April 14, 1978.

Becker, Gary S. "A Theory of Social Interactions." *Journal of Political Economy* November/December 1974, pp. 1063–93.

Bell, Daniel. *The Cultural Contradictions of Capitalism.* New York: Basic Books, 1976.

———. "A Report on England: The Future That Never Was." *Public Interest* (Spring 1978), pp. 35–73.

Bennett, William J. "Censorship for the Common Good." *Public Interest* (Summer 1978), pp. 98–102.

Berger, Peter L. "The Socialist Myth." *Public Interest* (Summer 1976), pp. 3–16.

Berger, Raoul. *Government by Judiciary: The Transformation of the Fourteenth Amendment.* Cambridge, Mass.: Harvard Univ. Press, 1977.

Bernardi, Aurelio. "The Economic Problems of the Roman Empire at the Time of Its Decline." In Cipolla, ed., *The Economic. . .*, pp. 16–91.

Best, Geoffrey. *Mid-Victorian England: 1851–1875.* London: Weidenfeld and Nicolson, 1971.

Bethell, Tom "The Wealth of Washington." *Harper's* (August 1978), pp. 41–60

Bhagwati, Jagdish N. "Introduction." In Bhagwati, ed., *The New International Economic Order: The North-South Debate.* Cambridge, Mass.: M.I.T. Press, 1977, pp. 1–24.

Bishop, John. "The Welfare Brief." *Public Interest* (Fall 1978), pp. 169–75.

Blaydon, Colin C., and Carol B. Stack. Income Support Policies and the Family." In Alice S. Rossi, Jerome Kagan, and Tamara K. Hareven, eds., *The Family.* New York: Norton, 1978, pp. 147–61.

Boak, Arthur E. R., and William G. Sinnigen. *A History of Rome to A.D. 565.* 5th ed. New York: Macmillan, 1965.

Bolkestein, H. *Economic Life in Greece's Golden Age.* New ed. Leiden: E. J. Brill, 1958.

Bonner, Robert J. *Lawyers and Litigants in Ancient Athens.* Chicago: Univ. of Chicago Press, 1927.

———. *Aspects of Athenian Democracy.* Berkeley: Univ. of California Press, 1933.

Borcherding, Thomas E., ed. *Budgets and Bureaucrats: The Sources of Government Growth.* Durham: Duke Univ. Press, 1977.

———. (a) "One Hundred Years of Public Spending, 1870–1970." In Borcherding, ed., *Budgets . . . .*, pp. 19–44.

———. (b) "The Sources of Growth of Public Expenditures in the United States, 1902–1970." In Borcherding, ed., *Budgets . . .*, pp. 45–70.

Bork, Robert H. *The Antitrust Paradox: A Policy at War with Itself.* New York: Basic Books, 1978.

Boulding, Kenneth E. *The Meaning of the Twentieth Century.* New York: Harper and Row, 1964.

———. *Economics as a Science.* New York: McGraw-Hill, 1970.

———. *The Economy of Love and Fear.* Belmont, California: Wadsworth, 1973.

———. "Equity and Distribution: The Interaction of Markets and Grants." In Martin Pfaff, ed., *Grants and Exchanges.* Amsterdam: North-Holland, 1976, pp. 5–21.

Brennan, Geoffrey, and Cliff Walsh. "Pareto-Desirable Redistribution in Kind: An Impossiblity Theorem." *American Economic Review* (December 1977), pp. 987–90.

Breton, Albert. "The Economics of Nationalism." *Journal of Political Economy* (August 1964), pp. 376–86.

Breyer, Stephen G., and Paul W. MacAvoy. "Regulating Natural Gas Producers." In Robert J. Kalter and William A. Vogely, eds., *Energy Supply and Government Policy.* Ithaca: Cornell Univ. Press, 1976.

Brittain, John A. *The Inheritance of Economic Status.* Washington, D.C.: The Brookings Institution, 1977.

Brittan, Samuel. "How British Is the British Sickness." *Journal of Law and Economics* (October 1978), pp. 245–68.

Brown, E. H. Phelps, with Margaret H. Browne. *A Century of Pay.* New York: St. Martin's, 1968.

Brown, Lester R. *The Twenty-Ninth Day: Accommodating Human Needs and Numbers to the Earth's Resources.* New York: Norton, 1978.

Browning, Edgar K. *Redistribution and the Welfare State.* Washington, D.C.: American Enterprise Institute, 1975.

———. "Welfare—A Reconstruction." *The Humanist* (March/April 1977), pp. 12–16.

———. "More on the Appeal of Minimum Wage Laws." *Public Choice.* Vol. 33, Issue 1 (1978), pp. 91–3.

Bruce, Maurice. *The Coming of the Welfare State.* Rev. ed. New York: Schocken, 1966.

Bruce-Briggs, B. "Prospect of a Planned America." In Chickering, ed., *The Politics . . .* , pp. 275–93.

———. *The War Against the Automobile.* New York: Dutton, 1977.

Brzezinski, Zbigniew. *Between Two Ages.* New York: Viking, 1970.

———. "America in the Technetronic Age." In George Kateb, ed., *Utopia.* New York: Atherton, 1971, pp. 127–50.

———. "Introduction" and "Appendix" in Crozier, ed., *The Crisis . . .*

Buchanan, James. "The Samaritan's Dilemma." In Phelps, ed., *Altruism . . .* , pp. 71–86.

——— (a) "Why Does government Grow?" In Borcherding, ed., *Budgets . . .* , pp. 3–18.

——— (b). "Commentary." In Campbell, ed., *Income . . .* , p. 99.

———. "Markets, States, and the Extent of Morals." *American Economic Review* (May 1978), pp. 364–68.

——— and Gordon Tullock. "The Politics and Bureaucracy of Planning." In Chickering, ed., *The Politics . . .* , pp. 255–73.

———. "The Expanding Public Sector: Wagner Squared." *Public Choice* (Fall 1977), pp. 147–50.

Burnham, James. *Suicide of the West.* New York: Day, 1964.

Cain, Glen G., and Harold W. Watts. "An Examination of Recent Cross-Sectional Evidence on Labor Force Response to Income Maintenance Legislation." In *Studies in Public Welfare.* Paper No. 13 ("How Income Supplements Can Affect Work Behavior"). Subcommittee on Fiscal Policy of the Joint Economic Committee, Congress of the United States. Washington, D.C.: February 18, 1974.

Calhoun, George M. *The Business Life of Ancient Athens.* New York: Cooper Square, 1926.

Campbell, Colin D., ed. *Income Redistribution.* Washington, D.C.: American Enterprise Institute, 1977.

Campbell, Donald T. "On the Genetics of Altruism and the Counter-Hedonic

Components in Human Culture." *Journal of Social Issues.* Vol. 28, No. 3 (1972), pp. 21–37.

Cantor, Norman F. *The Meaning of the Middle Ages: Promise and Reality.* Boston: Allyn and Bacon, 1973.

Carcopino, Jerome. *Daily Life in Ancient Rome.* New Haven: Yale Univ. Press, 1940.

———. "Rome Under the Antonines." In Sir Ernest Barker, introd., *Golden Ages of Great Cities.* London: Thames and Hudson, 1952, pp. 29–55.

Carson, Clarence B. *The Flight from Reality.* Irvington-on-Hudson, N.Y.: Foundation for Economic Education, 1969.

Chan, Wellington K. K. *Merchants, Mandarins, and Modern Enterprise in Late Ch'ing China.* Cambridge, Mass.: Harvard Univ. Press, 1977.

Chester, Eric. "Some Social and Economic Determinants of Non-Military Public Spending." *Public Finance.* No. 2 (1977), pp. 176–85.

Cheyney, Edward P. *An Introduction to the Industrial and Social History of England.* Rev. ed. New York: AMS, 1920.

Chickering, A. Lawrence, ed. *The Politics of Planning.* San Francisco: Institute for Contemporary Studies, 1976.

Church, R. A. *The Great Victorian Boom: 1850–1873.* London: Macmillan, 1975).

Cipolla, Carlo M. "Editor's Introduction." In *The Economic Decline of Empires.* London: Methuen, 1970, pp. 1–15.

———. *Before the Industrial Revolution: European Society and Economy, 100– 1700.* New York: Norton, 1976.

Clark, Colin. *The Conditions of Economic Progress.* London: Macmillan, 1957.

Coase, R. H. "Adam Smith's View of Man." *Journal of Law and Economics* (October 1976), pp. 529–46.

———. "Discussion." *American Economic Review* (May 1978), pp. 244–45.

Cochrane, Charles Norris. *Christianity and Classical Culture.* London: Oxford Univ. Press, 1957.

Cogan, John F. *Negative Income Taxation and Labor Supply: New Evidence from the New Jersey-Pennsylvania Experiment.* Santa Monica: Rand Corporation, February 1978. See also "New Evidence on Work Disincentives." *Challenge* (July/August 1978), pp. 53–54.

Cohen, David K., and Charles E. Lindblom. "Solving Problems of Bureaucracy: Limits on Social Science." *American Behavioral Scientist* (May/June 1979), pp. 547–60.

Cohen, Ronald. "Altruism: Human, Cultural, or What?" *Journal of Social Issues.* Vol. 28, No. 3, (1972) pp. 39–57.

Coleman, D. C. *The Economy of England: 1450–1750.* London: Oxford Univ. Press, 1977.

Coleman, James S. "Can We Revitalize our Cities?" *Challenge* (November/ December 1977), pp. 23–34.

Collard, David. *Altruism and the Economy: A Study in Non-Selfish Economics.* New York: Oxford Univ. Press, 1978.

Cornell, Nina W., Roger G. Noll, and Barry Weingast. "Safety Regulation," in

Henry Owen and Charles Schultze (eds.), *Setting National Priorities: The Next Ten Years*. Washington, D.C.: The Brookings Institution, 1976. 457–504.

Coser, Lewis A. "Introduction." In Lewis A. Coser and Irving Howe, eds., *The New Conservatives: A Critique from the Left*. New York: Quadrangle/New York Times, 1973.

Cotterell, Arthur, and David Morgan. *China's Civilization*. New York: Praeger, 1975.

Crain, W. Mark, and Robert B. Ekeland, Jr. "Deficits and Democracy." *Southern Economic Journal* (April 1978), pp. 813–27.

Crozier, Michael, et al. *The Crisis of Democracy*. New York: New York Univ. Press for the Trilateral Commission, 1975.

Dawkins, Richard. *The Selfish Gene*. New York: Oxford Univ. Press, 1976.

DeBary, William Theodore. "Common Tendencies of Neo-Confucianism," in Liu and Golas (eds.), *Change . . .* , 89–94.

DeBurgh, W. G. *The Legacy of the Ancient World*. London: MacDonald and Evans, 1947.

DeFina, Robert. *Public and Private Expenditures for Federal Regulation of Business*. Working Paper No. 22 (November 1977), Center for the Study of American Business, Washington University, St. Louis (Xerox).

Demsetz, Harold. "Discussion." *American Economic Review* (May 1970), pp. 481–84.

DeMuth, Christopher. "The Unheavenly City Revisited." *The Alternative* (November 1974), pp. 5–8.

Denison, Edward F. "Effects of Selected Changes in the Institutional Environment upon Output per Unit of Input." *Survey of Current Business* (January 1978), pp. 21–44.

Dickinson, Frank G. *The Changing Position of Philanthropy in the American Economy*. New York: NBER, 1970.

Dill, Samuel. *Roman Society from Nero to Marcus Aurelius*. Cleveland: World, 1956.

———. *Roman Society in the Last Century of the Western Empire*. New York: Meridian, 1958.

Dolan, Edwin G. "Discussion." In Selden, ed., *Capitalism . . .* , pp. 219–23.

Dolan, John P., and William N. Adams-Smith. *Health and Society: A Documentary History of Medicine*. New York: Seabury, 1978.

Doolitle, Frederick, Frank Levy, and Michael Wiseman. "The Mirage of Welfare Reform." *Public Interest* (Spring 1977), pp. 62–87.

Douty, Christopher M. "Disasters and Charity: Some Aspects of Cooperative Behavior." *American Economic Review* (September 1972), pp. 580–90.

Dubin, Elliot. "The Expanding Public Sector: Some Contrary Evidence: A Comment." *National Tax Journal* (March 1977), p. 95.

Dunlop, John T. "New Approaches to Economic Policy." *Regulation* (January/February 1979), pp. 13–16.

Dworkin, Ronald. "The DeFunis Case: The Right to Go to Law School." *New York Review of Books* (February 5, 1976), pp. 29–33.

Eberhard, Wolfram. *A History of China.* 4th ed. Berkeley: Univ. of California Press, 1977.

Ehrenberg, Victor. *The Greek State.* 2d ed. London: Methuen, 1969.

Eisenstadt, S. N., ed. *The Decline of Empires.* Englewood Cliffs, N.J.: Prentice-Hall, 1967.

———. "Intellectuals and Tradition." *Daedalus* (Spring 1972), pp. 1–19.

Elvin, Mark. *The Pattern of the Chinese Past.* Stanford: Stanford Univ. Press, 1973.

Engels, Friedrich. "Preface to the First German Edition." In Karl Marx, *The Poverty of Philosophy.* Moscow: Foreign Languages Publishing House, n.d.

Erasmus, Charles J. *In Search of the Common Good: Utopian Experiments Past and Future.* New York: Free Press, 1977.

Esman, Milton J. "Perspectives on Ethnic Conflict in Industrialized Societies." In Esman, ed., *Ethnic Conflict in the Western World.* Ithaca: Cornell Univ. Press, 1977.

Fabricant, Solomon. "Philanthropy in the American Economy: An Introduction." In Dickinson, *The Changing . . . ,* pp. 3–30.

Fairbank, John K., Edward O. Reischauer, and Albert Craig. *East Asia: Tradition and Transformation.* Boston: Houghton Mifflin, 1973.

Fairlie, Henry. *The Spoiled Child of the Western World.* New York: Doubleday, 1976.

Fawtier, Robert. *The Capetian Kings of France: Monarchy and Nation, 987–1328.* London: Macmillan, 1960.

Feldstein, Martin. "The Income Tax and Charitable Contributions: Part I—Aggregate and Distributional Effects." *National Tax Journal* (March 1975), pp. 81–100.

———. "The Income Tax and Charitable Contributions: Part II—The Impact of Religious, Educational, and Other Organizations." *National Tax Journal* (June 1975), pp. 209–26.

———, and C. Clotfelter. "Tax Incentives and Charitable Contributions in the United States: A Microeconomic Analysis." *Journal of Public Economics* (January/February 1976), pp. 1–26.

Ferguson, William Scott. "Athens: An Imperial Democracy." In Jill N. Claster, ed., *Athenian Democracy.* New York: Holt, Rinehart and Winston, 1967, pp. 11–19.

Ferkiss, Victor. *The Future of Technological Civilization.* New York: Braziller, 1974.

Ferrero, Guglielmo. *Characters and Events in Roman History.* New York: Putnam, 1909.

———. *Ancient Rome and Modern America.* New York: Putnam, 1918.

Finley, M. I. *Aspects of Antiquity.* New York: Viking, 1968.

———. *The Ancient Economy.* Berkeley: Univ. of California Press, 1973.

Forrester, Jay W. *Urban Dynamics.* Cambridge, Mass.: M.I.T. Press, 1969.

———. "Statement." U.S. Congress, House of Representatives, Ad Hoc Subcommittee on Banking and Currency, *Hearings on Industrial Location Policy.*

Part 3. October 7, 1970. Washington, D.C.: U.S. Government Printing Office, 1971, pp. 205–30.

Frank Tenney, *A History of Rome*. New York: Holt 1923.

———. *Aspects of Social Behavior in Ancient Rome*. Cambridge, Mass.: Harvard Univ. Press, 1932.

———. *Rome and Italy of the Empire*. Vol. 5. In Frank, ed., *An Economic Survey of Rome*. Baltimore: Johns Hopkins Press, 1940.

Franke, Herbert. "Chia Ssu-tsu-tao (1213–1275) A 'Bad Last Minister'?" In Arthur F. Wright and Dennis Twitchett, *Confucian Personalities*. Stanford: Stanford Univ. Press, 1962, pp. 217–34.

Frankfort, Henri, et al., *The Intellectual Adventure of Ancient Man*. Chicago: Univ. of Chicago Press, 1946.

Fraser, Derek. *The Evolution of the British Welfare State: A History of Social Policy Since the Industrial Revolution*. New York: Harper and Row, 1973.

Freeman, Roger A. *The Growth of American Government: A Morphology of the Welfare State*. Stanford: Hoover Institution, 1975.

French, A. *The Growth of the Athenian Economy*. New York: Barnes and Noble, 1964.

Fried, Charles. "Fast and Loose in the Welfare State." *Regulation* (May/June 1979), pp. 8–16.

Friedman, Barry L., and Leonard J. Hausman. "Welfare in Retreat: A Dilemma for the Federal System." *Public Policy* (Winter 1977), pp. 25–48.

Friedman, Lawrence M. "The Social and Political Context of the War on Poverty: An Overview." In Haveman, ed., *A Decade . . .* , pp. 21–47.

Friedman, Milton. *Capitalism and Freedom*. Chicago: Univ. of Chicago Press, 1962.

———. *From Galbraith to Economic Freedom*. Occasional Paper No. 49. London: Institute for Economic Affairs, 1977.

———. "Preface." In Simon, *A Time . . .* , pp. xi–xiv.

Furlong, James C. *Labor in the Boardroom: The Peaceful Revolution*. Princeton: Dow Jones, 1977.

Furniss, Norman, and Timothy Tilton. *The Case for the Welfare State: From Social Security to Social Equality*. Bloomington: Indiana Univ. Press, 1977.

Gabriel, Richard A., and Paul L. Savage. *Crisis in Command: Mismanagement in the Army*. New York: Hill and Wang, 1978.

Galbraith, John Kenneth. *The Affluent Society*. 2d rev. ed. Boston: Houghton Mifflin, 1969.

Garraty, John A. *Unemployment in History: Economic Thought and Public Policy*. New York: Harper and Row, 1978.

Garzetti, Albino. *From Tiberius to the Antonines*. London: Methuen, 1974.

Gaylin, Willard. "In the Beginning: Helpless and Dependent." In Gaylin et al., *Doing Good: The Limits of Benevolence*. New York: Pantheon, 1978.

Gellhorn, Ernest. "The New Gibberish at the FTC." *Regulation* (May/June 1978), pp. 37–42.

Gibbon, Edward. *The Decline and Fall of the Roman Empire.* New York: Viking, 1953.

Gilder, George. "Prometheus Bound." *Harper's* (September 1978), pp. 35–42.

Gimpel, Jean. *The Medieval Machine: The Industrial Revolution of the Middle Ages.* New York: Holt, Rinehart and Winston, 1976.

Glazer, Nathan. "Towards an Imperial Judiciary?" *Public Interest* (Fall 1975), pp. 104–23.

———. "Should Judges Administer Social Services?" *Public Interest* (Winter 1978), pp. 64–80.

Glotz, Gustave. *Ancient Greece at Work.* New York: Barnes and Noble, 1926.

———. *The Greek City.* New York: Barnes and Noble, 1929.

Goffart, Walter. "Zosimus, The First Historian of Rome's Fall." *American Historical Review* (April 1971), pp. 412–41.

Goldberg, Victor P. "Regulation and Administered Contracts." *Bell Journal of Economics* (Autumn 1976), pp. 426–48.

Goldfarb, Robert S. "Pareto Optimal Redistribution: Comment." *American Economic Review* (December 1970), pp. 994–96.

Goode, Richard. *The Individual Income Tax.* Rev. ed. Washington, D.C.: The Brookings Institution, 1976.

Goodrich, L. Carrington. *A Short History of the Chinese People.* New York: Harper and Row, 1969.

Gouldner, Alvin W. *The Future of Intellectuals and the Rise of the New Class.* New York: Seabury, 1979.

Grabowski, Henry G., and John M. Vernon. "Consumer Product Safety Regulation." *American Economic Review* (May 1978), pp. 284–89.

Graham, Jr., Otis L. *Toward a Planned Society: From Roosevelt to Nixon.* New York: Oxford Univ. Press, 1976.

———. "Planning the Society." *The Center Magazine* (May/June 1977), pp. 8–14.

———. "The White House Conference on Economic Growth." *The Center Magazine* (July/August 1978), pp. 52–59.

Gramlich, Edward M. "Impact of Minimum Wages on Other Wages, Employment, and Family Income." In Arthur M. Okun and George L. Perry, eds., *Brookings Papers on Economic Activity.* 2 (1976), pp. 409–61.

Grant, Michael. *The Army of the Caesars.* New York: Scribner's, 1974.

Gray, B. Kirkman. *A History of English Philanthropy.* New York: Kelley, 1905.

Greene, Kenneth V. "Attitudes Toward Risk and the Relative Size of the Public Sector." *Public Finance Quarterly* (April 1973), pp. 205–18.

Hadley, Herbert S. *Rome and the World Today.* 2d ed. New York: Putnam's, 1934.

Hands, A. R. *Charities and Social Aid in Greece and Rome.* Ithaca: Cornell Univ. Press, 1968.

Hardy, W. G. *The Greek and Roman World.* Cambridge, Mass.: Schenkman, 1970.

Harris, James F., and Anne Klepper. *Corporate Philanthropic Public Service Activities.* New York: The Conference Board, 1976.

Harris, Louis. *The Anguish of Change.* New York: Norton, 1973.

Hartwell, Robert. "Industrial Developments: The Coal and Iron Industries." In Liu and Golas, *Change . . .* , pp. 34–39.

Haveman, Robert H. "Introduction." In Haveman and Robert D. Hamrin, eds., *The Political Economy of Federal Policy.* New York: Harper and Row, 1973, pp. 3–8.

——— (a). "Poverty, Income Distribution, and Social Policy: The Last Decade and the Next." *Public Policy* (Winter 1977), pp. 3–24.

——— (b). *A Decade of Federal Antipoverty Programs: Achievements, Failures, and Lessons.* New York: Academic Press, 1977.

Hayek F. A. (a). *The Constitution of Liberty.* Chicago: Univ. of Chicago Press, 1960.

——— (b). "The Intellectuals and Socialism." In George Bide Huszar, ed., *Intellectuals.* Glencoe: Free Press, 1960.

———. *The Mirage of Social Justice.* Vol. 2. *Law, Legislation, and Liberty.* Chicago: Univ. of Chicago Press, 1976.

Heclo, Hugh. *Modern Social Politics in Britain and Sweden: From Relief to Income Maintenance.* New Haven: Yale Univ. Press, 1974.

———. "A Question of Priorities." *The Humanist* (March/April 1977), pp. 21–24.

Heichelheim, Fritz L. *An Ancient Economic History.* 3 vols. Leyden: Sythoff, 1958, 1964, 1970.

Hicks, Sir John. *A Theory of Economic History.* London Oxford Univ. Press, 1969.

Hilton, George W. "American Transportation Planning." In Chickering, ed., *The Politics . . .* , pp. 145–173.

Hirschleifer, J. "Economics from a Biological Viewpoint." *Journal of Law and Economics* (April 1977), pp. 1–52.

Ho Ping-Ti. "Early-Ripening Rice." In Liu and Golas, *Change . . .* , pp. 30–34.

Hochman, Harold M., and James D. Rodgers. "The Simple Politics of Distributional Preference." In Juster, ed., *The Distribution . . .* , pp. 71–107.

Hodgett, Gerald A. J. *A Social and Economic History of Medieval Europe.* London: Methuen, 1972.

Homer, Sidney. *A History of Interest Rates.* New Brunswick: Rutgers Univ. Press, 1963.

Hoos, Ida R. *Systems Analysis in Public Policy: A Critique.* Berkeley: Univ. of California Press, 1972.

Howard, Michael. *War and the Liberal Conscience.* New Brunswick: Rutgers Univ. Press, 1978.

Hsu I-T'ang. "Social Relief During the Sung Dynasty." In E-Tu Zen Sun and John De Francis, *Chinese Social History.* Washington, D.C.: American Council of Learned Societies, 1956, pp. 207–15.

Hucker, Charles O. *China's Imperial Past.* Stanford: Stanford Univ. Press, 1975.

Hughes, Jonathan R. T. *The Governmental Habit: Economic Controls from Colonial Times to the Present.* New York: Basic Books, 1977.

Hume, David. "Morality, Self-Love, and Benevolence." In Ronald D. Milo, ed., *Egoism and Altruism.* Belmont, California: Wadsworth, 1973, pp. 37–51.

Huntington. Samuel. "The United States. In Crozier et al., *The Crisis . . .* , pp. 59–118.

––––––. "Postindustrial Politics: How Different Will It Be?" In James William Worley, ed., *Prologue to the Future: The United States and Japan in the Postindustrial Age.* Lexington: Lexington Books for the Japan Society, Inc., 1974, pp. 89–127.

Hutchison. Keith. *The Decline and Fall of British Capitalism.* New York: Scribner's, 1950.

Inglehart, Ronald. *The Silent Revolution: Changing Values and Political Styles Among Western Publics.* Princeton: Princeton Univ. Press, 1977.

Ireland, Thomas R. "Charity Budgeting (Part I)." In Ireland and David B. Johnson. *The Economics of Charity.* Blacksburg: Center for Study of Public Choice, 1970.

Johnson. Harry G. "The Economics of Poverty: Discussion." *American Economic Review* (May 1965), pp. 543–45.

––––––. "Theoretical Model of Economic Nationalism in New and Developing States." *Political Science Quarterly* (June 1965), pp. 169–85.

Johnson. Paul. *Enemies of Society.* New York: Atheneum, 1977.

––––––. "Has Capitalism a Future?" *Wall Street Journal.* September 29, 1978.

Jones. A. H. M. *Athenian Democracy.* Oxford: Blackwell, 1964.

––––––. "The Social, Political, and Religious Changes During the Last Period of the Roman Empire." In Eisenstadt, ed., *The Decline . . .* , pp. 67–75.

––––––. *The Roman Economy: Studies in Ancient Economic and Administrative History.* P. A. Brunt, ed. Oxford: Blackwell, 1974.

Jordan. W. K. *Philanthropy in England: 1480–1660.* London: Allen and Unwin, 1959.

Juster. F. Thomas, ed. *The Distribution of Economic Well-Being.* Studies in Income and Wealth. Vol. 41 (Cambridge, Mass.: Ballinger for the NBER, 1977.

Kahn. Herman, and Anthony J. Wiener. *The Year 2000.* New York: Macmillan, 1967.

––––––, and B. Bruce-Briggs. *Things to Come.* New York: Macmillan, 1972.

Karl. Barry D. "Philanthropy, Policy Planning, and the Bureaucratization of the Democratic Ideal." *Daedalus* (Fall 1976), pp. 129–49.

Katona, George, and Burkhard Strumpel. *A New Economic Era.* New York: Elsevier, 1978.

Kendrick. John W. *Understanding Productivity: An Introduction to the Dynamics of Productivity Change.* Baltimore: Johns Hopkins Univ. Press, 1977.

Keniston. Kenneth, and the Carnegie Council on Children. *All Our Children: The American Family Under Pressure.* New York: Harcourt Brace Jovanovich, 1977.

Keyfitz. Nathan. "The Impending Crisis in American Graduate Education." *Public Interest* (Summer 1978), pp. 85–97.

Keynes, John Maynard. "Economic Possibilities for Our Grandchildren." In *Essays in Persuasion.* London: Macmillan, 1931.

Kiechle, Franz K. "Technical Progress in the Main Period of Ancient Slavery."

In F. C. Lane, ed., *Fourth International Conference on Economic History.* Paris: Mouton, 1973.

Klein, Burton H. *Dynamic Economics.* Cambridge, Mass.: Harvard Univ. Press, 1977.

K'o, Ch'ang-Chi. "The Problem of Hired Labor," in Liu and Golas (eds.), *Change . . .* , 44-51.

Kracke, Jr., E. A. "Change Within Tradition." In Liu and Golas, eds., *Change . . .* , pp. 9-15.

———. "Sung K'ai-feng: Pragmatic Metropolis and Formalistic Capital." In John Winthrop Haeger, ed., *Crisis and Prosperity in Sung China.* Tucson: Univ. of Arizona Press, 1975, pp. 49-77.

Krauss, Melvyn B. "Stagnation and the 'New Protectionism.'" *Challenge* (January/February 1978), pp. 40-44.

Kristol, Irving. *Two Cheers for Capitalism.* New York: Basic Books, 1978.

Krueger, A. O. "The Political Economy of the Rent-Seeking Society." *American Economic Review* (June 1974), pp. 291-303.

Laistner, M. L. W. *A History of the Greek World from 479-323 B.C.* 3d ed. London: Methuen, 1957.

Landes, David S. *The Unbound Prometheus: Technological Change and Industrial Development In Western Europe from 1750 to the Present.* London: Cambridge Univ. Press, 1969.

Landes, William M., and Richard A. Posner. "Altruism in Law and Economics." *American Economic Review* (May 1978), pp. 417-21.

Lapham, Lewis H. "The American Courtier." *Harper's* (October 1978), pp. 9-17.

Latouche, Robert. *The Birth of the Western Economy.* New York: Harper and Row, 1961.

Lee, Mabel Ping-Hua. *The Economic History of China.* New York: Columbia Univ. Press, 1921.

Lekachman, Robert. "The Case for Controls: Most Prices Are Already Controlled but Not by the Government." *New Republic* (October 14, 1978), pp. 18-21.

Levine, A. L. *Industrial Retardation in Britain: 1880-1914.* London: Weidenfeld and Nicolson, 1967.

Levine, Robert A. *The Poor Ye Need Not Have with You.* Cambridge, Mass.: Harvard Univ. Press, 1976.

Levitan, Sar A., and Robert Taggart. *The Promise of Greatness.* Cambridge, Mass.: Harvard Univ. Press, 1976.

Levy, Jean-Philippe. *The Economic Life of the Ancient World.* Chicago: Univ. of Chicago Press, 1964.

Li, Don J. *The Ageless Chinese.* 2d ed. New York: Scribner's, 1971.

Lilley, William, III, and James C. Miller III. "The New Social Regulation." *Public Interest* (Spring 1977), pp. 49-66.

Lindbeck, Assar. "Stabilization Policy in Open Economies with Endogenous Politicians." *American Economic Review* (May 1976), pp. 1-19.

Lindblom, Charles E. *Politics and Markets: The World's Political-Economic Systems.* New York: Basic Books, 1977.

Lin Yutang. "Experiments in State Capitalism." In Meskill, ed., *Wang . . . ,* pp. 62–76.

Lipset, Seymour Martin. "The New Class and the Professoriate." *Society* (January/February 1979), pp. 31–38.

——— and Richard B. Dobson. "The Intellectual as Critic and Rebel: With Special Reference to the United States and the Soviet Union." *Daedalus* (Summer 1972), pp. 137–98.

——— and Earl Raab. "The Message of Proposition 13." *Commentary* (September 1978), pp. 42–46.

Lipson, E. *The Economic History of England.* Vol. III. *The Age of Mercantilism.* 6th ed. London: Black, 1956.

Liu, James T. C. *Reform in Sung China.* Cambridge, Mass.: Harvard Univ. Press, 1959.

———, and Peter J. Golas, eds. *Change in Sung China.* Lexington: Heath, 1959.

Lo, Jung-Pang. "The Rise of China as a Sea Power," in Liu and Golas (eds.), *Change . . . ,* 20-29.

Louis, Paul. *Ancient Rome at Work.* New York: Barnes and Noble, 1972.

Lynn, Jr., Laurence E. "A Decade of Policy Developments in the Income Maintenance System." In Haveman, ed., *A Decade . . . ,* pp. 55–117.

Macaulay, J., and L. Berkowitz, eds. *Altruism and Helping Behavior.* New York: Academic Press, 1970.

McCloskey, Donald *Economic Maturity and Entrepreneurial Decline: British Iron and Steel, 1870–1913.* Cambridge, Mass.: Harvard Univ. Press, 1973.

MacDonald, Maurice, and Isabel V. Sawhill. "Welfare Policy and the Family," *Public Policy* (Winter 1978), pp. 89–119.

McKean, Roland N. "Economics of Trust, Altruism, and Corporate Responsibility." In Phelps, ed., *Altruism . . . ,* pp. 29–44.

MacMullen, Ramsey. *Roman Government's Response to Crisis: A.D. 235–337.* New Haven: Yale Univ. Press, 1976.

MacRae, C. Duncan. "A Political Model of the Business Cycle." *Journal of Political Economy* (April 1977), pp. 239–63.

Maddox, John. *The Doomsday Syndrome.* New York: McGraw-Hill, 1972.

Manne, Henry G. "Corporate Altruism and Individualistic Methodology." In Selden, ed., *Capitalism . . . ,* pp. 128–42.

———. "Individual Constraints and Incentives in Government Regulation of Business." In Siegan, ed., *The Interaction . . . ,* pp. 23–34.

———, and Henry G. Wallich. *The Modern Corporation and Social Responsibility.* Washington, D.C.: American Enterprise Institute, 1972.

Marris, Robin. "Is Britain an Awful Warning to America?" *New Republic* (September 17, 1977), pp. 23–28.

Marx, Karl, and Friedrich Engels. *The German Ideology.* New York: International Publishers, 1947.

Maslow, Abraham H. *Eupsychian Management.* Homewood: Irwin, 1965.

———. *Motivation and Personality.* 2d ed. New York: Harper and Row, 1970.

Masters, Stanley and Irwin Garfinkel. *Estimating the Labor Supply Effects of Income-Maintenance Alternatives.* New York: Academic Press, 1977.

Mathias, Peter. *The First Industrial Nation: An Economic History of Britain, 1700-1914.* New York: Scribner's, 1969.

Mazzarino, Santo. *The End of the Ancient World.* New York: Knopf, 1966.

Mazzolani, Lidias Storeni. *The Idea of the City in Roman Thought: From Walled City to Spatial Commonwealth.* Bloomington: Indiana Univ. Press, 1970.

Meadows, Donella H., Dennis L. Meadows, Jorgen Randers, and William N. Behrens III. *The Limits of Growth.* New York: Universe, 1972.

Meiggs, Russell. *The Athenian Empire.* London: Oxford Univ. Press, 1972.

Meltzer, Allen H., and Scott F. Richard. "Why Government Grows (and Grows) in a Democracy." *Public Interest* (Summer 1978), pp. 111-18.

Mencius. Trans. and introd. by D. C. Lau. Baltimore: Penguin, 1970.

Meskill, John, ed. *Wang An-shih.* Boston: Heath, 1963.

Mesthene, Emmanuel G. *Technological Change.* Cambridge, Mass.: Harvard Univ. Press, 1970.

Michell, H. *The Economics of Ancient Greece.* 2d ed. New York: Barnes and Noble, 1957.

Midgley, Mary. *Beast and Man: The Roots of Human Nature.* Ithaca: Cornell Univ. Press, 1979.

Mill, John Stuart. *Principles of Political Economy.* New York: Kelley, 1965.

Miller III, James C. "Lessons of the Economic Impact Statement Program." *Regulation* (July/August 1977), pp. 14-21.

Mills, Edwin S. *The Economics of Environmental Quality.* New York: Norton, 1978.

Mincer, Jacob. "Unemployment Effects of Minimum Wages." *Journal of Political Economy* (August 1976, Part 2), S87-104.

Mishan, E. J. *The Economic Growth Debate: An Assessment.* London: Allen and Unwin, 1977.

Miyazaki, Ichisada. "The Reforms of Wang An-Shih." In Meskill, ed., *Wang . . . ,* pp. 82-90.

Molnar, Thomas. *The Decline of the Intellectual.* Cleveland: World, 1961.

Monsen, R. Joseph, and Anthony Downs. "Public Goods and Private Status." *Public Interest* (Spring 1971), pp. 64-76.

Montesquieu. *Considerations on the Causes of the Greatness of the Romans and Their Decline.* New York: Free Press, 1965.

Murphy, Brian. *A History of the British Economy: 1086-1970.* London: Longmans, 1973.

Murray, Gilbert. *Five Stages of Greek Religion.* 2d ed. New York: Columbia Univ. Press, 1925.

Mussen, Paul, and Nancy Eisenberg-Berg. *Roots of Caring, Sharing, and Helping: The Development of Prosocial Behavior in Children.* San Francisco: Freeman, 1977.

Muth, Richard. *Public Housing: An Economic Evaluation.* Washington, D.C.: American Enterprise Institute, 1973.

————. "Housing and Land Use." In Chickering, ed., *The Politics . . .* , pp. 175–91.

Myrdal, Gunnar. *Beyond the Welfare State.* New Haven: Yale Univ. Press, 1960.

Needham, Joseph. *Clerks and Craftsmen in China and the West.* Cambridge: Cambridge Univ. Press, 1970.

Nelson, Ralph L. *Economic Factors in Corporate Giving.* New York: NBER, 1970.

Nichols, Albert L., and Richard Zeckhauser. "Government Comes to the Workplace: An Assessment of OSHA." *Public Interest* (Fall 1977), pp. 39–69.

Nisbet, Robert. *Twilight of Authority.* New York: Oxford Univ. Press, 1975.

————. "The Dilemma of Conservatives in a Populist Society." *Policy Review* (Spring 1978), pp. 91–104.

Nivison, David S. "A Neo-Confucian Visionary: Ou-yang Hsiu," in Liu and Golas (eds.), *Change . . .* , 74-78.

North, Douglass C. "Structure and Performance: The Task of Economic History." *Journal of Economic Literature* (September 1978), pp. 963–78.

———— and Robert Paul Thomas. *The Rise of the Western World.* Cambridge: Cambridge Univ. Press, 1973.

Nutter, G. Warren. *The Growth of Government in the West.* Washington, D.C.: American Enterprise Institute, 1978.

Okun, Arthur M. "Discussion." In Campbell, ed., *Income . . .* , pp. 61.

Orfield, Gary. *Must We Bus? Segregated Schools and National Policy.* Washington, D.C.: The Brookings Institution, 1978.

Orr, Daniel. "Toward Necessary Reform of Social Security." *Policy Review* (Fall 1977), pp. 47–65.

Orr, Larry L. "Income Transfers as a Public Good: An Application to AFDC." *American Economic Review* (June 1976), pp. 359–71.

————. "Income Transfers as a Public Good: Reply." *American Economic Review* (December 1978), pp. 990–94.

Owen, Bruce M., and Ronald Braeutigam. *The Regulation Game: Strategic Use of the Administrative Process.* Cambridge, Mass.: Ballinger, 1978.

Owen, David. *English Philanthropy: 1660–1960.* Cambridge, Mass.: Harvard Univ. Press, 1964.

Paglin, Morton. "Poverty in the United States: A Reevaluation." *Policy Review* (Spring 1979), pp. 7–24.

Pareto, Vilfredo. *The Rise and Fall of the Elites.* Totowa, N.J.: Bedminster, 1968.

Peacock, Alan T., and Jack Wiseman. *The Growth of Public Expenditures in the United Kingdom.* 2d ed. London: Allen and Unwin, 1967.

Peltzman, Sam. "The Effects of Automobile Safety Regulation." *Journal of Political Economy* (August 1965), pp. 677–725.

Percival, John. *The Roman Villa: An Historical Introduction.* Berkeley: Univ. of California Press, 1976.

Petit, Paul. *Pax Romana.* Berkeley: Univ. of California Press, 1976.

Phelps, Edmund S. *Altruism, Morality, and Economic Theory.* New York: Russell Sage, 1975.

Pirenne, Jacques. *The Tides of History.* Vol. I. New York: Dutton, 1962.

Poggi, Gianfranco. *The Development of the Modern State: A Sociological Introduction.* Stanford: Stanford Univ Press, 1978.

Polanyi, Karl. *The Livelihood of Man.* Harry W. Pearson, ed. New York: Academic, 1977.

Pole, J. R. *The Pursuit of Equality in American History.* Berkeley: Univ. of California Press, 1978.

Pollak, Robert A. "Interdependent Preferences." *American Economic Review* (June 1976), pp. 309–20.

Pollard, Sidney, and David W. Crossley. *The Wealth of Britain, 1085–1966.* London: Batsford, 1968.

Pryor, Frederic L. *The Origins of the Economy: A Comparative Study of Distribution in Primitive and Peasant Economies.* New York: Academic Press, 1977.

Pugh, George Edgin. *The Biological Origin of Human Values.* New York: Basic Books, 1977.

Ravitch, Diane. "The 'White Flight' Controversy." *Public Interest* (Spring 1978), pp. 135–49.

Reece, William S. "Charitable Contributions: New Evidence on Household Behavior." *American Economic Review* (March 1979), pp. 142–51.

Reynolds, Morgan, and Eugene Smolensy. "The Fading Effect of Government on Inequality." *Challenge* (July/August 1978), pp. 32–37.

Rivlin, Alice M. "Discussion." *American Economic Review* (May 1966), pp. 395–98.

Roberts, David. *Victorian Origins of the British Welfare State.* New Haven: Yale Univ. Press, 1960.

Roberts, Marc J. "Is There an Energy Crisis?" *Public Interest* (Spring 1973), pp. 13–37.

Robinson, Cyril E. (a). *History of Rome.* New York: Crowell, 1965.

——— (b). *History of Greece.* New York: Crowell, 1965.

Rochlin, Gregory. *Man's Aggression.* Boston: Gambit, 1973.

Rodgers, James D. "Explaining Income Redistribution." In Harold M. Hochman and George E. Peterson, eds., *Redistribution Through Public Choice.* New York: Columbia Univ. Press, 1974, pp. 165–205.

Roebuck, Janet. *The Making of Modern English Society from 1850.* New York: Scribner's, 1973.

Rokeach, Milton. *The Nature of Human Values.* New York: Free Press, 1973.

Rose, Richard, and Guy Peters. *Can Government Go Bankrupt?* New York: Basic Books, 1978.

Rostovtzeff, M. *The Social and Economic History of the Roman Empire.* Vol. I. 2d ed. Oxford: Oxford Univ. Press, 1957.

———. *Greece.* London: Oxford Univ. Press, 1963.

Rostow, W. W. *How It All Began: Origins of the Modern Economy.* New York: McGraw-Hill, 1975.

Rousseau, Jean Jacques. *The Social Contract and Discourses.* New York: Dutton, 1950.

Rowley, Charles K., and Alan T. Peacock. *Welfare Economics.* New York: Wiley, 1975.

Salter, F. R. *Some Early Tracts on Poor Relief.* London: Methuen, 1926.

Sansom, Robert L. *The New American Dream Machine.* Garden City: Anchor, 1976.

Sayers, R. S. *A History of Economic Change in England: 1880–1939.* London: Oxford Univ. Press, 1967.

Schiller, Bradley R. "Income Transfers as a Public Good: Comment." *American Economic Review* (December 1978), pp. 982–84.

Schlesinger, James R. "Systems Analysis and the Political Process." *Journal of Law and Economics* (October 1968), pp. 281–98.

Schnitzer, Martin. *The Economy of Sweden: A Study of the Modern Welfare State.* New York: Praeger, 1970.

Schultz, Theodore W. "Investing in Poor People: An Economist's View." *American Economic Review* (May 1965), pp. 510–20.

Schultze, Charles L. *The Public Use of Private Interest.* Washington, D.C.: The Brookings Institution, 1977.

Schumpeter, Joseph A. *Capitalism, Socialism, and Democracy.* 3d ed. New York: Harper and Row, 1950.

Schwartz, Robert A. "Personal Philanthropic Contributions." *Journal of Political Economy* (November/December 1970), pp. 1264–91.

Seabury, Paul. "Trendier Than Thou," *Harper's* (October 1978), pp. 39–52.

Seidman, David. "The Politics of Policy Analysis" *Regulation* (July/August 1977), pp. 22–37.

Selden, Richard T., ed. *Capitalism and Freedom.* Charlottesville: Univ. Press of Virginia, 1975.

Senese, Donald J. "The IRS and the Private Schools: The Power to Tax Involves the Power to Destroy." *Policy Review* (Spring 1979), pp. 67–83.

Shattuck, John. "Scarce Resources and Civil Liberties." *The Center Magazine* (January/February 1978), pp. 18–19.

Shiba Yoshinobu. *Commerce and Society in Sung China.* Trans. Mark Elvin. Michigan Abstracts of Chinese and Japanese History. No. 2. Ann Arbor: Center for Chinese Studies, University of Michigan, 1970.

Shils, Edward. "The Intellectuals and the Powers." In Philip Rieff, ed., *On Intellectuals.* Garden City: Doubleday, 1969, pp. 25–48.

Siegan, Bernard, ed. *The Interaction of Economics and Law.* Lexington: Lexington, 1977.

Silver, Morris. "The Relationship Between Nationalism and Per Capita Gross National Product: Comment." *Quarterly Journal of Economics* (February 1967), pp. 155–57.

———. "Political Revolution and Repression: An Economic Approach." *Public Choice* (Spring 1974), pp. 65–71.

———. "Towards a Consumption Theory of Political Democracy." In Robert D. Leiter and Gerald Sirkin, eds., *Economics of Public Choice.* New York: Cyrco, 1975, pp. 140–53.

———. "Economic Theory of the Constitutional Separation of Powers." *Public Choice* (Spring 1977), pp. 95–107.

Simon, William E. *A Time for Truth.* New York: Reader's Digest, 1978.

Simmons, Harvey. "System Dynamics and Technocracy." In H. S. D. Cole, et al., *Models of Doom: A Critique of the Limits of Growth.* New York: Universe, 1973, pp. 192–208.

Sirkin, Gerald. "Resource X and the Theory of Retrodevelopment." In Robert D. Leiter and Stanely Friedlander, eds. *Economics of Scarce Resources.* New York: Cyrco, 1976, pp. 193–208.

Smeeding, Timothy M. "The Antipoverty Effectiveness of In-Kind Transfers." *Journal of Human Resources* (Summer 1977), pp. 360–78.

Smith, Morton. *The Ancient Greeks.* Ithaca: Cornell Univ. Press, 1960.

Smolensky, Eugene. "Investment in the Education of the Poor: A Pessimistic Report." *American Economic Review* (May 1966), pp. 370–78.

———, Leanna Stiefel, Maria Schmundt, and Robert Plotnik. "Adding In-kind Transfers to the Personal Income and Outlay Account: Implications for the Size Distribution of Income." In Juster, ed., *The Distribution . . .* , pp. 9–44.

Southwick, Jr., Lawrence. "Income Transfers as a Public Good: Comment." *American Economic Review* (December 1978), pp. 977–81.

Spall, Hugh. "Income Transfers as a Public Good: Comment." *American Economic Review* (December 1978), pp. 985–89.

Spencer, Herbert. *The Principles of Psychology.* Vol. II. New York: Appleton, 1897.

———. *The Data of Ethics.* New York: Collier, 1901.

———. *The Man versus the State.* Ed. and introd. by Donald Macrae. Baltimore: Penguin, 1969.

Starr, Chester G. *Civilization and the Caesars.* Ithaca: Cornell Univ. Press, 1954.

———. *The Ancient Romans.* New York: Oxford Univ. Press, 1971.

———. *The Economic and Social Growth of Early Greece: 800–500 B.C.* New York: Oxford Univ. Press, 1977.

Starr, Roger. *America's Housing Challenge.* New York: Hill and Wang, 1977.

———. "Controlling Rents and Razing Cities." *The American Spectator* (October 1978), pp. 21–24.

Sternlieb, George, and Robert W. Burchell. *Residential Abandonment.* New Brunswick: Rutgers Univ. Press, 1973.

Stigler, George J. "Director's Law of Public Income Redistribution." *Journal of Law and Economics* (April 1970), pp. 1–10.

———. "The Intellectual and His Society." In Selden, ed., *Capitalism . . .* , pp. 311–21.

Stobart, J. C. *The Grandeur That Was Rome.* 4th rev. ed. New York: Praeger, 1961.

Sumner, William Graham. *Folkways.* Boston: Ginn, 1906.

Tollison, Robert G. "Does Antitrust Activity Increase Economic Welfare?" In M. Bruce Johnson, ed., *The Attack on Corporate America: The Corporate Is-*

sues Sourcebook. New York: McGraw-Hill, for the Law and Economics Center of the Univ. of Miami, 1978, pp. 294–98.

Toutain, Jules. *The Economic Life of the Ancient World.* New York: Barnes and Noble, 1951.

Toynbee, Arnold J. *A Study of History.* Vol. V. New York: Oxford Univ. Press, 1962.

Trever, Albert A. *History of Ancient Civilization: The Roman World.* Vol. II. New York: Harcourt, Brace, and World, 1939.

Tufte, Edward R. *Political Control of the Economy.* Princeton: Princeton Univ. Press, 1978.

Tullock, Gordon. "The Charity of the Uncharitable." *Western Economic Journal* (December 1971), pp. 379–92.

———. *Private Wants, Public Means: An Economic Analysis of the Desirable Scope of Government.* New York: Basic Books, 1970.

———. "Altruism, Malice, and Public Goods." *Journal of Social and Biological Structures.* Vol. 1, No. 1 (1978).

Tumlir, Jan. "The Unintended Society: Some Notes on Nozick." *Eastern Economic Journal* (January 1978), pp. 27–40.

Tussman, Joseph. *Government and the Mind.* New York: Oxford Univ. Press, 1977.

Tyrell, Jr., R. Emmett, ed. *The Future That Doesn't Work: Social Democracy's Failures in Britain.* Garden City: Doubleday, 1977.

Unger, Roberto Mangabeira. *Law in Modern Society.* New York: Free Press, 1976.

van den Haag, Ernest. "Economics Is Not Enough—Notes on the Anticapitalist Spirit" *Public Interest* (Fall 1976), pp. 109–22.

van Houtte, J. A. *An Economic History of the Low Countries, 800–1800.* New York: St. Martin's, 1977.

Veblen, Thorstein. *The Engineers and the Price System.* New York: Viking, 1921.

———. *The Theory of the Leisure Class.* New York: Modern Library, 1934.

Viljoen, Stephan. *Economic Systems of World History.* London: Longman, 1974.

Voegelin, Eric. *The New Science of Politics.* Chicago: Univ. of Chicago Press, 1952.

Von Martin, Alfred. *Sociology of the Renaissance.* New York: Harper and Row, 1963.

Wagner, Richard E. "Economic Manipulation for Political Profit: Macroeconomic Consequences and Constitutional Implications." *Kyklos.* Vol. 30 (1977), Fasc. 3, pp. 395–410.

Walbank, F. W. "Trade and Industry Under the Late Roman Empire in the West." In M. M. Postan and E. E. Rich, eds., *Cambridge Economic History of Europe.* Vol. II. Cambridge: Cambridge Univ. Press, 1952, pp. 33–88.

———. *The Awful Revolution.* Toronto: Univ. of Toronto Press, 1969.

Wallace, Phyllis A. "Impact of Equal Opportunity Laws." In Juanita M. Kreps, ed., *Women and the American Economy: A Look to the 1980s.* Englewood Cliffs, N.J.: Prentice-Hall, 1976, pp. 123–45.

Walters, Alan A. "Commentary." In Campbell, ed., *Income* . . . , pp. 213–16.

Watt, Kenneth E. F., et al. *The Unsteady State: Environmental Problems, Growth, and Culture*. Honolulu: Univ. Press of Hawaii for the East-West Center, 1977.

Weaver, Paul H. "On Adversary Government and the Liberal Audience." In Chickering, ed., *The Politics* . . . , pp. 307–24.

———. "Regulation, Social Policy, and Class Conflict." *Public Interest* (Winter 1978), pp. 45–63.

Weber, Max. *The Agrarian Sociology of Ancient Civilizations*. London: New Left Review Editions, 1976.

Weidenbaum, Murrary I. "On Estimating Regulatory Costs." *Regulation* (May/ June 1978), pp. 14–17.

——— and Linda Rockwood. "Corporate Planning versus Government Planning." *Public Interest* (Winter 1977), pp. 59–72.

Weintraub, Sidney. *Capitalism's Inflation and Unemployment Crisis: Beyond Monetarism and Keynesianism*. Reading: Addison-Wesley, 1978.

Weisbrod, Burton A. *The Voluntary Nonprofit Sector: An Economic Analysis* Lexington: Heath, 1977.

———. "Toward a Thoery of the Voluntary Nonprofit Sector in a Three-Sector Economy." In Weisbrod, ed., *The Voluntary* . . . , pp. 51–76.

———, and Stephen H. Long. "The Size of the Voluntary Nonprofit Sector: Concepts and Measures." In Weisbrod, ed., *The Voluntary* . . . , pp. 11–49.

Welch, Finis. "The Rising Impact of Minimum Wage Legislation." *Regulation* (November/December 1978), pp. 28–37.

Westermann, William L. *The Slave Systems of Greek and Roman Antiquity*. Philadelphia: The American Philosophical Society, 1955.

Wiener, Anthony J. "Growth as Ideology." *Society* (January/February 1978), pp. 49–53.

Williamson, H. R. *Wang An-Shih*. 2 vols. Westport: Hyperion, 1973.

Wilson, Edward O. *Sociobiology*. Cambridge, Mass.: Harvard Univ. Press, 1975.

———. *On Human Nature*. Cambridge, Mass: Harvard Univ. Press, 1978.

Wilson, James Q. "The Mayors vs. the Cities." *Public Interest* (Summer 1969), pp. 25–37.

———. and Edward C. Banfield. "Public-Regardingness as a Value Premise in Voting Behavior." *American Political Science Review* (December 1964), pp. 876–87.

Young, J. Z. *Programs of the Brain*. Oxford: Oxford Univ. Press, 1978.

Zimmern, Alfred. *The Greek Commonwealth: Politics and Economics in Fifth Century Athens*. 5th ed. rev. London: Oxford Univ. Press, 1931.

INDEX

233